PARC 83

Introduction

Computer graphics have been fascinating industrial designers for a number of years now, and architects have always been at the forefront of applications developments. With the cost of hardware now falling rapidly, the potential of computer graphics techniques is only now being realised.

The proceedings, published in this volume, include forty papers from contributors from Europe, the United States and Australia as well as the UK, all of whom have practical experience of designing, planning, teaching, researching, administration or computing. If your interests lie in using computers, especially computer graphics, in your professional life, you will enjoy and benefit from the following pages.

These papers, presented at the international Online conference PARC 83 examine, in detail how to apply computer graphics techniques to architecture. They have been written by many of the world's leading experts in the field and provide concise, detailed information on how to apply the latest techniques. The papers have all been prepared with the needs of the practising architect in mind and will be of considerable use and value to all in the field.

Online Conferences Limited has established a unique reputation as the world's premier organiser of significant and prestigious events concerned with the business implications of leading-edge technology. During the last 12 years it has co-ordinated over 300 highly respected events in the UK, on the Continent of Europe and in North America.

The proceedings of most of these conferences have been published by and are available from Online Publications Ltd. A fully descriptive catalogue is available upon request.

Online Conferences Limited
Pinner Green House, Ash Hill Drive, Pinner, Middlesex,
HA5 2AE, UK
phone: 01 868 4466 Int'l phone: 44 1 868 4466
Telex: 923498 ONLINE G

iv

PROGRAMME COMMITTEE

Mr J Amkreutz, Director, I3P Consulting Engineers, Netherlands
Mr P Bredsdorff, Director of Research, Building Research Institute, Denmark
Mr J Chalmers, Partner, Bensasson & Chalmers Partnership, UK
Mr R D'Arcy, Partner, D'Arcy Race Partnership, UK
Prof C Eastman, Professor, Carnegie Mellon University, USA
Mr B Evans, Executive Editor, Architects' Journal Computer Club, UK
Dr J Gero, Associate Professor, University of Sydney, Australia
Mr J Lansdown, Chairman, System Simulation Ltd, UK
Prof T Maver, Professor, ABACUS, Strathclyde University, UK

Contents

Education

Authors

POSSIBILITIES OF LOW COST COMPUTER SYSTEMS

Jonathan Greig
Senior Lecturer in Architecture
Polytechnic of Central London
UK

Computing is within the purchasing power of every office. The possible uses of low cost microcomputers in architects offices are explained, and the equipment needed to cover each of the areas of application is gone into.

Jonathan Greig qualified as an architect at the Architectural Association. He worked in Paris, Milan and Berlin before practicing in London. He has taught at the AA, the Bartlet, Canterbury and the University of Virginia. He was a consultant to the Home Office and the DHSS and now to several architectural practices as well as to the Architects Journal on Computers in Architectural Education. He was co-author of their series on computing.

Low Cost Computing

Low Cost in computing is becoming ever more low cost! The power per pence is increasing, the physical size reducing, and the cost of equivalent equipment dropping each year.

Every office can now afford a computer, but what can it do, are there useful programs for architects, and what will it all cost?

There are three principle areas in which computing can be effective in architectural practice, and these will be covered in turn, together with the available programs and the equipment that will be required for each area apart from the basics of microcomputer, keyboard, display and storage devices for information and programs.

MANAGEMENT

DESIGN TOOLS   GRAPHICS

Management

The most obvious application in the area of management is word processing. This can be used for standard letters, statutory applications, specifications and reports. The programs are cheap, available on virtually any microcomputer, and the benefits immediate. Alterations are easy and fast to make, and even spelling can be checked on some systems.

The only additional equipment needed is a letter quality printer.

Other management tasks that a computer can carry out are in the financial management of the office. Accounts, invoices, VAT, payrole can all be done with standard programs.

In addition, filing can be handled by the computer. Records of clients, jobs, contacts, drawings etc. are all easily put onto a computerised filing system.

If a lot of information is to be stored, then it is possible that additional storage systems will be required that have far greater capacity than the usual floppy disk.

Design Tools

Design tools refer to those tasks that we carry out often in the office, such as calculations of environmental and structural aspects of our designs. Programs exist that will do many of these tasks for us - though the legal liability for the accuracy of the results rests with the user!

The only extra item of equipment required for these sort of programs is a cheap "dot-matrix" printer.

Another aspect of this area is the development of computer "expert systems" - that is a program that has had imparted to it the expertise of a consultant or group of consultants, and can be used as such through a question and answer routine.

There is also available a vast amount of information on readily accessible libraries relating to the profession, and the new RIBA scheme is one example of this, where product information can be called up, prices ascertained, and even ordered through Prestel.

This type of service requires a communications device known as a Modem, and probable a special automatic dialing machine to access the data. You also have to subscribe to the particular service that you require.

Graphics

On the border of low cost computing is our last area of graphics. If we think of it in simple terms, there is a great deal of benefit to be gained from seeing information in a visual manner.

In the pure sense, graphics systems are concerned with production drawings, but these systems are still outside the range of what we are considering as low cost computing. There are however, some very good and simple programs that allow the development of plans, and the inspection of them in three dimensions. It can also draw details that will be used repeatedly. It is also possible to use the computer to measure areas with great accuracy, and programs exist to do this.

For this type of application a plotter will be required, and also a "digitiser" with which to enter the graphical data into the computer.

Other more simple uses of graphics are more easily implemented, and cost less. It is useful to be able to produce diagrams for reports, simple drawings of the thermal and moisture graphs through a wall and job planning diagrams such as PERT charts.

While a plotter would give better results for these applications, a more sophisticated dot matrix printer can also produce crude graphics that might well be acceptable.

Overlaps

The most interesting application of computers comes when we overlap these three areas and see what the implications might be. There are no programs readily available to do this, but it is well within the possibilities of low cost computing.

One could imagine a system where the records of hours worked would automatically be assigned to the appropriate job, invoices, based on percentage or hourly rate fees, sent out on standard letters, and at the same time the progress of the job through the office monitored with regard to the original time and cost estimate. This could all come together to produce monthly reports on the office finances, with graphs if required, and deal with deadlines on a continuously updated office diary. The possibilities are enormous.

As another example, if drawing, specification and cost information could be cross linked through the computer, then automatic taking off and costing could be available at every stage of the design, and linking in other design tools, such as environmental and structural checks could also be carried out from the earliest moment of design.

Conclusions

All this may seem idyllic, but it is not far away from reality and these facilities should soon be available on low cost computers.

There are problems with the compatability of equipment, which are now beginning to be eliminated by better design of computers and their peripherals.

There is the problem of the programs that are not yet readily available, and need to be developed. They are also expensive.

There are   problems with the training of staff and in changing the methods of working in offices.

The trend is inevitable, and soon every architectural office will have to involve itself in the process of computing.

MANAGEMENT

Wordprocessing
    letters
    reports

Accounts
    invoicing
    VAT
    PAYE
    accounts

Records
    clients
    contact

Letter Quality
Printer
Mass Storage

Calculations
    thermal
    lighting
    structural

Space/
    Planning

Databanks

Expert/
    Systems

Drawing
    Records

Job Programm-
    ing

Specification

Job costing

Integrated
    programs

PERT

Job Planning

Reports

Diagrams

Taking Off

Databanks

Finance
    diagrams

Office
    program

Office diary

Production
Drawings

Perspectives

Diagrams

Measurement

Sketches

Modelling

Details

Dot Matrix
Printer
Modem

DESIGN
TOOLS

GRAPHICS

Plotter
Digitizer
C Printer

MICROPOWER ASSISTED DRAFTING FOR LOCAL AUTHORITY STANDARD DRAWINGS

J R Woolley
Research & Development Architect
A J Smith
Group Leader Quantity Surveyor
Derbyshire County Council
UK

The background to the office structure is reviewed. The particular requirements of standard drawing production are outlined in the context of drawing office production generally. The development of the chosen program is discussed, the end results evaluated.

Richard Woolley is a Research and Development Architect at Derbyshire County Architect's Department. His responsibilities include technical support and the provision of office guidance notes, good practice details and specifications. In liaison with Adrian Smith he has been involved in departmental computer developments since 1975.

Introduction: Background

Housed in a 130 year old Hydro in Matlock, Derbyshire County
Architect's Department is a multi-discipline practice of Architects,
Quantity- and Land Surveyors, Mechanical, Electrical and Structural
Engineers.

In 1967 the Department began to use the IBM main frame computer
facilities for the production of Bills of Quantities. In 1973,
C.A.R.B.S. (Computer Aided Rationalised Building System) was
successfully used for drafting and Bills of Quantities for the
C.L.A.S.P. system of steel framed buildings. A perspective drawing
facility was also available but was found at that time to be too
tedious to be of benefit. Further, the system was not suitable for
traditional building details.

In 1980 we developed a perspective system (hidden lines removed)
from a program devised by Leeds Polytechnic, to run on the IBM main
frame. Also in March 1980, the first stand-alone micro was
installed for text processing followed by a second machine for the
design of building services.

Since the late 1960's the Department has had a set of good practice
details. Undoubtedly beneficial, these standard drawings need to
be kept up to date in line with design improvements, new British
Standards and Building Regulations. This has always been a
difficult and unpopular task.

By late 1981 a major exercise was needed to bring the standard
drawings into line with changing office requirements. During the
previous ten years computer developments had been monitored but
none of the larger systems was economically feasible for the task
in question. Then "P.A.D." (Power Assisted Drafting), now known
as "Autoplan", was discovered at a L.A.M.S.A.C. seminar in December
1981. It was the only available system which met the Department's
needs at an affordable price.

Installation

The hardware equipment was purchased "off the shelf" in April 1982.
A Commodore 8032 CBM, 8050 disk drive, 4022 printer and an A3 size
Watanabe WX 4636 plotter were unpacked, plugged together and working
in a very short time.

Because some computing equipment was already in use, a suitable
room was already available, with adequate power points and
diffused lighting.

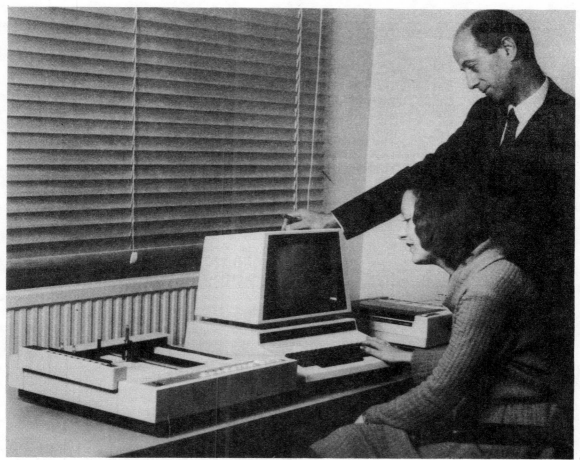

The System in Use

Training

Instruction on how to use the drafting system took the form of seven
tutorials. As first users in an office environment most expertise
was gained by trial and error. However a good liaison with the
system developers enabled the system to be developed to suit the
Department's requirements.

Whilst the Department had some computing expertise available neither
the architect nor the technician had any significant prior knowledge
of computers, furthermore the assistant had no architectural
experience.

Use of the System

The re-drafting of the standard drawings was originally undertaken as a joint project with another County Authority. Derbyshire had some useful existing data, the other party had some spare technical drawing capacity.

Although it took about two months to develop the drafting technique to the level required for the production of standard drawings, within six months the original target had been met. Then, due to unforeseen problems the other County Department had to drop out of the joint scheme, which left the remaining work, further justifying the use of the drafting system.

The original good practice drawings, known as R.T. (Rationalised Traditional) drawings consisted of A2 size tracing film sheets many of which had more than one detail per sheet.

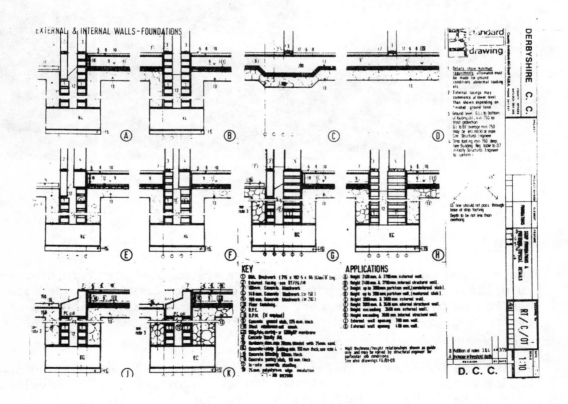

The stencil-lettered drawings were dyeline copied for issue together with contract drawings, often with details crossed out. To gain the advantage of faster improved photocopying techniques (and save paper) the more conveniently sized A3 drawing was opted for which could then be further photo reduced to A4 size for reference purposes.

Use of the System (cont)

This meant that considerably more lettering was required to annotate
the individual detail. With "Autoplan" this problem has been considerably alleviated due to the facility to store and re-use
individual words/figures or complete sets of notes.

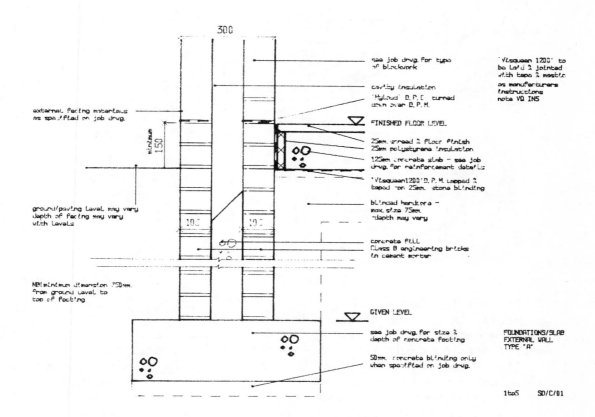

1 to 5 Standard Drawing Plotted at 1 to 12

The screen displays alphanumerics only, the plotter displays graphics.
The ability to use the plotter as a drafting machine rather than
working "on screen" has the particular advantage that the drafts-
person works in a way very close to the traditional drawing method.
For example, when it is necessary to insert break lines into a
detail drawn at an angle to the horizontal, it is simple to place
an adjustable set square on the plotter, draw in a feint line and

Use of the System (cont)

then digitise or trace over the feint line.

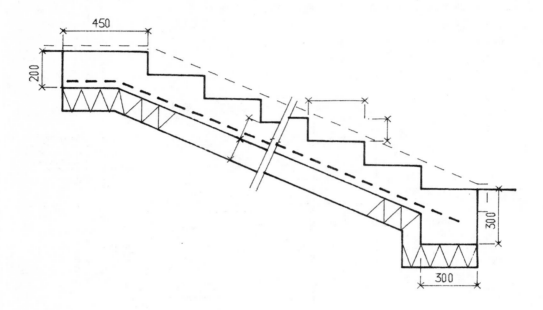

There is a further advantage in direct drafting which is not
generally taken into consideration when discussing methods of
drawing data input and that is to do with the clear overview of the
detail drawing as it evolves. Because of the clarity of the drawing it is possible to identify any errors in the drawing content
efficiently and to quickly correct the error as it is seen.
Conventional methods of checking drawings after production fall
down when in the interests of issuing a drawing the scrutineer's
eye tends to see what it expects to be correct.

A total of 75 standard A3 drawings are currently in use having been
drawn/checked, printed and issued in approximately 100 man days.
During the production time alterations and improvements to the
program have been assimilated without undue stress and although the
latest compiled version of the program has involved certain significant differences in working method previously adopted, the changes
are appreciated particularly the faster input/alteration facility
and the increased space for text input.

Use of the System (cont)

Text handling has seen the most significant improvement since the
first version of the program which had no facility for carriage
return. Now up to 200 characters can be entered where previously
the number was limited to 80, i.e. the screen width. The first
version of the text font incorporated in the Watanabe plotter had
kinked serifs and poor spacing qualities which the program author
changed with a new microchip for the plotter to suit the
Department's requirements.

setting blocks 150mm. long x8x12mm.high
(100mm. from each corner)
to be Iroko pre-drilled with 2mm. bit
to take 2.6x30 galvanised
clout-headed nails 3No per block
 N.B! an additional setting block
will be needed for panes larger
than 1sq.m.fixed centrally on cill

Text produced from the original font microchip

Although this paper is particularly concerned with standard drawing
production, it is of significance to note that a "wire-line" perspective program "Autoview" was supplied with the "Autoplan" program
which has been used to produce internal perspectives of four building projects. The individual architect users found "Autoview"
easier to use than 'Leeds perspective program''(see introduction),
and capable of drawing more complicated shapes albeit in "wire-line"
only.

"Autoplan" has also been used for non-architectural tasks, e.g. the
production of printed micro-film aperture cards.

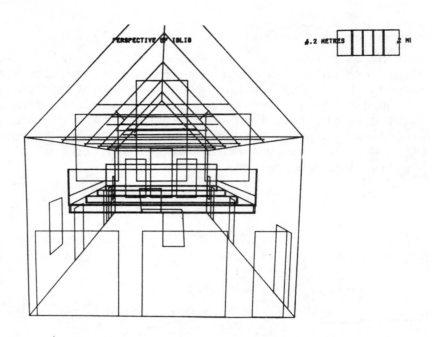

PERSPECTIVE OF IBLIB   4.2 METRES   2 MI

AUTOVIEW   17/8

"Autoview" Wire-Line Perspective

Effects on the Department

As Derbyshire had recently taken on an assistant to look after the
existing equipment, the assistant (referred above under Training)
was already conversant with the back-up services required, e.g. disk
security, time allocation and overall guidance to those members of
the Department who are beginning to show interest in the system and
computer aids in general.

In Retrospect

Experience has found the equipment to be reliable. There have been
no major breakdowns. Programs have proved to be robust and apart
from minor temporary "bugs" the system has achieved what was required
and more besides.

The original proposal to buy the system had to be justified in a
written report to a County Council Advisory Panel. Part of that
report reads "The drafting effort (as distinct from the design
effort) involved in the current re-drawing process has been assessed
as approximately £12,000 including overheads. If we were not to
purchase this system then either additional staff would be required
for a short period or technician resources would need to be re-
allocated from fee-earning work undertaken by the Department.
Neither of these alternatives is considered to be desirable.

In Retrospect (cont)

Maintenance of the standard drawings currently requires an architectural technician for approximately 3 man months per year at an
annual cost of about £3,000. Purchase of this system should reduce
this to no more than 1 man month per year thus releasing the technician to be used on fee-earning jobs." A subsequent report confirms
that targets have been met and the system purchase has been justified.

The initial re-drafting brief called for A4 sized detail drawings.
Fortunately the decision was made to pay £2,500 for an A3 plotter
capable of drawing at 40 cms per second, using wick pens and ball
point pens. The nett swept area of the plotter is less than A3 -
this size is just large enough to suit the perspective program. At
the time of purchase an A1 size plotter cost about £13,000. Today
this size is available for one quarter of that cost. An A2 size
plotter would be an ideal general purpose device for layouts and
perspective drawings.

At the time of writing the 32K Commodore CBM is pushed to the limits
of its capacity even with the 'Mark 3' Autoplan microchip. It is no
mean feat to have achieved the shape manipulation devices, scale
changes, automatic dimensioning, arrows, hatching and in-program
editing facilities with the existing hardware and the enhanced
program is 'downwards' compatible with the earlier versions such
that it is possible to interchange details, for example, from the
old version of the program "PAD" to the new version "Autoplan".

With regard to the bulk of the drawings executed via "PAD" a conversion program is available but Derbyshire is waiting for the outcome
of the programmer's appraisal of its use before embarking on conversion work. The chief advantage of converting the old data would
accrue if another architect's practice wanted to use Derbyshire's
details. In the meantime the two versions are in use, the one
rather like a 'dialect' of the other, however, all current work
utilises the "Autoplan" program.

Conclusions and Future Development

The decision to purchase the "PAD" system was taken before the
arrival of the Architects' Journal's series on low-cost computing.
There is much sound advice in the series, in particular the warning
against "paying a lot of money to be a (developer's) guinea pig".
Fortunately Derbyshire went into the guinea pig situation with open
eyes, initially taking the program on approval and subsequently
deriving what was hopefully a two-way benefit with the programmers.
It is sobering to note that had the full cost of the program had to
have been found without a thorough understanding of its capabilities, the Department probably wouldn't have been able to justify the
finance.

Conclusions and Future Development (cont)

Since July 1983 Derbyshire has subscribed to a £200 annual maintenance agreement with the programmers. The Department is considering the acquisition of an expansion board to the Commodore to allow
for the acceptance of further program enhancements.

Whilst difficult to conceive as yet micro-systems like "Autoplan"
are possibly going to converge with the mini-powered C.A.D. systems
to achieve the common goal of a wider availability of useful
computer aided drafting, together with the ancillary design aids of
area/volume checks, daylight and thermal evaluations et al. In the
meantime "Autoplan" is fulfilling a useful role in the overall
strategy at Derbyshire County Council.

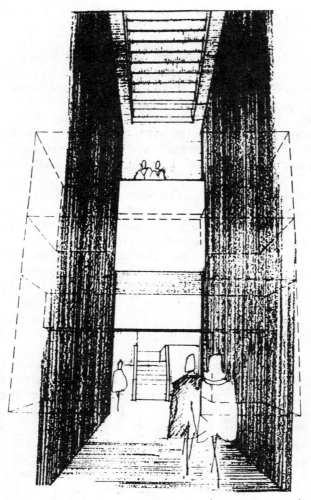

Architect's sketch produced from Autoview
wire-line within one day

TOWARDS AN END USER VIEW OF DESIGN SYSTEMS

R J Walters
Principal Assistant Architect
Oxford Regional Health Authority
UK

Based upon detailed reporting of CAD use on hospital projects an
end user view of design systems is developed. From the recorded
user experience system development, implementation, performance in
use and effects upon design practice are assessed. Aspects of
user technique are developed. Current systems are found to be
flawed but satisfactory results may be obtained under the right
conditions. These are identified. The range of factors required
in the development of an end user view of design systems also
identified.

Roger Walters is a project architect at
Oxford RHA with a long standing interest
in CAD applications to health building
design. His responsibilities have included
CAD use on Milton Keynes DGH and other
major capital schemes. Formerly, he was
an architect with the health service in
Scotland and a research fellow with
ABACUS, University of Strathclyde.
Currently, he is working on a PhD thesis
evaluating user experience of CAAD.

An evaluation of the use of OXSYS/BDS* on Milton Keynes DGH is presented together with an assessment of CAD use (both BDS and GDS) on health building projects at Oxford RHA. The paper summarises a detailed report (WALTERS 83). The paper is presented in 4 parts, an introduction, results of a detailed case study and an assessment leading towards an end user view of current design systems.

INTRODUCTION

Factors and methods are developed for a case study approach to system evaluation (See Table 1). System design considerations (eg MITCHELL and OLIVERSON 78) and cost benefit analysis (eg CHASSEN and DOW 79) provide other approaches of design system evaluation. Approaches are seen to be interdependent but the case study approach is the least well developed and is under represented within CAD literature.

Key issues for system design and use can be identified in terms of:
a   the capacity and robustness of the system
b   the completeness of the geometric model
c   facilities for non-geometric information
d   facilities for maintaining data consistency
e   the right conditions for use
f   the design of the user interface and the handling of input
g   the imposition of a procedural model of design.
Design systems may be seen as a compromise.

CASE STUDY

MKDGH provides the focus for both extensive building system and CAD development at ORHA. It is the culmination of development effort and, in spite of the building system, the project provides a demanding context for CAAD because it is, like most design projects, characterised by a lack of stability of user practices. Briefing, CAD development, building system development, contractual arrangements and staffing all contribute a demanding design context.

In the course of sketch and detailed design development a number of OXSYS models are developed then abandoned. Programme changes can be seen to cause difficulties in design team working but additional difficulties are faced in terms of:
a   data development
b   management of information for processing
c   management learning
d   staffing and training.

After sketch design, exploitation of the drawing system may be found but modelling applications are limited. The OXSYS model is not always the definitive record of the design nor is the image often shared between design team members.

Automatic detailing (OXSYS specific sub-systems) is not exploited due to the over simplified procedural model imposed and due to the lack of stability of building system development on most super-structure elements. Powerful drawing and scheduling facilities (BDS sub-systems) are demonstrated but production quality applications are limited to particular sub-elements (eg doors and ironmongery).

Maintaining the design description in the face of design development can be seen to be a demanding task consuming a greater resource than the initial description.

Project design costs can be seen to be within fee scale. CAD costs require a favourable treatment of development costs, and a charge to the office (rather than 1 project) for full hardware, training and user support costs to break even.

Cost/benefit based on OXSYS/BDS experience at ORHA may be summarised as follows:

a a favourable view of CAD use achieved in terms of cost/ effectiveness within the design process is dependent upon an incomplete assessment of CAD costs
b a commercial view of CAD and project costs, with CAD costs charged as used (utilisation assumed maintained through other projects) shows overall design costs within fee scale
c the effect of utilisation on overall costs appears crucial
d benefits within the design process are limited to specific tasks and tend by themselves to be marginal
e CAD can be seen to promote effective design working at the early design stages where large potential benefits in terms of improved product can be claimed
f recovery of development costs is dependent upon a high value being attached to improved design
g the difference between commercial costs and development costs are such that the cost of pioneering is substantial
h the greatest benefits are in the product but the value that can reasonably be attached and when it may be considered realised are contentious.

Given this pattern to benefits the design management perspective and the client relationship are crucial factors in any assessment.

Design team working can be seen to suffer from a lack of shared models of design procedure. An uneven pattern of acceptance is found within the design team. CAD can be seen to reinforce client consultations. The case study confirms the intractibility of hospital briefing problems and highlights the inadequacy of conventional costing in CAD evaluation.

From CAD use on the project it is possible to draw a number of broad conclusions regarding user technique both in terms of system management and system use. Management learning, project co-ordination and user proficiency are important in user technique.

a   a realistic match between objectives set and available resources
    in terms of data development and trained users must be set.
    The extent of modelling must be determined by the level of
    user training and the access available to the description at
    periods of peak workload.

b   project management must account for the lack of robustness in
    CAD methods of working in the face of uncertainty over design
    development and procedure especially at detailed design stage.

c   system support for handling a steady flow of minor amendments
    is good. System support for larger scales changes is poor.
    Project management must allow for mixed system support over
    design development.

d   careful timing of OXSYS/BDS modelling in relation to other
    project activities is needed. Co-ordination activities giving
    rise to design changes are in general best completed prior to
    detailed modelling. Notably,
    1   development/co-ordination of structural layout
    2   development/co-ordination of fire planning
    3   development/co-ordination of architectural/engineering
        design solutions.

e   significant differences exist in user proficiency between
    naive and average and average and expert users of the system.
    Factors of 2-3 times may be present between each group.

f   use is most efficiently accomplished by a specialist group of
    users. However, vulnerability to the turnover of key staff
    is such that adequate cover is essential.

g   most users need only to be taught a limited set of system
    commands but training must be structured to meet the differing
    needs of project leader, CAD co-ordinator and system users.

h   a concern for technique must be developed. It must take
    account of what should be modelled, when it should be modelled,
    what level of detail developed and what structure for data
    should be adopted for data.

i   management of utilisation is crucial to overall cost/
    effectiveness.

The importance of CAD on MKDGH can be seen in the CAD and design
management issues raised.

ASSESSMENT

Based upon the CAAD material presented here and upon other ORHA
experience (notably Wexham 70 EMI/MI beds WALTERS 82) a personal
view of system performance in use is developed. In practice, it
is frequently difficult to differentiate between system
performance and the adequacy of user practice facing the issues
raised. Assessment is complex, needs careful qualification and
is often apparently contradictory.

OXSYS/BDS Development
a system development represents an extraordinary achievement but at a price
b system can be seen to be unique, ambitious, well conceived and a software development at the limits of conventional computing technology and reliant upon simplifying assumptions.

Implementation
a software development problems were not as difficult as initially expected. Implementation has however generated more difficulties than was anticipated because of the user technique necessary to support data consistency and because of the CAD and design management issues raised
b OXSYS/BDS development is conceptually advanced but (with hindsight) over ambitious and premature in relation to:
1 knowledge of design and of the nature of user practices
2 performance of available implementation tools
3 cost of available suitable hardware
4 level of development of design standards and data
5 knowledge of the effects upon design practices.

Performance in Use
a OXSYS/BDS rationale (resource distribution and shared image) does not take adequate account of the limitations of traditional techniques and of design team attitudes. It remains an objective rather than an accomplishment
b OXSYS/BDS is restrictive in the system concepts, implementation tools and user interface design employed but the system is powerful and shows improvement upon traditional techniques.
c choice of implementation tools is crucial. The most restrictive implementation acceptable within the context has to be taken
d system support for the content (as opposed to the fabric) is better due to the lack of relational complexity
e system facilities provided for high level input and data consistency unusual and much needed but current facilities inadequate in practice
f detailed design systems associated with the fabric are generally not robust enough to withstand building system development. BDS systems more useful than Oxford Method specific facilities; beam and ductwork design systems excepted
g OXSYS/BDS and GDS each have their own particular performance profile against key issues for system design and use. (See Table 2)

Effects in Practice
a CAD methods are not robust in the face of uncertainty over design development. Currently, they are tools for recording rather than developing orderliness. They do not support multiple options or tentative decisions.
b lack of any shared model of design procedure prevents more widespread acceptance and also prevents realisation of full

benefits of application across professional boundaries.

c whilst design systems can be found wanting so also is the design team's current ability to use them.

d high development costs must be set against more than 1 major project and benefits from the product. These benefits are not easily quantified.

e use on selected projects continues to be justified. Systems are restrictive but they have still to be fully exploited.

f CAD can be seen to be a comparatively small part of the overall design working but requires much of the design process to be organised around CAD use to achieve results. It tends therefore to have an exaggerated effect upon design practice.

g explicit validation of sub-systems is seldom possible. In this situation individual professional attitudes are important.

h distinct patterns of benefits exist; savings from process, are less than, capital cost savings, are less than, revenue cost savings. Within the process there are both direct and indirect savings. Direct savings show a high PR on specific tasks but tend to the marginal overall and are realisable in the longer term. Measurement of productivity is difficult.

i system use has important training and staffing considerations. User learning must be seen as not only operator skills, but also system management, database management and design management, each with its own timescale. Learning is completed over a range of projects.

j project development cycles and the currency of user practices can be seen to be in conflict with both hardware and software lifecycles. Software maintenance costs, where there is a close relationship to user design practices, are prohibitive.

k as with the building system, there is with CAD an inertia which requires the maintenance of procedures and standards in order to exploit previous investment. The cost of system evolution may be seen to be crucial in this context.

Overall Assessment

a the difficulties raised should not necessarily limit wider acceptance of systems but should help develop a mature, coherent end user view of design systems generally. This view is urgently needed.

b system use, whether integrated or drawing system, raises a number of related database management, design management and policy issues which are of strategic importance to design practice.

c a difficulty exists in maintaining a balanced view of design systems. There is no reason to suppose, in spite of the reporting of the issues raised by system use, that BDS and GDS are not state of the art of software. They are the best available. In particular BDS has not received the recognition it deserves due to the initial restriction to orthogonal geometry and to confusion in its relation to Oxford Method. The same level of criticism has also to be applied to other design systems and to traditional methods to maintain a balanced view.

END USER VIEW

Detailed case studies are necessary for the development of an independent assessment of systems. Further detailed case studies covering a wider range of systems and projects are required to refine an end user view. However, current systems (and implementation strategies) appear flawed. They:

a are inevitably compromised in their system design
b provide insufficient support for design development and data integrity maintenance
c provide insufficient support for the evolution of user design practices
d cost too much to develop, implement and more particularly evolve (only possible through user group).

The state of the art in practice suggests that:

a satisfactory (sometimes spectacular) results may be obtained under the right conditions (see Table 3) keeping CAD objectives limited to specific tasks, operating within limiting factors and exploiting the distinct pattern of actual benefits.
b current systems provide an improved design representation but only at a low level of abstraction.
c research in support of the relational complexity in building description (as opposed to geometrical modelling) is required.
d research in support of computer aided integrity maintenance facilities is required.
e new software techniques which can economically support design development and the evolution of user design practices are required.
f current systems are better suited to engineering product design than to building design problems.

The end user view of systems is dependent upon:

a an assessment of current systems in practice
b insight into system design trade-offs
c an assessment of the rate of development of current research topics.

Given the developments that remain outstanding and the wide range of disparate topics that support any CAD system, each with its own development timescale, a period of transition may be anticipated where results may be had with somewhat inadequate systems whilst newer systems are awaited. The need is for a "growth path" (BIJL 82) but it should not be suggested that users are presented with easy choices. Individual investment decisions are compromised by the need for high and immediate returns on investment in current systems and the need to anticipate future developments. A mature end user view of systems can be seen as a vital guide within this context.

ACKNOWLEDGEMENT

I am grateful to design team colleagues at Oxford RHA for access to and discussion of their CAD work. Also, I acknowledge the interest and the financial support of the DHSS Building and Engineering R and D Committee (Project Code W75/SY/465F). The views expressed are, however, the author's alone and do not represent past or present views of either ORHA, ARC or DHSS.

REFERENCES

BIJL 82
Bijl, A., "The Future for Architects with Small Means and Large Ambitions", EdCAAD Paper 17, March 1982.

CHASSEN and DOW 79
Chassen, S.H., and Dow, J.W., "The Guide for the Evaluation and Implementation of CAD/CAM Systems", CAD/CAM Decisions, On-line Publications, 1979.

MITCHELL and OLIVERSON 78
Mitchell, W.J and Oliverson, M., "Computer Representation for 3D Structures for CAEADS", CERL Technical Report P-86, February 1978.

WALTERS 82
Walters, R.J., "CAD Case Study: Wexham Park Hospital 70 EMI/MI Beds", ORHA Internal Report, May 1982.

WALTERS 83
Walters, R.J., "Milton Keynes DGH: CAAD Case Study and Assessment", Report for the DHSS BERD Committee, May 1983.

* ABBREVIATIONS

ARC	Applied Research of Cambridge Ltd
BDS	Building Design System, ARC modelling system
CAAD	Computer Aided Architectural Design
DHSS	Department of Health and Social Security
EMI/MI	Elderly Mentally Infirm/Mentally Ill
GDS	General Draughting System, ARC drawing system
MKDGH	Milton Keynes District General Hospital
ORHA	Oxford Regional Health Authority
OXSYS	Oxford System for CAD, BDS plus building system detailed design systems
PR	Productivity Ratio

TABLE 1

CAAD Case Studies - FACTORS and METHODS

		Method
PHASE 1 : RECORD/MONITOR		
Scheme	– brief, programme – design team	
Design Objectives	– product – service	

CAD Objectives	– system design functions utilised
	  – management
	  – evaluation
	  – drawing
	  – modelling
	– desired pattern of benefits
	  – direct – prod gain
	  – indirect – speed/co-ord/etc.	

Application	– non trivial case – scope re system functions and design/CAD objectives relationship to other design activities – ad hoc or integrated	
Hardware	– resource available – cost	Audit
Software	– range available – system design criteria – acquisition costs or development costs	Audit
Support	– maintenance, user support	Audit
System/User Interface	– record response reliability utilisation cost – CPU Disk I/O " typical working sessions (interaction) Disk Space – numbers of users	CAD Costing System
Users	– skill levels – levels of previous experience – previous training	
Data	– Library information – information development costs – organisation/structure information – manual, automated/CAD library	
Input	– manual information. – relationship to traditional practices.	
Output	– record output – evaluations – drawings schedules – users/relationship to other manual/documentation. – design team.	Log
Organisation	client – fees control – who uses arch – working relations – who supervises project team – responsibilities/roles – procedures	
Project	– overall resources by design stage – programme – monitor design process	
Record	– ease/difficulty in using system. – ease/difficulty in creating/maintaining model and processing. – specific features that seem important.	Office Costing System
PHASE 2 : REVIEW		

Cost Benefit Analysis	– complete analysis of – risks taken
	  – benefits received
	– analyse Productivity Ratios
	  Learning Curves
	– tabulate assumptions re basis economic factors
		Chassen and Dow

Review Performance Against Objectives	– product – service – office cost – CAD cost	
Review System Performance	– reliability – resource budget – programme – relationship to other design activities	
Review Project Performance	– manual + computing	

Note unusual/interesting findings	– efficiency
	– employment
	– organisation/roles/design team working
	– users : skills/stress
	– design process/new tasks/new procedures/
	  new roles
	– product
	– relationships CAD users/design team/
	  client
	– unexpected benefits	

Note lessons learned	– project organisation – office – data – user technique	
Note difficulties still to be resolved	– hardware – software – data – users/user support – organisation – relationships	Log

TABLE 2

Criterion/Issue	OXSYS/BDS	GDS
COMPLETENESS	• 3D but strictly orthogonal. Modelling of function.	• 2D only otherwise full. No modelling of function.
CAPACITY/ROBUSTNESS	• Demonstrated adequate for large projects. • Low redundancy in design representation. • Poor multi-user access. • Reliability high.	• Demonstrated adequate for large projects by others. • High redundancy in design representation. • Good user access. • Reliability high.
PROCEDURAL MODEL, OR DESIGN	• System concepts of zones and components imposed. • No alternative concepts may be implemented eg non-discreet elements. • Design decision sequence imposed by need to define components and data. • System support for design development weak except for handling large bulk of minor amendments.	• System concept of objects imposed but may not be rigorously applied except when convenient. • Any drawn abstraction available for use at user discretion. • No decision sequence implied, however, similar sequence may be expedient. • System support for design development better, earlier manipulation.
INPUT/USER INTERFACE	• Command language powerful but tedious. • Worst feature of development.	• Command language powerful but tedious but with codes an improvement. • Little better as dependent upon EOS implementation.
DB FACILITIES	• Very powerful facilities for handling attribute data and for report generation especially when: 1 integrated with zone system, 2 component property data exploited.	• Good facilities by draughting system standards but poor in relation to BDS.
APPLICATIONS	• Major advantage of modelling approach but most applications lie on professional boundaries. • Extensive facilities, evaluations, detailing, visualisation, schedules. • Further applications possible.	• Visualisation and report generation current applications. • Further applications reply on extensive additional input.

Criterion/Issue Contd...	OXSYS/BDS	GDS
INTEGRITY MAINTENANCE	• Clash checking for components and zones on input. System procedural requirements assist in making model generally accessible and aid updating.	• No system facilities. • Drawings tend to be personal – updates by others less easy and more likely to undermine any structure imposed on drawn information.
	• Multi-user support from system.	• Office or project user practices must be imposed to make multi-user. • For drawn information integrity easily maintained but for reports taken then integrity maintenance difficult with several users and dependent upon agreement on user procedures.
	• For drawn information data integrity easily maintained but for scheduled output integrity maintenance must be provided by user.	
RIGHT CONDITIONS	• Applications dependent upon design team agreement on practices. • Limiting factors curtail pattern of desired benefits. – high indirect benefits – high potential	• Use self-contained. • Limiting factors less critical effect on pattern of potential benefits. – high direct benefits – lower potential
	• Total training/support cost high but may be structured. • Workload low in relation to project cost and peaks.	• Lower total training. • Workload high and reasonably distributed.

TABLE 3 — RIGHT CONDITIONS FOR CAD

GENERAL
- project selection – size and repetitive element
- level of user commitment and technique
- level of user experience and data development
- limited objectives and right conditions
- record rather than develop solution

MANAGEMENT CONTROL
- CAD integral to design organisation
- office and project management control essential pre-requisites

JOB COSTING
- review project costing procedures to monitor re-investment
- determine level of detail required to monitor effects of CAD introduction

CAD COSTING
- cost benefit framework
- determine workstation rates, peak/off-peak, relation to office overheads, target utilisation
- integrate with job and office costing

PLAN OF WORK
- identify new procedures, eg option evaluation room layout documentation, arch/eng drawing co-ordination. Clarify level of service, roles, resources, responsibilities, liabilities, programme and agree conditions and fees
- relationship to other projects and library data development; long term objectives

PROJECT PROCEDURES
- project information structure: primary and secondary; co-ordinating framework for manual and CAD information; CI/SfB, overlays
- drawn information structure: relationship to library data, data standards and structure
- personal information or agreed conventions; updates
- drawing practice; CCPI conventions
- relational information; implied or explicit
- pre-requisites for stage F (STYLES 82)
- handling of 2 records
- agreement on practices, within office, within architect's design team

ORGANISATION/WORKING RELATIONSHIPS
- office structure: number of staff, same or different staff, flatten pyramid
- core teams for CAD and library
- new roles: designer of design systems, db manager/ CAD co-ordinator, systems manager
- design team working; integrated working of design team, review of existing procedures re. co-ordination, agreement on roles, resource allocation and costs and responsibilities for abortive work, local or institutional agreement
- client relationship; improved access to design process, option evaluation, PR

PROGRAMME/RESOURCES
- workstation utilisation and allocation: shift use, available staff, Productivity Ratio on workload, co-ordination with project programme and build up of library data
- form of interaction: designer, system operator or both
- resource management, handling peaks

ACCUMULATION OF USER EXPERIENCE
- user technique: see case studies
  MHDG 8.3 User technique
  Wexham 3.4.1 Preparation of Input
  Wexham 3.5.1 Updates and Procedure
- manage period of transition
- make simple, low boffin factor
- learning completed, data developed over a range of projects

TRAINING
- timing: in relation to production – off peak ; in relation to installation – secure benefits of mature leaving curve
- topics: system operation, system management ; database management, design management
- investment in people, career structures to keep key staff
- staff assignments to maintain fluency

SUPPORT
- hardware and software maintenance agreements
- documentation
- trouble shooting, daily management, security
- professional support

COMPUTER-AIDED DRAFTING
FOR A
MAJOR UK MANAGEMENT CONTRACT

C J Blow
Associate
Scott, Brownrigg & Turner
UK

CAD is responsive by speed, accuracy and consistency to demanding drawing office work schedules. Parallel working of design and construction teams demands simultaneous maintenance of many types of drawings, and demand is accentuated in a management contract. Heathrow Terminal 4, currently under construction and valued at £200 million, has benefitted from CAD.

Chris Blow is Associate responsible for Drawing Office Computer Systems at Scott, Brownrigg and Turner, one of the largest UK architectural practices. He has been concerned with work for the British Airports Authority at Heathrow Airport since 1976 and since 1980 has been responsible for selecting, installing and managing two CAD systems in the practice's Guildford and London offices.

Introduction

This paper is specifically about computer-aided drafting but really it concerns a great deal more than an electronically aided replacement for the conventional drawing board.

Computer-aids can either merely speed up traditional ways of doing things or can actually improve the product or the process by making possible better communications such as could not be achieved conventionally at reasonable cost.

The combination of a basically low-technology industry and large projects with complicated communications patterns offers the opportunity for a major contribution by computer-aids.

Simple Drawings of Three-Dimensional Complexity

The building professions rely upon plans, sections and elevations. Traditionally plans are drawn at one level per floor of the building, with limited use of multiple drawings either redrawn or copied at the appropriate moment to produce ceiling layouts, etc. However, multiple drawings of this sort are costly to change: an amendment on one will affect others which must consequently also be altered by hand. Thus the limitations of traditional drawings militate against efficient communications.

The ideal bridge between design and production in building, long recognised by researchers, is the elemental drawing; one which gives the sub-contractor a diagram of his work area showing what is to be fixed and what it is to be fixed to, eliminating redundant information. The right combination of these elemental drawings needs to be chosen.

A Structured Set of Elemental Drawings

For each level of a normal framed construction building the following related elemental general arrangement plans would need to be maintained simultaneously:

1. Structural framing plans.

2. Superstructure plan: suspended floor or roof.

3. Drainage layout.

4. Superstructure plan: internal and external walls.

5. Wall and floor finishes plan.

6. Ceiling plan.

7. Co-ordinated services (mechanical and electrical comprising heating and ventilating ductwork, piped services and electrical).

These drawings in turn refer to assembly details and a wide range of component schedules as needed by designers, contractors and suppliers.

Parallel working of design and construction teams, and the letting of each elemental contract to a different contractor under the direction of a management contract, accentuates this demand for simultaneous maintenance of drawings.

Heathrow Terminal 4

Improved drawing processes, with elemental drawings and supporting component schedules, have been achieved by Scott, Brownrigg and Turner, a large UK architectural practice, with computer-aided drafting.

The system adopted is GDS (General Drafting System), supplied by Applied Research of Cambridge. The Practice installed two systems in mid 1980 in the London and Guildford offices.

The Guildford system was immediately devoted to architectural work on Heathrow Terminal 4. This project is one of the largest current UK construction projects, valued at £200 million and being built for the British Airports Authority under a management contract.

Detailed design of the project commenced immediately on installation of GDS and all long-life multi-purpose general arrangement drawings have been produced by GDS. Over the intensive period of work of two and a half years up to March 1983, 1500 such drawings were produced in 13,000 workstation hours together with certain component schedules generated automatically from the graphical data. The most important thing is that six types of drawing have been maintained from one co-ordinated set of data. Only one of the seven types of drawing has been maintained separately, due to difficulty in sharing common drawings with structural engineers.

In addition to the principal working drawings, derivatives have been used for both a full planning authority presentation and a public relations exhibition. In co-operation with the British Airports Authority's own Engineering Department, now themselves GDS users, and Consulting Engineers, accurate setting out of roads and aircraft pavements has been incorporated in SBT's architectural drawings for multi-disciplinary use. Tailor-made plots have been supplied to Mechanical Engineers, themselves now GDS bureau-users, for the addition of ductwork layouts, etc. Thus, as well as in speed and accuracy of drawing, collaborating designers have benefitted from CAD. Ultimately teams of designers using the same or compatible systems will reap the full benefit of CAD.

Staff, Training, Management and Team Structure

One keynote of the system from the user's point of view is the fact that it can be, and has been, run by architects with virtually no previous experience of running a computer system. This has the benefit of convenience and economy as well as the concealed benefit, in a non-computer-orientated organisation, of avoiding the tendency to empire-building or elitism.

The wish to avoid elitism and achieve the widest use and application of CAD does not however discourage expertise with CAD. Some members of SBT's team have developed skill with the generation of component schedules and three-dimensioned visualisation, as just two of many adjuncts to the basic drafting system. Others have developed a knowledge of the BASIC language, with the help of personal microcomputers and use self-programmed routines within GDS to speed repetitive work.

Trained architects, who play a co-ordinating role when assembling and developing drawings in GDS, are backed up by assistants. It is SBT's policy to offer training to any member of staff who shows interest. Accepting the cost of this venture as an intrinsic part of practice development, the value of training job leaders and managers in CAD is important in order that the use of its power may be well controlled.

The work on Heathrow Terminal 4 has been done by eight staff, each with a specific role in the team. Members of the CAD team are full members of the project teams as well.

Overall Practice C.A.D. Application

Now, with 25,000 workstation hours and many projects achieved, SBT aims to produce all long life multi-purpose drawings by CAD.

Work is extending into the site analysis and scheme design stage and direct input of survey data is being exploited.

The truly general application of GDS is illustrated by the wide range of drawings produced. 'Quality as well as quantity' was one of SBT's criteria in selecting GDS initially, with infinitely variable line styles and character styles at the designers finger tips as well as the most ambitious geometrical constructions imagineable. One of SBT's GDS drawings was accepted by the Royal Academy Summer Exhibition in May 1982, the first such computer-aided architectural drawing to achieve that distinction.

A Footnote on Equipment

Each system initially had a Prime 150 computer as CPU, with 48 megabytes of storage available for drawings and data and half a megabyte of memory. Peripherals comprised Benson 1322 plotters, Decwriter printer/consoles and one Tektronix 4014 workstation to each system. With two principal offices in London and Guildford, the advantages of SBT of two identical systems lay in the ability to exchange staff, workstations and drawings.

The demand for CAD in SBT's Guildford office has led to the sixfold expansion of the system, while the London Office has similarly expanded to three stations. The Guildford Prime 150 has been upgraded to a 550 and a Benson 36 inch electrostatic plotter added to support the high demand for plotting generated by six workstations.

The CAD systems are complementary to Wang word processing systems and a central Kienzle management accounting system, and links are planned between these systems.

COMPUTER AIDED MODELLING AND EVALUATION IN AN ARCHITECTURAL PRACTICE WITH SPECIAL REFERENCE TO THE SCRIBE SYSTEM

Paul Nicholson
Chapman Lisle Associates
UK

Computer aided architectural modelling and evaluation is a tool for use from the earliest stages in building design and is beginning now to be taken seriously by practice after a decade of incubation in the Universities.

This paper looks at the ideas behind modelling and evaluation, and their introduction in practice. It discusses the value of such tools, their implications for the design team, the client, the architectural process and the product and how future developments might make them even more effective.

<u>Paul Nicholson</u> qualified as an Architect in 1982. He studied at the Polytechnic of the South Bank, London, where he is currently a design tutor and lecturer in CAAD in the Department of Architecture. He is a Project Architect with Chapman Lisle Associates, London, and responsible for implementing CAAD in the office.

INTRODUCTION

There is a healthy scepticism among architects about computer aided architectural design - CAAD. Despite an attitude that computers are wholly numerate, logical and representing the antithisis of creativity and therefore a likely constraint on design freedom, there appears to be more than a casual interest in the application of computer graphics.

This interest might wane were it not for a growing realisation within the profession that the role of the architect as a key figure in the design process is being eroded by the rise and emancipation of the variously disciplined building consultant. Architects can only blame themselves for this situation for in the pursuit of a superficial quality or "delight" they have delegated the design of the substantial "firmness" and "commodity". However, some architects are looking to CAAD as a means of properly handling their recalled responsibilities in an attempt to improve the product and maintain control over the process.

The Problem

The architectural design process is highly complex for it does not have a clearly defined goal. The problem definition proceeds with its attempted solution. Unlike pure engineering, the strictly pragmatic criteria do not dominate the solution. Cultural, contextural and aesthetic criteria are equally important concerns and have as much to do with a balance of expectation with surprise, style and symbolism as with the simple provision and expression of a structure to modify the climate. [1] However, the design of a building is based as much on informed decisions made on measurable or 'quantiative' criteria as from subjective decisions about quality or on 'qualitative' criteria. The complexity results from our lack of understanding of the relationship between building volume, surface area, orientation, solar gain, heat loss, cooling effects, daylighting, sun penetration, noise transfer, climate, altitude and prevailing winds. Banham argues: [2]

> It is probably true that an intelligent commercial glass house operator today, judiciously metering temperature, moisture and carbon dioxide levels in the atmosphere around his out of season chrysanthanums has more environmental knowledge at his finger tips than most architects ever learn.

We cannot be expected to carry in our head an appreciation of the inter-relationships of these concepts but each time we design a building we are making decisions about them based on little more than a hunch or a very naive understanding of their effects.

If architecture is the "modifying interface" between a natural, intrinsic environment and an artificial, imposed environment then it is only reasonable to expect that its behaviour or performance was determined at the design stage. This requires both a quantitative and a qualitative understanding of the problem and therefore the tools to make these clear and aid project development. Without these tools the building is generally not seen as an "environmental modifier", the real modification being achieved by the crude installation of mechanical devices. Indeed consultants are equipping themselves with computers to help solve the problems that architects through their architecture have set them. This is both an uneconomic and undesirable method of working and furthermore results in the unnecessarily profligate consumption of energy.

CAAD can provide the tools for both quantitative and qualitative analysis. Moreover, they can be used at the early design stage where the decisions made about a scheme are usually the most significant [3]. It is usually these initial decisions that the architect may take for himself without realising their full implications.

Timber stage for musical performances. Anniversary exhibition "700 Years of Turko" 1929, by Alvar Aalto.

Architecture as a "modifying interface".

Clearly then the quantitative aspects of design need to be analysed at the early design stage in order that the solution to the client's problem will be an efficient "site modifier" where the relationship between fabric, structure, and layout can provide a "passive" but coarse modification of the site environment and the use of plant to provide "active", fine control.

Modelling

Computer modelling allows the design team to set up a geometric model of the building in the computer. Using various input techniques the three dimensional coordinates of the end points of lines that define the geometry are stored in the computer, translated by the program and displayed as a two dimensional image on the television screen. Since the "model" is three dimensional it is possible to manipulate the image to give any desired projection of all or some of the "building". This is called visualisation. It is extremely useful for allowing a thorough understanding of the building geometry and tends to increase spatial appreciation and stimulates the design process rather than suffocates it. Visualisation also helps in explaining the scheme to those outside the design team and is especially useful when dealing with lay people who find it difficult to interpret conventional orthographic drawings as a three dimensional building.

Evaluation

Once the geometric data is in the computer, the surfaces, planes and volumes may be assigned codes that refer to their non-geometric attributes such as their cost, construction, thermal, acoustic, reflective and structural properties. These are stored in a specification file that is generated separately.

Various programs interrogate the geometric model and the specification file and calculate costs, heat loss, acoustic performance or sun lighting. Indeed any measurable analysis possible on a real building can be mimicked using computer aided evaluation providing:

a) there are prediction and calculation methods available and

b) the specification file has the relevant data.

As the design proceeds, there will be changes to the specification codes and the geometry but the analysis or evaluation programs operate on current data and therefore they can remain pertinent to the scheme throughout the whole design evolution.

Prototypes

What the design team are able to create is a "building prototype". It begins as a coarse, three dimensional idea and is gradually refined as the design process provides more detail. The prototype may include the site, levels, neighbouring buildings, trees and geographical features.

Architectural design must be as much an empirical skill as a studied skill since we can only really learn about the problems by doing, testing, analysing and doing again. The concept of a prototype then, by its definition encourages feedback and analysis.

In evaluating a "prototype" the accuracy and amount of information offered must be relative to the data available for analysis and the level of definition of the geometric model. At the early stages it being necessary to examine overall trends in quantitative criteria whilst much later on a more accurate breakdown of the analysis may be required.

The Role of Micro Computers

The type of computer modelling and evaluation suggested above requires very complex programs. However, it is just this type of modelling that is becoming available on "personal" computers. It is not an indication of the smaller practices clutching at straws or using a crutch to prop up their lack of creativity but an indication of the economics of design aids. If an architect is expected to pay the equivalent of five years salary of an assistant for a useful draughting system he will demand something that makes a very substantial saving in the running costs of his office. Arguments about quality of design are not convincing at this level of cost. If the use of the computer is aimed at improving design quality then the overall costs should be low enough to make the economic considerations of much lower priority [4]. Microcomputers are cheap to buy and cheap to run and therefore they do not require frantic use to remain economic. "Thinking time" can be as productive as "active times" and these should not be squeezed to suit the computer use. Indeed Green considers that the smallness and cheapness of microcomputers is a virtue rather than a handicap.

* * *

SECTION 2

SCRIBE is a micro computer based modelling and evaluation package. It currently runs on the Apple II computer with the option of a high resolution, plug-in board and monitor. The complete system with software would cost under £5,000. An A3 plotter would cost an additional £800-£2,000.

We have had an Apple system in our office for 3 years, for financial administration and word processing. In addition it was decided to investigate the graphics potential of the system, with a view to offering a modelling capability at the early design stage. We finally chose the SCRIBE system, and initially bought the standard resolution modelling package. This seemed to pack a lot of useful programming into a small computer and demonstrated that the micro had a role at the early stage, as a "graphics tool" to augment the traditional drawing board activities. We used it for such tasks as determining the effect of a scheme in relation to its surrounding buildings by modelling the street, and also to help appreciate the scale of a cafetria in a large warehouse project.

Initially though, whilst SCRIBE provided some interest in terms of novelty value, the slow speed of operation and the low resolution, prevented it's enthusiastic use in the office. This was overcome later when we bought, the speeded up, high resolution version, complete with evaluation modules. Since then, we have been using the SCRIBE 3D modelling in practice on several schemes and are currently evaluating the thermal modules.

The 14 programmes in SCRIBE can be divided into 3 groups:-

1)   A 3D spatial modelling package which includes both the building description program and the visualisation programs.

2)   A steady state thermal modelling program which can calculate heat loss and fabric costs.

3)   A dynamic thermal modelling and simulation program for passive solar design modelling.

Whilst each package may be used independently of the others, they are all compatible and can use the same building data base. This is where the benefit of a modelling and evaluation system is really appreciated.

SKETCH TAB

The three dimensional modelling package SKETCHTAB permits the description to the computer of the building. On setting up the screen, it shows a grid of dots and a scale up the left hand side. There are two methods of input:-

a)   games paddles or joystick
b)   graphics tablet

In practice we found the games paddles to be cumbersome and
preferred the use of the graphics tablet. The major advantage being
that a drawing can be "traced off" from it very quickly and
accurately. The scale of the tablet can be adjusted to suit the
drawing. This permits the description of both very large dimensions
and fine detail within the same model, enhancing the actual
resolution of the screen - the model being stored at "full scale".

Initially it is important to decide just how much detail it is
necessary to model. For instance to calculate floor areas or costs
for a feasibility study, it might only be necessary to give external
walls and heights and the major horizontal planes, floors and
roofs. However, for a detailed thermal analysis it would be
important to model all those elements that will have a thermal
effect on the building, dividing it up into zones of differing
temperature, showing the thermally massive elements, glazing, etc.
If visualisation is the main reason for modelling then window
shapes, staircases and even landscaping might be described.

Input

A plan is taped to the graphics tablet and the cursor on the screen
shows the location of the stylus or pen on the tablet. At each line
intersection a code is typed on the keyboard which relates the
graphic element to the specification file. Subsequent lines with
the same specification are entered by placing the stylus on the end
points and pressing the space bar. New lines not connected with old
ones, or with a different specification are given new codes. The
"plan" is rapidly generated in this way. Heights are entered via
the keyboard. Codes less than 70 refer to plane elements which,
given a height, extrude the planes vertically. Differing heights
may be entered individually and the base levels may be changed.
With practice a complicated 3D object can be entered very quickly.
There is also a facility to "recall" a previously "stored" 2 or 3D
element and position it in the new model. Once it is fixed in
position however its subsequent removal or repositioning is more
difficult. At any time hitting H or P on the keyboard will
instantly give a perspective or projection of the 3D image. This
projection can be anything from an elevation to an axonometric,
depending on the coefficient set. These two features allow rapid
appraisal of the 3D model, particularly when checking how much of
the scheme has so far been modelled.

A part of the model can be zoomed in on using the expansion facility
and manipulated very easily. Altering the base levels at which
objects are stored permits the whole model to be stored, but only
those elements in which one is interested need be displayed. This
facility was used to great effect on one sports centre. The project
consisted of the phased demolition of the existing temporary timber

framed huts that made up the club and the phased construction of the
new club buildings. Because of the proximity of new with old
building and the problems of access to each phase, it was decided to
model both the existing huts and the new buildings using SCRIBE and
then selectively display the model to indicate the phasing. This
proved to be particularly useful when explaining to the contractor
the development and how much room he would have for his operations.
The computer modelling took about 90 minutes. Later we developed
each phase as a separate model in order to show more graphic detail
and use as a basis for simple cost and thermal analysis.
Visualisation also permitted the impact of two covered tennis courts
to be assessed from the adjoining housing and using the perspective
drawings produced with the system we could determine the most
suitable shape and colour.

During the "input" of the building any of the visualisation routines
may be used. These are:

    (a)   Perspective and projection with hidden line removal or
          solid modelling - HIDEM

    (b)   successive rotated projections - ROTAB

    (c)   parallel projections as "seen" by the sun - SOLPRO

HIDEM allows full, partial or no hidden line removal and solid plane
modelling. In practice solid modelling can only usefully be used
with a colour graphics system and then the addition of form and
solidity to the geometry significantly aids visualisation. Hidden
line removal is often regarded as an unnecessary luxury since their
removal can be carried out manually by tracing over a wire frame
image, but a complicated image such as SCRIBE might produce on a
monitor is often far clearer when hidden lines have been removed.
The high resolution version also allows 3 point wire frame
perspectives permitting "bird's eye" and "worm's eye" views. In
addition the range of projections from elevation and section to
axonometrics are also possible with hidden line removal. Together
with plan viewing this makes orthographic projections from the 3D
model an extremely simple operation. This implies a 3D to 2D
draughting capability but in practice the amount of information
conveyed by most orthographic drawings is beyond the scope of this
system. However, these "drawings" can form the starting point for
draughting packages. Indeed, SCRIBE, includes a 2D drawing program
which allows any projected image to be developed and annotated.
These can then be saved for either printing on a dotmatrix printer
or better, "drawn" on a plotter. In practice A3 sketch scheme
drawings are very common. It is the finiteness of a plotted image
that some architects object to while a coarse dotmatrix image
appears transient and capable of evolution.

ROTAB rotates the building model in increments of angle displaying successive perspectives. The height and angle can be specified. The facility is most effective with a simplified model so that the image is not too confusing. It is an interesting distraction to have at project meetings but it has a real value in that it encourages a 3D understanding of the building that many clients claim they do not possess until they walk in the front door on the first day of occupation.

SOLPRO is similar to ROTAB except that it mimics a heliodon. It produces successive parallel projections of the building as the sun would "see" it throughout the day. The program requires to know the time interval, the date, latitude and orientation so that it can calculate the locus of the sun and then project from it. This is particularly useful for examining the shading effects of nearby structures and planting. On the Maldon sports centre we used this routine to determine the most effective location for a sun terrace and pool glazing in relation to the other sports volumes. It also helped us determine the height of planting required to provide visual privacy from a car park but solar penetration the scheme. The surrounding objects and planting were diagrammatically modelled using SKETCHTAB and therefore included in the projections.

SPECALC

The second module in SCRIBE is the steady state thermal modelling and cost package - SPECALC. It is more efficient and accurate to use this package after using SKETCHTAB to define the building. SPECALC can then interrogate the building data automatically to derive the quantities for subsequent calculation and evaluation. For this reason it is imperative that if the evaluation routines are to be used the various rules affecting how elements are coded during their input are rigourously adhered to. Codes are divided up into three groups for calculation purposes.

a)   Those defining mass elements and whose various properties such as capacitance and cost are derived from their volume.

b)   Those defining vertical planes and whose parameters are derived from their areas.

c)   Roofs and sloping planes where the volume or area may be computed depending on their 3D geometry.

There are also rules regarding the allocation of codes to elements at differing locations, orientations and within other codes, for example - windows in walls.

After listing all the building data a summary is produced giving a total area or volume for each code used. This is followed by the definition of costs and "U" values for each code. The cost figure has to be chosen carefully. Although an element might refer to an external wall its associated cost must include all those components of the wall that might attract a cost. For example, a wall might comprise:

a)   Aluminium cladding   @   £^{w}/m2
b)   Insulation   @   £^{x}/m2
c)   150mm Blockwork   @   £^{y}/m2
d)   2 coats emulsion paint @   £^{z}/m2

Therefore, total cost for code = £w+x+y+z/m2 or for mass elements a cost/m3.

It is not that costs should be accurate but should be relatively accurate to each other so that cost comparisions between different schemes will be based on the same assumptions. After some research it was decided that the measured rates in the Cost Datafile's provided the best guide to item prices. Specialist items such as patent glazing require specialist quotations. We are currently building up a standard specification file of commonly used materials which includes thermal properties and cost. These is no provision within SCRIBE for calculating "U" values so hybrid composites need evaluating separately using their thickness, resistivity and a calculator.

Further information required by SPECALC includes ventilation rates and clarification of the disposition of coded elements relative to each other and the external area. Output consists of:-

a.   the total heat loss/hour/^{o}C
b.   the total heat loss/24 hours/^{o}C
c.   the gross loss/hour/20°C (hourly heating load including ventilation loss)

d.   total cost
e.   total cost/m2

It is a simple procedure to change the data including the building model and run the program again. The benefit of having a direct relationship between building model, material properties and costs means that the "what if" approach to design is a powerful raison d'être.

We have used these analyses in researching the effects of using alternative materials in terms of cost and thermal performance, sizing a heating system and comparing volume shape to cost and performance. Output figures should be regarded in relation to the building models that they refer to. While their accuracy appears finite, they can only be as accurate as the model that represents reality.

SPIEL

The final module in SCRIBE is based around a multi-node dynamic thermal simulation program. This permits an accurate thermal analysis of special passive solar elements such as trombe walls and conservatories. However, it can also be used to provide a more rigorous thermal analysis of conventional structures. By taking into account solar radiation, orientation, latitude and heat transfer within the building including occupancy gains, a much more detailed picture of the thermal behaviour of the building and the specific effects of such elements as rooflights and shading devices can be determined.

For use of this module to be effective, there is a lot of data required. The building can be divided in up to ten nodes or heated spaces and their characteristics and relationships described. Glazings are given particular attention, their orientation, amount of shading and the associated internal absorbances given in order that incident solar radiation and consequent gains can be included in the calculations.

Satisfactory use of this module is dependent on a thorough understanding of the building and an accurate model of it which includes all those elements that will have a thermal effect. These include the thermally "massive" and the thermally "minimal" elements.

We have used this module to explore the design of a shading system for south-east facing glazing on a swimming pool. It was a trial and error process - suggesting a system, modelling it, testing it and altering it and at the same time being able to assess visually the implications including its appearance from inside and outside.

Conclusions on Using SCRIBE

Visualisation with SCRIBE is proving extremely useful and use tends to generate further ideas for use. Familiarity with the thermal modules is bringing confidence in their use and encourages an empirical understanding of the scheme. When this "quantitative" understanding is matched by the qualitative appreciation through visualisation the resulting knowledge about the project must help in its subsequent development.

Using SCRIBE in the office has borne out our expectations of modelling on a micro computer. It is an excellent "tool kit" for use on feasibility studies and small jobs where a "tool" is required to help solve a problem. As a tool kit is does not make any real claim to replace the drawing board but rather augment the traditional skills alongside it.

* * *

SECTION 3

SCRIBE and Beyond

SCRIBE was initially developed to model passive solar designs and predict energy consumption and thermal behaviour in buildings. Typical of simulation programs it requires a lot of data to be reliable and useful and at the early design stage this might prevent it from being used more effectively. Default values do not help as they serve to devalue the real data. Further the many tables, results and summaries obtainable from evaluation routines have to be carefully interpreted before taking "what if" action.

If information on thermal behaviour was presented graphically, many trends could be examined simultaneously. If this were possible during graphic and/or parameter manipulation then it would provide truly interactive feedback.

This suggests simulation with a degree of optimisation. Simulation with numerical output has its role but it must not suffocate design exploration, knowledge and understanding must not be confused with information. A degree of optimisation will surely encourage and to some extent stimulate design exploration.

Modelling and evaluation techniques promote a new outlook on the way buildings should be designed, by understanding where and how energy is consumed we can begin to investigate ideas for "energy harvesting". Further, innovation and conceptual leaps need not be suffocated by these processes, indeed innovation comes from a thorough examination of the problem and a freedom of though applied to its solution.

The architect's ability to both qualitatively and quantitatively evaluate a scheme at the early stages in design places the role of his consultants in a different light. With a knowledge of the general principles involved he can test his building prototype and develop an insight into the inter-disiplinary relationships between structure, environment, fabric and form. It follows that interaction with his consultants must be on a qualitative level. This faces the consultants with a tremendous challenge, their role being based more on developing a conceptual and strategic dialogue with the other members of the design team and less concerned with tactics and quantitative aspects as formerly. Far from computers eroding the already fragile position of the architect they may just be their salvation. On the other hand it is the subjective, qualitative role of our variously disciplined consultants that is going to be their saving grace, not their ability to crunch numbers.

Futures

SCRIBE packs a lot of power into a small computer and already it and its rivals are causing us to at least think about designing differently. This is surprising because despite its sophistication it still represents the model 'T' Ford in the development of CAAD. Developments must be directed to improving the interaction with the building model before increasing the sophistication of the model analyses.

Artificial intelligence must hold the key to improved interaction with the building model, this will enable a dialogue in the architect's graphic language not the computer's graphic language to be developed. Once this has been established then the frontiers of CAAD development can be properly pushed forward. Coupled with this must be a new initiative in humane interface design. The keyboard and its associated tablet and VDU are ergonomically cumbersome and interactively hostile combination. Ruffle has dispensed with the keyboard in his highly "friendly" Perspective Programme. This must mark the trend towards better interfaces.

Finally

I do not believe, as an architect, that it is possible to hold an opinion on the role of CAAD without an opinion on the design and nature of architecture. Architectural design in the end still comes down to good designers and bad designers whether they happen to be sitting in front of drawing boards or digitisers. But in the schools of architecture there is a growing awareness that an informed quantitative debate produces confidence in the students and leads to a more serious debate on the qualitative issues. This, I submit, is the most significant implication of CAAD - the ability to help clarify the design problem and stimulate research in the design process towards a general improvement in the product.

REFERENCES

1.   Hutt, Barry, 'The place and nature of environmental evaluation in a computer aided building design system', thesis for Master of Engineering, University of Liverpool, November, 1975.

2.   Banham, Rayner, 'The Architecture of the Well Tempered Environment', Architectural Press, London, 1969.

3.   Anson, M. and Fuller, R.S. 'Evaluating Building Alternatives at the Planning Stage'. Build International, 8. 1975. Applied Science Publishers Ltd, England, 1975.

4.   Green, Cedric, 'Three dimensional and thermal modelling of passive solar buildings on graphic microcomputer systems', working paper, Ecotecture Group, Department of Architecture, University of Sheffield,1983.

CAD IN THE LARGE PRACTICE

Richard Griffin
Associate
YRM Architects & Planners
UK

This text briefly describes how YRM uses its CAD system to enhance the architectural and engineering services it provides on its projects.

It covers the CAD system we have and how we use it and describes the assembly of data to provide drawings for a major project.

Richard Griffin is an Associate of YRM Architects and Planners, London. As an architect he is project manager for a District General Hospital now under construction in Hackney. He is responsible for the Intergraph CAD system at YRM and was closely involved in its selection and implementation. He studied at the Architectural Association in London and joined YRM in 1970. His recent experience with CAD at YRM includes work at Gatwick Airport, Qaboos University in Oman and Homerton Hospital in London.

Introduction

We have been using our in-house CAD system since February 1982.
Before then we used bureau services to assist with the production
of design and contract drawings on several major projects in the UK
and overseas.

The following description of our system and how we use it relates
particularly to our basic 2D graphics work. The majority of this type
of work is done during the detail design and production drawing
stages of projects. We use our system in both 2D and 3D but currently
only use 3D for more detailed studies. The 3D facility which we have
provides 'full 3D' surfaces modelling with full perspective hidden
line removal and shading. The 2D system is sophisticated and easy-
to-use, providing all of the facilities we require for accurate and
coordinated 2D drawings.

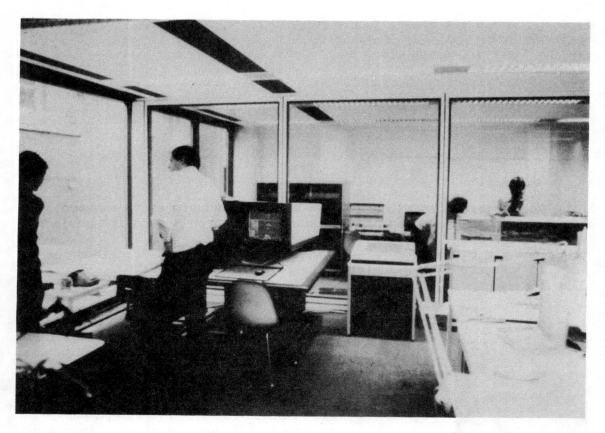

YRM's System

We have an Intergraph CAD package based on the VAX 11/750 cpu which
comprises 5 graphics workstations, 4 alphanumeric terminals, an A3
electrostatic hard copy unit and an A0 electrostatic plotter.

Input:
The graphics workstations have dual raster screens and can display up
to eight views of a design file simultaneously. In 2D work, this
facility allows both general and detail views to be displayed
simultaneously, without the need to update frequently the general view.
Zoom and pan facilities allow fast review and comfortable searches
of data. In 3D work the dual screens are normally set up to display
a plan and two or more elevation views and one whole screen is
reserved to display isometric or perspective views. The system is
substantially menu-driven with both on-screen and tablet menus
available. These can be developed to suit particular projects or
applications. The command structure, as presented to the workstation
user, is simple and easy to use, being controlled by a cursor pad.
This unit also controls the cursor cross (or data point) on the
screen. The unit provides an extremely 'friendly' interface with the
machine and all our workstations are located in normal open plan
office areas.

workstation   cursor and menu

Storage:
Requirements for data storage vary from project to project. We
currently use two 300 mb disc-drives for the bulk of our 'live' storage.
Backup and archiving is carried out on tape.

hard copy unit   AO plotter

Output:
Instantaneous 'hard copy' is available from the centrally located
A3 plotter. Scale plots up to AO size are available from the AO
plotter. Once a first plot is set up, further copies can be produced
in minutes.

Alphanumeric data can also be printed out on a fast dot-matrix
printer which doubles as the system console. Letter quality printing
is produced on a daisy-wheel printer.

Software:
The software we are currently using is in four parts; Graphics,
Database, Word Processing and Thermal Analysis. The first two are
standard Intergraph products and can be developed and linked to
provide graphic and non-graphic data, specifications and schedules.
The others are 'third-party' software packages run on the VAX and
using separate terminals. The ability to run such software at the
same time as running graphics and without interfering with the
standard operating system has proved to be important. Many other
applications packages are available, both within the Intergraph
environment and from other sources. These include Digital Terrain
Modelling, Structural Analysis, Building Services packages and many
others. Currently, our graphics requirements are provided for
by the basic Interactive Graphics package. However, we are developing
higher levels of this to provide for our particular applications.

Using the System

Apart from the central processor room, which is separated from the
open office area by an acoustic screen, the system and its terminals
are distributed around the office and integrated with project team
areas.

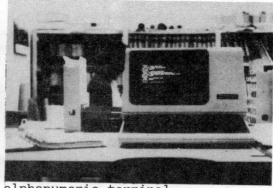

graphics workstation   alphanumeric terminal

Training:
Initially, training was given to six people and lasted one week.
These people were selected from one project team, Gatwick Airport,
and were heavily involved in the development of graphics standards
and a general graphics database. We had no previous experience
of CAD in-house and deliberately set out to develop working methods
to suit our own needs. We did not purchase an 'architectural'
system.

We have now trained some 40 architects and engineers; that is almost
one quarter of our professional staff. In-house training in basic
2D graphics now takes about 1½ days. Work on live projects, in
teams already using CAD, starts immediately after training.

Once the basic concepts such as 'design file', 'command menu' and
'data point' are understood, the system relies only upon simple
English language. Some terms such as 'cell', meaning graphics
component, have been chosen by Intergraph to avoid conflict with the
vocabulary of disciplines other than architecture. However, users
very soon become acquainted with such oddities.

Manuals:
Since Intergraph rely on the basic VAX (VMS) operating system, the
comprehensive manuals on running a VAX system are available to the
System Manager. The manuals necessary for reference at workstations,
though less complex, are comprehensive. However, it is very rarely
necessary to refer to either set of manuals unless complex routines
or development of the system are being undertaken. Individual
project teams using the CAD system develop their own 'user handbooks'.
These are developed in conjunction with the System Manager to ensure
that general office standards are represented.

System Management :
We do not employ any specialist computer staff and have drawn the
few 'experts' that we have from our architectural staff. We have
always believed that the system should be driven by its application
and not vice-versa. However the System Manager role has been
developed and is filled by an architect who, having worked for some
time with the system on a project, developed an interest in a more
central role. Apart from being responsible for the day-to-day
running of the system, he has obtained more detailed training in
programming and database management and has specific interests in
developing the system.

File Structure :
The 'design file' structure necessary to the operation of the system
can be compared with any carefully organised correspondence filing
system. Owners of files, or 'project sets' of drawings, have
certain privileges to access such files. The files are protected
in such a way that they cannot be inadvertantly damaged or read
by the wrong person. This normally allows only the 'creator' of a
file, or set of drawings, to read, write,execute or delete a particular
file. The project team with whom he works will normally have access
rights to that same file but only to read it. Even this access can
be restricted and the system is protected by a comprehensive User
Identifications Code format with passwords known only to individual
users.

Setting up Files :
When setting up files for a project the team members who will
use the system are first described to the system by 'Username' and
'Password'. They are also allocated a code, usually the project's
job code, which will allow them direct access to the files of that
particular project without having to tell the system such details
every time they 'log on'.

The design files required for a particular job must be put into a
directory. When this directory has been set up, every new file
created will automatically be added to that directory. Files are
classified by the 'device' name of the particular disc drive on
which the project is to reside, an identification code the same as
that of the users of the file, the name of the file and a convention
representing its type.

Once the two elements of the file structure, (the users and the files)
are set up, the detail of the coding and structure are 'transparent'
to the users.

Assembly of Data

The illustrations in the remainder of this paper have been selected
from our early work on production drawings for Gatwick Airport North
terminal. To ensure maximum clarity at such a small scale, the
examples shown are deliberately simple.

The illustrations below show typical design files 'merged' to permit
a combined 'plot' or drawing. The left hand illustration shows the
whole area of one level of the pier structure. The right hand
illustration shows the terminal building design file attached to it
as 'reference' file.

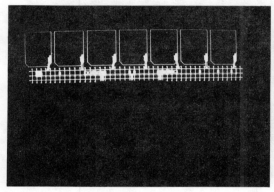
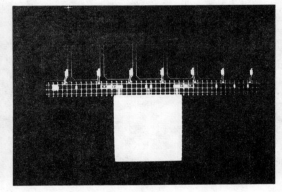

pier   pier and terminal

The system permits one active file to be worked on while up to three
'reference' files are attached, for display or plotting. We use the
reference file system on projects where other disciplines are producing
their drawings on the system. Files are created for each discipline;
structure, fabric, services, drainage. 'Write access' is assigned
only to the appropriate discipline. The files can then be used as
reference to each other and to produce coordinated drawings.

The illustrations below show parts of the same design file used to
produce drawings of progressively larger scale. The 'design plane'
or total design area, in 2D, would extend 43 kilometres in x and y
if a resolution or accuracy of 1 to 1/100 of a millimetre were
required. Working units can be set up to allow greater accuracy or
larger design areas.

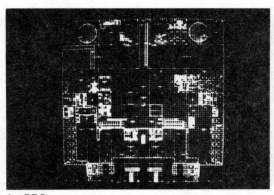

1:250

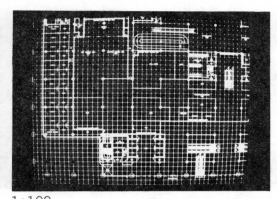

1:100

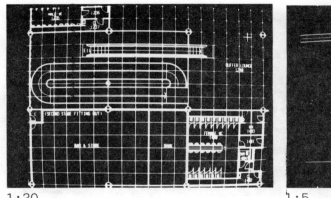

1:20

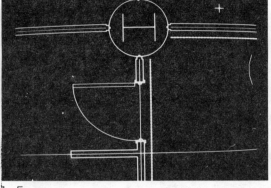

1:5

In these illustrations, the same level of detail has been drawn
consistently over the whole building to allow drawings of very large
scale to be extracted from one design file. Clearly, this level of
detail or accuracy will not necessarily be required on some projects.
However, the CAD system allows it and designers will naturally tend to
use it.

'Overlay' drafting :
The Intergraph system allows information to be shown on any of 63
'levels' within the same design file or drawing. Using 'reference
files' 252 levels can be developed. In practice this technique
is similar to 'overlay' drafting and has the profound advantage
over the 'root negative' system in that the assembled 'levels', or
layers, can be individually modified and the whole assembly of levels
're-assembled' at will.

In the case of location plans, the levels are assigned to specific
items of information. For example, the first few levels carry
grids and their reference, the next carry structure, the next external
and internal walls, and so on. The levels can be 'switched' on and
off to make up location plans for various purposes. Any up-dating
necessary can be carried out only on the level affected and the whole
design plane reassembled. This system can be readily understood by
users and compared with existing drawing methods.

Graphics Techniques :
Lines, circles, arcs and other geometrical shapes, including pre-drawn
symbols and lettering, are placed on the 'design plane' using
accurate placement methods. They can be input as x and y (and z, in 3D)
coordinate references related to real (full size) dimensions. However,
they are usually placed by moving the 'data point' or cursor on the
screen and using reference grids and dimensional 'locks' to correct
errors from free-hand use of the cursor. They can be locked
to positions, angles or levels and to objects already placed on the
design file or reference file. A chair could be placed on a setting
out grid. A light fitting could be placed on a grid and in the correct
relationship with a ceiling tile on a 'reference file'.

Graphics Libraries :
Pre-drawn graphic objects or 'cells' are stored in libraries and
retrieved by code or by selection from an on-screen menu using the
cursor. The illustrations below show part of a typical library and a
cell from it.

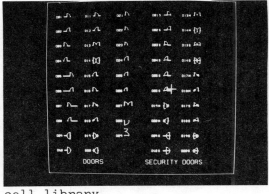 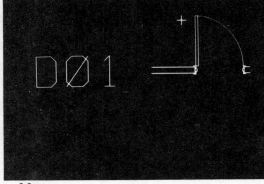

cell library   cell

Cells are placed by their pre-defined origins onto the level on which
they were created or on to any other level if required. They are
created on any of the 63 levels available and can contain different
graphics at each level for different purposes. For example, the
illustrations below show how a door symbol can be constructed as a
'multi-level' cell to provide different graphics at floor and ceiling.

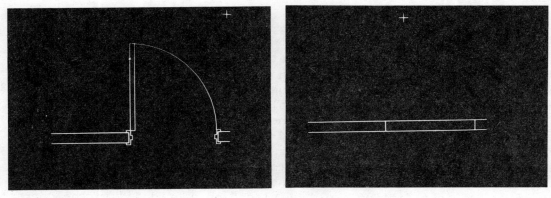

door at floor   door at ceiling

A complete 'design file' will be made up of many 'multi-level cells'
each of which will have been placed only once. As different levels are
switched on or off the appropriate graphics for the various symbols
will automatically appear.

Assembly of Drawings :

Final prints or plots are made up by extracting the required section
of the design file together with any reference files and placing it in a
separate 'issue' file. The appropriate structural grid and other
information common to several drawings is attached from further reference
files. The following illustrations show the various components as they
are assembled to produce the final drawing :

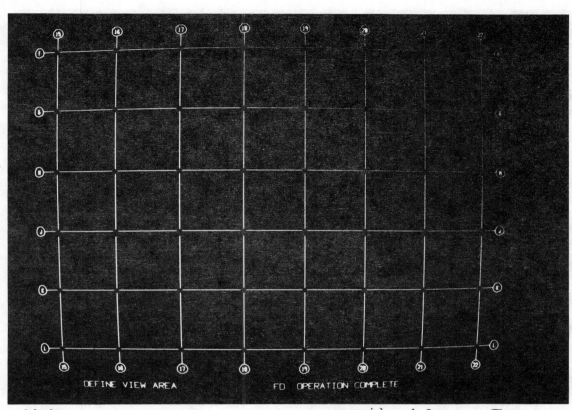

DEFINE VIEW AREA   FD OPERATION COMPLETE

grid ▲   grid and frame   ▼

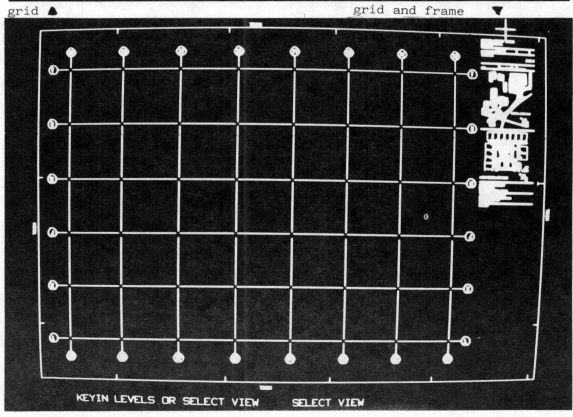

KEYIN LEVELS OR SELECT VIEW   SELECT VIEW

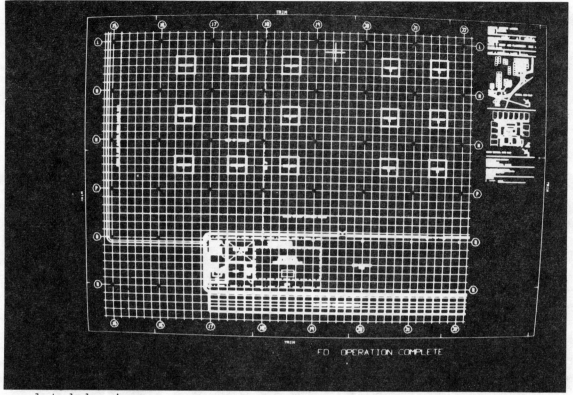

completed drawing

The 'empty' title block is retrieved with the drawing frame and a particular level of it filled out to form the completed title block :

empty title block   completed title block

The completed title block is built up using the various layers in a separate file called 'drawing' which is then attached to the 'issue' file. This assembled 'file' is then plotted by completing a standard 'Plot Request Form' which is then sent to the plotter.

The entire procedure is 'menu-driven' and can be varied to suit
different applications or projects. Initial plots take about 20 minutes
to set up and produce. Subsequent plots from the resultant 'spool' file
can be produced in one or two minutes.

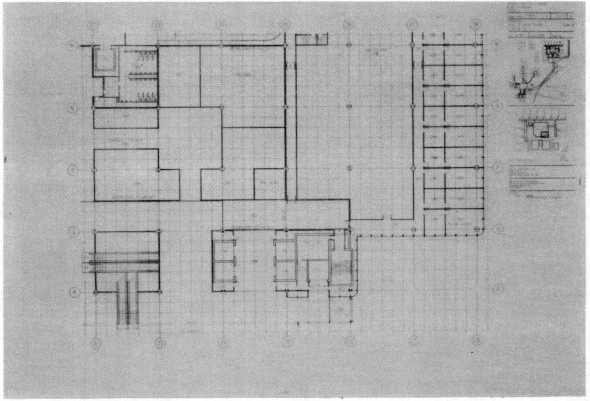

completed plot

The completed plot above was taken at an early stage of the project.
The two illustrations which follow show a developed floor plan
of the same area and a coordinated ceiling plan of that area produced
using reference files containing ceiling and lighting information.

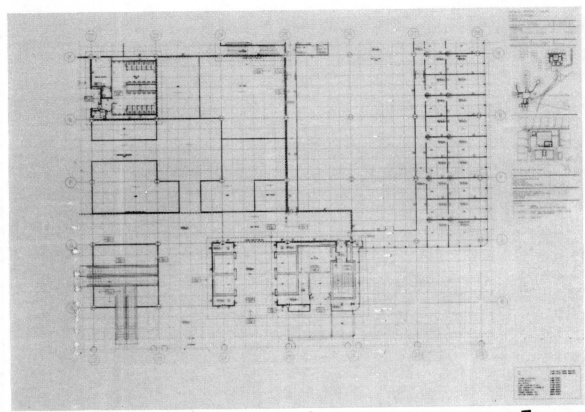

developed floor plan ▲

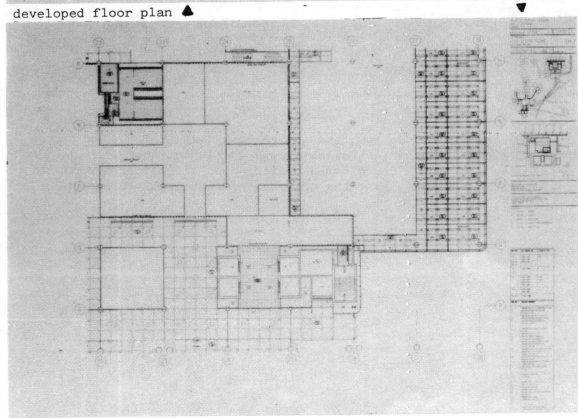

Design files and completed plots are stored on disc for live access during design work and on tape for archive purposes. Some of our clients also require negatives of plots to be stored in their 'mechanical' form.

tape safe

plan can

Conclusion:

Finally, it must be stressed that this paper describes only the basic methods behind a very sophisticated information medium.

We have achieved and improved on all those manual techniques we wished to emulate using CAD. Our analysis of the system's performance has shown it to be fast, efficient and cost-effective. As we become more and more proficient at the basic methods, we naturally wish to progress to more complex applications so that the service we can offer is further enhanced by the medium available.

IMPLEMENTION EXPERIENCES OF DESIGN APPLICATIONS

L Kraal
Data Processing Manager
EGM Architects
Netherlands

The introduction of the computer as an aid in the design process will enable the architect to act as all-round coördinator in the collection, management and employment of all necessary data. For every step in that process computer programs will be required.
GOAL, by ABACUS, is such a computer program, developed for use in the early stages of the design.
The selection, implementation, adaption and introduction of GOAL within EGM Architects in the Netherlands is here described and some experiences of practical use are presented.

Leen Kraal is Data Processing Manager at EGM Architects in the Netherlands. Originally he was a building technician within the EGM organisation, but when in 1975 the need arose for computer knowledge within the practice, he was re-educated as a specialist in this field to fulfill that requirement. Since then he has combined his experience as building technician and computer expert in order to develop or implement a wide variety of packages on the EGM computer.

1.   EGM's philosophy for computer-use

1.1. The role of the architect

The architect has a very important role in the design process, which is often very complex. The job of an architect itself has become more complicated over the years, but the knowledge required to perform the task has remained at the same level.

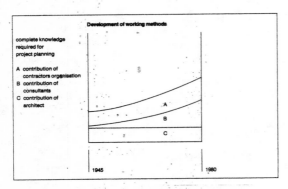 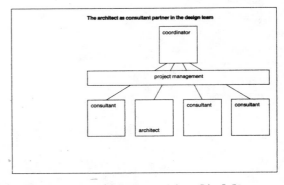

This is partly reflected in the existence of specialists in fields that formerly were part of the expert-tasks of the architect. These include such as, quantity surveying, structural engineering, environmental engineering etc.

Before an architect can take responsibility for the design and realise the design within the limits of the project budget, he has to be at the centre of the information-processing for as many disciplines of the design-team as possible.
This can not be achieved without a great deal of effort. Therefore it is necessary that the architect takes care of this development in order to achieve the necessary standard of knowledge required for this job. The introduction of the computer as an aid in the design process will enable him to develop this knowledge and accept the role of all-round coördinator.

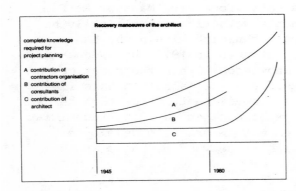 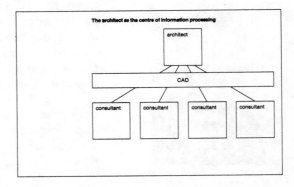

1.2. Clarification of procedures

In order to control the quality of the design process it is absolutely necessary to make obvious the steps within the process. Every specialist or consultant requires to know what is expected of him and when. Also the sources of data and the relations between the several types of data need to be clarified.

1.3. The quality of the information

The processing of information during the design process is often careless. The result is that solutions are developed upon the basis of incomplete and inaccurate information. This leads quite often to a tremendous waste of time, both for client and architect.

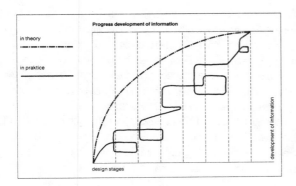

Although the design procedures for most projects are basically the same, architects somehow seem to be unaware of that fact. His work consists for a great deal of the processing of information. Studies within EGM have proved that especially the processing of information during design consists of 80% of routine actions. From this the conclusion can be drawn that the work can be systematised to a high degree.

1.4. The use of computers in the design process

It will be clear, that the use of a computer in the collection, management and employment of all the necessary data is inevitable. The computer can be used either to improve the quality of the design or to increase the productivity of the design office. Within EGM we concentrated upon the former although we expect that the introduction of the computer as a drafting aid, in our case, is within the immediate future.

2.   In search of a program

2.1. The need for a design aid

About 4 years ago EGM received the commission for the design of a new
University Hospital. Although we had experience in the design of
general hospitals, we considered this commission as an extraordinary
task, given the complexity and size of such a project. At that time we
began to consider the introduction of the computer as an aid in the
early stages of the design process.

2.2. The feasibility study

A committee was formed consisting of designers, technicians and myself
as a representative from the computer department. This committee
started out to set the objectives for both the selection of the
program and of the feasibility study itself. From the beginning it was
clear that such a program would be far too complex to develop ourselves.
At that time we were introduced to ABACUS by one of our colleagues who
happens to be a Scottish architect graduated from Strathclyde
University in Glasgow, and who was familiar with ABACUS. He introduced
us to the Markus/Maver model of the design process, which appealed to
us as being very practical and sympathetic to the principal that the
design process is considered a process of an interactive nature.

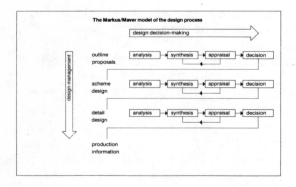

In addition we were confronted by another well-known model, in which
we could confirm that the most important decisions are taken in the
very early stages of the design process but very few resources
applied.

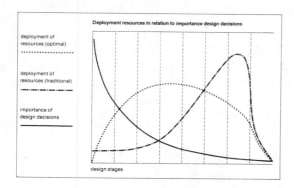

Both models were adopted by the committee as the basis for further investigations. Within the models we found a very pragmatic approach to the design process. We considered both models as being clear, very natural and self-evident.

Although we had a very quick look at a few other systems, in practice we concentrated upon those of ABACUS. In the end we decided to select GOAL and BIBLE as a basis for our own developments.
GOAL is a computer program to be used at the early stages of the design of a building. It presents detailed analyses of spatial, functional, environmental and economical performances.
BIBLE enables the user to view a building design in perspective or in parallel projection on a display terminal or to produce plots of selected views.
Our interest in ABACUS also attracted us to HELP and SPACES2, although I must say these in fact helped us to the extent in making our choice easier.

Now, $2\frac{1}{2}$ years after the decision was taken, we are able to evaluate our cooperation with ABACUS. We had, and still have, a lot of questions and demands, some rather naive in the beginning and some very valuable. We overestimated the responsiveness of such a scientific institute as ABACUS. We expected that when an error was found in the software they would immediately respond with a proper correction.
This turned out to be untrue. Once a computer program is developed it appears that the scientist loses interest in that particular program; the problem is solved, the challenge met. However, this does not imply that in practice the program will fulfil its requirements. Although a program which is tested during development and appears to be alright, it may still contain errors when it is used in practice.
Perhaps these errors are no longer really interesting from a scientific point of view, but if the scientific institute sells the software in practice, it must be aware that the required software quality has to be of a higher standard than when it is only used for research.

Therefore the institute should try to gain as much information as possible from the results with practical use, in order to improve the quality of the software and as such also to improve the quality of its teaching aids.

Of course both ABACUS and EGM had to get used to a coöperation between science and practice and it took some time before it was clear what we could expect from each other, eventually resulting in a good partnership.

3.   Evaluation of the implementation process

3.1. Implementing the software

Implementing software on a computer which is not of the same type as the one for which the software was developed is not an easy task. Conversion in general is an activity which costs always more time than was predicted. We decided for several reasons, to convert the software not only to make it run on our computer but also to convert it from FORTRANIV to FORTRAN77.
The lack of experience with FORTRAN in our office at that time created quite a few problems. But with the assistance of ABACUS we were able to solve a lot of these problems within a reasonable period of time.
A lot of time was lost due to a poor quality of the FORTRAN77 compiler on our computer at that time, which contained several bugs. After having received a new version several months later, most of these problems were corrected and thus we were able to do the programming more efficiently.

3.2. Performance tests

The next thing we ran into was the impractical way some program routines were written or the way in which some problems were solved within the software. A lot of routines were written by students who had no idea as to the real requirements in practice.

Another inconvenience we discovered was the time needed to run the programs. It is a fact that a DEC10 is a much larger machine than a Burroughs B1800, and it is also a fact that ABACUS had never used large projects for testing as we had in practice. Therefore we had no idea what to expect of run-times, once we were able to use the program. During the first test-runs with big geometry files, we were shocked by the amount of time necessary to perform certain calculations. It took us several weeks to optimize the program to run faster.

A very annoying aspect was the amount of internal memory required to
store the data in. For example we were not able to store all relevant
geometry data of the University Hospital at one time in internal
memory. Partly this was due to the computer we used at that time, and
partly to the way in which the geometry is described in GOAL.

The typical hardware constraints we met were solved at the beginning
of 1983 when the B1800 with 512 KB of internal memory was replaced by
a B5900 which is about 6 times faster and has 3 MB of internal memory.

3.3. Updates and new versions of GOAL

As early as at the time of our selection of GOAL, we made an agreement
with ABACUS to extend its possibilities.

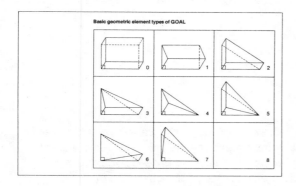

The most important of these was the extension of the number of
different geometrical shapes and the possibility to display functional
lay-outs of floor-plans including polygons.

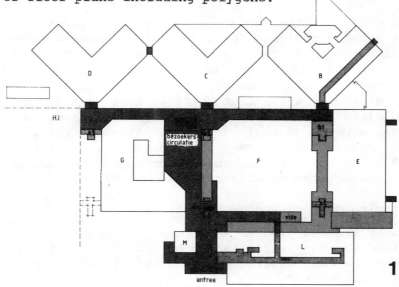

While ABACUS was developing these features we decided to implement the version which was available at that time to allow a start in testing and to gain some experience. While half-way through the implementation of that version, we received an intermediate version from ABACUS. Immediately we started to implement that version and thus more or less forgot the objectives of achieving a test-version as soon as possible. Later we found that this was a mistake.

When finally testing the graphic manipulation section of GOAL we were not satisfied with the results and the quality of the software. This led to the decision to rewrite that part of GOAL ourselves because ABACUS had no resources to do so. Although this cost a lot of extra time, we found the effort very worth while. We learned a great deal of how graphics can be manipulated and how GOAL was built. In the end we were able to look through GOAL and extend its possibilities with hardly any effort. At the end of everything, our GOAL, as it runs on our computer now is a mixture of ABACUS software and EGM-experience.

4.   Evaluation of the introduction process

4.1. Differences in education

Even working the way we do at EGM, where we try to involve the users during the design, development and implementation of systems right from the beginning, we met a lot of opposition when we started to introduce the new tools to the architects. We thought that, like ourselves, the architects would become enthusiasts when they learned what the possibilities of the program were, but it turned out to be very difficult to explain to the architects the real purpose of GOAL. In our opinion this is for a great deal due to differences in education between British and Dutch architects.

We have found that in the education in the Netherlands there is too much emphasis being put upon the design in the narrow sense of the word; the elevations and the layouts. As soon as Dutch architects have to look at the more technical aspects of their design they become less interested. It takes some time and a lot of discussion before they become gradually aware that there is more to a design than only layouts and elevations. More and more they understand that looking at the technical aspects of their design is basically not a new idea, but that it is something they always do intuitively. By using design aids such as GOAL, however they are able to do so more objectively, more accurately, more systematically and more quickly.

4.2. Introducing GOAL to the architects

GOAL is a very complex program and therefore hard to explain in a short session. You can tell a lot about it and demonstrate it even a few times but the real understanding comes through effective use.

So we thought it would be a good thing to carry out a few experiments and report the results in order to give the architects real insight to the possibilities of GOAL.

Whatever we tried, we did not succeed. The designers were repelled by the, for them, unknown aspects covered by GOAL and for which they had to gather basic data, for instance for the environmental performances. So they used only the graphics module of GOAL and thus not using the program any further than area and volume calculations.

The reactions were enthusiastic, but they were only enthusiastic about the very sophisticated and spectular way in which they had carried out their usual job.

Again and again during meetings, tests, try-outs etc., we found that the objectives of GOAL were greatly misinterpreted. We discovered that the designers started to see GOAL as a burden which made their job more complex instead of easier.

4.3. Technical analysis of GOAL

We decided therefore to do an objective study and prove on paper that GOAL was really a very useful tool to be used for almost every design. The study was carried out by technicians from the staff-group and, perhaps not so surprisingly, the results of the study were exactly the opposite of the results of the experiment carried out by the designers. The technicians hardly noticed the graphic manipulation but concentrated entirely on the energy and cost calculations. Their conclusion was that GOAL was meant to determine the influence of energy costs on the total running costs. They concluded that, even the parts of GOAL which did not appear to have anything to do with energy, still were intended as basic data for the energy calculations. However, GOAL was still regarded by them as a very useful tool, despite its few shortcomings.

After this exercise the managements' reaction was one of dismay, if that really was all there was to GOAL, then a big mistake had been made. Very intense discussions have taken place since then. Eventually, everybody agreed that GOAL was the major tool for the architect to use in future design.
A working committee was formed to function as an interface between the users and the computer department. The committee also started to develop a workshop for the architects to teach them the use of GOAL in practice.

4.4. Workshops

In the workshops which require 4 sessions, we work with groups consisting of 4 or 5 architects.
In the first session we introduce them to the hardware and to GOAL. We also present them with a brief for a small project, a sports centre, and ask them to make a sketch design before the next session.

In the second session we ask each of them to give us an impression of the design he or she has made. Then we go to the CAD room and digitise the design as input within a few minutes and type in all other relevant data. We try to run a first appraisal of the design within half an hour. This we consider as a very important event. We attempt to give the architects a very positive impression at their first 'meeting with the computer'. We attempt to prove to them that it is not difficult at all to do an appraisal of a design, thus encouraging them. The results of the appraisal are then discussed with an environmental engineer and a specialist from the costing department. The 'pros and cons' of their design are pointed out and suggestions for improvements are made. At the end of the session we send them away to study alternative solutions. At the next session, we allow them to type in all their suggested changes themselves and let them run GOAL, with our assistance. The whole session is spent making changes to the design and thus interactively they are gradually improving their own designs. In the fourth and last session we answer all sorts of remaining questions and then draw conclusions.

Of course we do not expect that, after attending the workshop, the architects can use GOAL independently. They still require some assistance when they want to use GOAL for the first time on a real project, but at least they are then aware of the scope of GOAL, how they can use it and in what ways they have to contribute themselves.

This way of introducing GOAL, by means of a workshop turned out to be very succesful. The architects were in general quite anxious to take part and a few even felt frustrated by the fact that they could not have taken part earlier.

The full effect of the workshops can not be estimated yet because we have only just started the series. In general, we have the impression that after attending the workshop the designers are enthusiastic and that our message has come across.

4.5. Other introduction experiences

From the preceding statements the impression may have been given that by definition every architect was unwilling to use GOAL. Fortunately that was not true, although the majority of them were reluctant. A few were very positive from the beginning, either because they were involved from the beginning or because they were convinced themselves that CAD could be useful to them. From their experiences we learned a lot and we were able to 'repair' a few of the problems in GOAL and make it more user-friendly.

We also learned that some of the architects could be introduced to GOAL more easily if we first allowed them to work with BIBLE. This program is more clearly a useful tool for the architect. It allows him to do a three dimensional appraisal of his design, where the output of the program is purely in graphic form, the architects own language.

The only danger of BIBLE is that it encourages the architect to play with it. We accept this to a certain extent, because the more the architects spend their time behind the terminal, the more they get used to it. After using BIBLE the architects were more willing to use GOAL.

At first the introductions and demonstrations were given by personnel from the computer department. Somehow this was not the most effective method, for it appeared that the architects did not trust them. At a later stage we found an architect who wanted to become involved very closely in developing CAD. Now he gives demonstrations, writes the Dutch manuals, assists the architects and prepares the material for the workshops. Through him, we now have an easier approach to the architects' education.

Going through such an introduction process with all its difficulties, it is absolutely essential that the management of the firm gives the people in the field enough flexibility to act as they think fit. On the other hand, they must keep themselves informed of what is happening. The management in our firm, mainly consisting of architects, have to lead the way and stimulate their designers to make use of tools in which a great deal has been invested. For a better understanding, the directors too have to attend the workshops and become really convinced of the benefits of the tools.

5. Experiences of practical use

5.1. Area and volume calculations

As stated at the beginning we decided to buy GOAL because we acquired the commission for a large University Hospital. Apart from this University Hospital we are designing several other hospitals and therefore we considered the purchase of GOAL of significant importance to our firm.

Due to several circumstances we were not able to use GOAL completely in the design process of the total University Hospital, since the design of most of the building was already in a too advanced stage. For such a scale of project as an University Hospital, (200.000 m², 600.000 m³), with constructional costs totalling in excess of 537 million Dutch guilders (£ 125.000.000), it is easy to realise that it is necessary to keep control of the areas and volume of the building as the project develops. Our client asks for a monthly calculation of areas and volume in order to know that the developing project is not going to overreach the total target cost.

The area calculations include floors, walls and roofs thus giving the envelope of the building and its capacity. On the basis of this calculation the control of the budget is achieved against such as a 'gross area'/'net required area' ratio on a cost per m² basis.

With GOAL we can achieve such an enormous calculation within 8 hours of work by one operator, whereby manually it takes two quantity surveyors one week to reach the same conclusion.

```
AREA ANALYSIS AND VOLUME CALCULATIONS              30-aug-83 12:00
GEOMETRY    : HOTEL DESIGN (GEOMETRY 1)      HOTEL         GOAL 2.95
AREAS (M2) / VOLUME (M3)

COMPONENT       EXT.FLR   INT.FLR   TOT.FLR  EXT.WALL    ROOF   VOLUME


  1 RESTAURANT    147.0       0.0     147.0      78.0     0.0    441.0
  2 LOUNGE        109.3       0.0     109.3      78.0   109.3    327.8
  3 KITCHEN        75.0       0.0      75.0      36.0    27.0    225.0
  4 FOYER         258.0       0.0     258.0      33.0    96.3    774.0
  5 ADMINISTR'    270.0       0.0     270.0     121.5     0.0    810.0
  6 STEAKBAR      155.0       0.0     155.0     100.5   127.0    465.0
  7 FUNCTIONS     252.0       0.0     252.0     129.0   252.0    756.0
  8 BEDROOMS      101.3    1410.8    1512.0     834.0   756.0   4536.0

TOTAL             101.3U   1410.8    2778.3    1410.0  1367.5   8334.8
                 1266.3GROUND

WALL TO FLOOR RATIO                 0.51
VOLUME COMPACTNESS                  0.55
AREA DEVIATION MAX. 0.5000 % ,AVERAGE 0.1341 %
```

5.2. Environmental analyses

The original energy model in GOAL as it was developed by ABACUS has been modified by Architech AB, a subsidiary environmental engineering practice of EGM, to cover the need for specific calculations required in the Netherlands. The output has been modified to present information about the environmental performance of the building in such a way, that an architect, who is not primarily an environmental engineer, receives a general impression of the most important aspects.

```
ENERGY ANALYSIS GENERAL                            30-aug-83 12:03

GEOMETRY    : HOTEL DESIGN (GEOMETRY 1)      HOTEL         GOAL 2.95
CONSTRUCTION: HOTEL CONSTRUCTION 1           HOTEL
PROJECT     : HOTEL SITE: GLASGOW            HOTEL


AREAS:
TOTAL GROUND FLOOR       :     1266. [m2]
TOTAL EXTERNAL FLOORS    :      101. [m2]
TOTAL ROOF               :     1368. [m2]
TOTAL EXTERNAL WALLS     :     1410. [m2]
TOTAL ENVELOPE           :     4145. [m2]

TOTAL VOLUME             :     8335. [m3]

AVERAGE U-VALUE          :     1.51 [W/m2.K]
ENVELOPE/VOLUME RATIO    :     0.50 [1/M]
THERMAL INSULATION INDEX :       3. [-]
```

The information involves a thermal insulation index, called I(t)-value which is used in the Netherlands as a quick reference to the thermal quality of the building envelope. Often the target value is already given in the project brief and as such can be used easily by the architect himself. However, the architect is not specialised in environmental calculations. Therefore it will take him at least a few hours to do a similar calculation manually. By using GOAL the architect will receive the information with hardly any effort within minutes, and moreover he is able to test several design solutions very quickly, against the I(t)-value given in the brief.

Another interesting feature which is of much use to the architect is a performance impression per external surface. It enables him to make a quick analysis of the effect of the materials he wants to use in the external walls. In fact this is the first step in the energy-analysis of the design, which gives the architect general information about the energy losses and gains per surface. This step in the energy-analysis can result in changes in the design, e.g. adjustment of percentage glazing in specific locations.

```
ENERGYANALYSIS:PERFORMANCE PER EXTERNAL SURFACE (WINTER) 30-aug-83 12:04
GEOMETRY     : HOTEL DESIGN (GEOMETRY 1)          HOTEL          GOAL 2.95
CONSTRUCTION: HOTEL CONSTRUCTION 1                HOTEL
PROJECT      : HOTEL SITE: GLASGOW                HOTEL

BUILDING ORIENTATION :     0 DEGREES
             Qtrans   Qsolar    Qt+Qz
   SURFACE   W/M2     W/M2      W/M2      AREA     KW

   NORTH     63.4      0.0      63.4      492.     31.19
   EAST      49.8     -4.7      45.1      213.      9.60
   SOUTH     68.5   -105.9     -37.4      492.    -18.40
   WEST      48.9     -4.5      44.4      213.      9.46
   ROOF      12.7      0.0      12.7     1368.     17.44
   FLOOR     29.8      0.0      29.8      101.      3.01
   GRND       6.3      0.0       6.3     1266.      8.01

AVERAGE      27.6    -19.5      14.5

                     TOTAL               4145.     60.31
```

Through a further analysis per surface and per spatial function, the architect is able to check which external surface causes specific problems. Either he may select other materials for that function, or he may change the requirements of a specific department or room in the same location.

```
ENERGYANALYSIS: EXTERNAL SURFACE HEAT LOSS    (WINTER)  30-aug-83 12:05
GEOMETRY     : HOTEL DESIGN (GEOMETRY 1)       HOTEL           GOAL 2.95
CONSTRUCTION: HOTEL CONSTRUCTION 1             HOTEL
PROJECT      : HOTEL SITE: GLASGOW             HOTEL

BUILDING ORIENTATION :    0 DEGREES
                                Qtrans    Qsolar    Qt+Qz
                                W/M2      W/M2      W/M2      AREA      KW
COMPONENT             SURFACE
     8  BEDROOMS      NORTH     64.5       0.0      64.5      336.0    21.67
     8  BEDROOMS      SOUTH     64.5    -100.0     -35.5      336.0   -11.93
     8  BEDROOMS      ROOF      12.3       0.0      12.3      756.0     9.26
     7  FUNCTIONS     NORTH     71.9       0.0      71.9       54.0     3.88
     5  ADMINISTR'    NORTH     71.9       0.0      71.9       51.0     3.66
     7  FUNCTIONS     ROOF      13.7       0.0      13.7      252.0     3.44
     8  BEDROOMS      FLOOR     29.8       0.0      29.8      101.3     3.01
     6  STEAKBAR      EAST      71.9     -10.0      61.9       45.0     2.78
     1  RESTAURANT    WEST      79.6     -12.0      67.6       40.5     2.74
     6  STEAKBAR      SOUTH     79.3    -119.3     -39.9       40.5    -1.62
     8  BEDROOMS      EAST      35.3      -1.6      33.7       81.0     2.73
     8  BEDROOMS      WEST      35.3      -1.6      33.7       81.0     2.73
     7  FUNCTIONS     EAST      71.9     -10.0      61.9       42.0     2.60
     5  ADMINISTR'    SOUTH     71.9    -100.0     -28.1       40.5    -1.14
     4  FOYER         SOUTH     78.4    -140.0     -61.6       33.0    -2.03
     2  LOUNGE        WEST      71.9     -10.0      61.9       34.5     2.13
     2  LOUNGE        SOUTH     71.9    -100.0     -28.1       28.5    -0.80
     5  ADMINISTR'    GRND       6.5       0.0       6.5      270.0     1.76
     6  STEAKBAR      ROOF      13.7       0.0      13.7      127.0     1.73
     4  FOYER         GRND       5.8       0.0       5.8      258.0     1.51

                     AVERAGE PER SURFACE        14.5

                     TOTAL                               4145.0    60.31
```

There are plans within EGM and Architech AB for further modifications of the energy model within GOAL towards a degree/hour method (dynamic model). For this significant modification a coöperation pact will be established with both Eindhoven University and ABACUS.

6.   Conclusions

At this stage, we at EGM can draw conclusions in an arbitrary order:

- Cooperation between a University and a professional practice can be very fruitful. EGM considers its relation with ABACUS as being very useful. The combination of 'pure theory' and 'pure practice' may result in tools of a high quality for the benefit of both architects and scientists.

- Introduction of CAD-tools to architects is a very difficult task. We believe it may be achieved by doing it gradually. First introduce the tools that appeal to them most and later involve them in the 'heavier' aids. In all situations we must be aware that they have to be helped across the threshold. Ours is the task to break the barriers without disturbing the relations. Let users do the introduction rather than specialists. Introduction through work-shops proves to be very effective.

- Do not forget the ordinary draftsman who sees all these things happen and will become afraid of the future because he knows that the era of computer aided drafting is at hand.

- Mid-carreer education concerning the use of computers becomes more important than ever before.

- The emphasis we put on improvement of quality rather than increasing the productivity, results both internally in terms of higher efficiency and externally in terms of being more attractive for the clients. Using the computer to achieve this makes a positive impression on them.

- Using 'sophisticated computer aids' has helped to make EGM not only one of the largest but also one of the leading offices in the Netherlands. We have become involved in general developments and thus try to develop trends rather than simply follow them.

- And in conclusion it must be stated that we underestimated the problems possible when attempting an implementation such as this for CAD software.

HAVING A GO

H Michael Cummings
Partner
Cummings Eland Partnership
Chartered Architects
UK

3 years ago this practice started to experiment from a base of curiosity into the use of a small computer. The results are compared with the expectations. This review is directed at the practitioner with little or no experience of computing

 <u>Michael Cummings</u> is a partner in a medium sized provincial practice. He has been a lecturer in Management at Manchester Polytechnic and a practising Architect since 1963. His present practice was formed in 1980 and is involved in a very wide range of building types. A significant part of his role as partner is in settling disputes as a practising member of the Chartered Institute of Arbitrators.

Background

In 1980 the practice of Cummings Eland Partnership
commenced. The firm was the Manchester office of a
National practice. Because of philosophical differences
and ages a separation was mutually agreed to be mutually
beneficial. This background and painful birth
generated an excitement which was important.

The Office

The personnel was in the 25-40 age group and much youth-
ful enthusiasm was generated by an Associate who had
experimented with computers as a student.

The two partners had different views, one wildly
optimistic, the other interested but sceptical.

Aims

This paper is aimed at many similar practices who may be
sceptical about the uses of computers. They may be
frightened by the "box of tricks".

Motivation

A good fee outlook and plenty of optimism for the future
success of the practice led to a search for better
organisation.

Much publicity was directed to the selling of micro
circuitry and "chips" were becoming commonplace. Not
willing to be left behind it was decided to investigate
the market.

Les Andrew, our associate, was helpful in directing the
partners to seminars and exhibitions to see computers
working. It became an obsession to get "hands on"
experience.

Our efficient secretary was completely negative about
our new found interest.

Expectations

After much investigation it was decided that we should
make a gradual and low key incursion into computers.

As a new office of twelve people, obvious and well
trodden paths were open.

Payroll

Most small and simple computers will run a payroll. We had our salaries in a manual system run efficiently by a semi-qualified accountant. On the computer all this could be simplified and under our own control.

Book-Keeping

A manual double entry book keeping system had been in existence for ten years. It was felt that more information could be made available if reduced to disc (the storage medium).

Job Records

We saw and were impressed by the costing records which applied costs to time spent and calculated work in progress at the touch of a switch.

Education

Most important of all was the need to learn. This educational role was felt to be almost as important as the aggregate of the others. Once installed it was expected that all the opportunities would become apparent.

The constant question was "what will it do?" The answer could only be given by "Having a go!"

Having a Go

The decision to install and the choice was based on software availability. We were also close to a supplier of National repute and decided after much procrastination on an Apple II plus three disc drives and a superb daisy wheel printer. This was on the basis that the printer could be interfaced with more sophisticated hardware in the future.

The choice has now widened and some of the home computers are nearly as powerful as our original Apple. We did not regret that decision.

Electronics are (and were) moving so rapidly that it is inevitable that equipment purchased today will be out-dated next week; we did appreciate this problem but still wanted to learn.

The merits of the Apple against the competition have not been evaluated because we have had no experience with anything else.

Software

We bought payroll, Ledger Accounts and a primitive word processing programme came free.

Reaction

To the outside world we became wizz kids overnight, even though we could do very little except to play games. We nearly lost one millionaire client because we beat him in a business game of investment and he became so upset he walked out in a temper. We spent some time giving demonstrations to our colleagues and becoming more facile on the keyboard.

The sceptical partner kept asking "what can it do?"

Changes

In a small office suite the equipment was installed in a private office. This was not very satisfactory because it became too exclusive. It should have been more accessible to all the staff.

Fear

The exclusivity produced fear. This among the women who hated the idea of their jobs being mechanised and staff who thought it was a plot to take over their jobs.

Acclimatisation

After-hours games playing helped to familiarise some of the staff and the fear began to dissipate. However the secretarial staff did not respond to the enthusiasm and the whole enterprise began to sour.

It was then decided to appoint a person to learn to use the computer for all the administrative tasks for which it had been acquired. This was a disaster. The appointment produced jealousy and the appointee, a university graduate, was simply not able to perform the task. After a year we gave up.

A transformation then occurred. The original secretary became a computer buff. We acquired an even more sophisticated word processing system and started producing specifications, standard letters and pro-formas. This activity virtually absorbed all the computer time.

Record Keeping

Payroll was a waste of time. The amount of information required at the keyboard was so complex and time consuming that we never "went live". This task is now undertaken by a bureau who, through our accountants, produce pay slips and year end records.

Job Costing

Once again the imputting of information is laborious. The task is essential to a well run business but we have not yet been able to tackle the problem. Great discipline is required and must logically follow a manually kept system.

Accounts

It was found to be impracticable to devote computer time to this task and we continued with the manual system.

Success

We can perform tasks which we did not previously undertake

Beams   Simple steelwork design

Heat Loss/Condensation Prediction Simply undertaken on an Apple

Word Processing   80% of time is taken up by this.

Expectation

We were expecting too much. A computer has no motivation and enthusiasm. It cannot work for you, it can only make the operator feed in information. It cannot tidy untidy records. Before imputting information the information must be ready and in order. One piece of information missing and hours of work can be wasted.

A muddled office cannot be tidied by a computer.

Conclusion

We did the right thing. We now know much more about what
can and cannot be achieved by micro circuitry. We could
not do without our Apple now!

The Future

We would like to consolidate our position and think more
about our next step. We are still looking at other
installations and have been singularly unimpressed. The
next generation of computers must be better and more
sophisticated like valve radios compared with
transistors.

Computer language is crude and esoteric and should not be
so. As a design tool computers will become more
significant and software is being produced rapidly. So
far we have found that photocopiers are more efficient
but this situation will not last for long. It is
important to keep updated on the changes as costs and
therefore value for money keep improving.

ORGANIC COMPUTING

Lucien Kroll
Atelier d'Urbanisme et
d'Architecture L Kroll
Belgium

An industrialized system is used for the construction of 110 dwellings in Emerainville (Paris). The built landscape is generally mastered by the sewage pipes, the motor circulation, the building process (prefabrication series and the crane path...), and not by the sympathy people should discover in living together. In order to avoid that form of a 'new town', the architects used all possible differentations: participation of the inhabitants, simulation, different materials, variety of the plans, the volumes, the positions, etc. In order to handle these complexities, they used a CAD system and tried not to be the victims of that tool.

Lucien Kroll is an architect, he leads his Atelier d'Urbanisme et d'Architecture in Brussels. Her is mostly known for his attitudes of encouraging participation of future users and, at the same time, of organizing it results in a technological way: building of organizing its results in a technological way: building industry, CAD...'Les Facultes Medicales' in Woluwe, Brussels for the Catholic University of Louvain are well known around the world of architecture. These days, he is busy in France and the Netherlands. Among other buildings in progress are: '
'Les Vignes Blanches' in Cergy Pontoise, designed with the inhabitants, the rehabilitation of the 'ZUP de Perseigne' in Alencon, Normandy, etc

Already the industrialisation of architecture has produced some
not very likeable objects, yet here she goes trying to take on
board the computer as fast as possible: already in the name of
rational mechanisation, tenderness and loving care have been
massacred. And now are we going to build more, more quickly, and
even more unthinkingly?

Architects (like politicians and priests) are perhaps the last
ones who wish to put forward their feelings amongst everyday
realities.   They begged the industry to "seize the opportunity of
building".   The Industry has done so and has chased the architects
away. Today architects tinker with computers. Are they again
cutting down the branch on which they are sitting? Certainly I am
not so much worried about the interests of architects as I am
about architecture, but it is they who are again doing it the
best.   Several generations of ingenious people have demonstrated
that in the landscape with their heavily prefabricated concrete.

Who is winning?

Whilst electronic construction information systems are grafted on
directly to industrialised systems (in a few seconds one can
telephone the machine which commands a million elements necessary
for the construction of a ZUP *) where on earth will there be room
for architecture.   The architect will be an assistant to the
commercial service, like a salesman or a watercolourist (we know
that the contribution to industrialised products by industrial
designers has been negligible ...). It is not the architects who
are being asked for advice when an industrialised building system
is being conceived.

The concept of industrialisation, assisted by the use of a
computer could fairly easily ensure a certain diversity (cars have
it a little: seats, colours, small embellishments, options, etc).
But it would only be an artificial diversity, a commercial one;
it would never be instinctive, atavistic or religious.   One
mustn't believe that the tools are neutral, that things are done
simply, clearly, "that the best always wins ..".   It is in reality
the struggles of the antediluvian animal races for their survival.
One either wins by massacring the others or by adapting oneself
more quickly. In our present day, the power (money is just an
illusion) is diffused amongst the electorate, then uniformly
centralised by the politicians and administered by the
administrators whether public or private. It is the one who is
closest to the chief who is right.   The big companies are joining
up with the major builders, the new industries are going to do it
very quietly.   What weight do the architects have amongst such
giants when virtue is one of their least noticeable attributes.

*   Zone d'Urbanisme Priorite = ZUP

They could marginalise themselves, refuse to comply, or fall in line, cheat it or simply run faster.

The client?

But how? And relying on what social movement? Who are they speaking on behalf of? The welfare state, technical knowledge, nostalgia, the ware machine, Robinson Crusoe, "Work - good health - Patriotism, a fascist novel on a musical comedy, Thoreau, William Morris, General Motors etc. They have the choice ... The CAO (Computer Assisted Conception) is only a more clever instrument than the others; it's not the tool which makes architecture. That comes from the demands of society. But is society being listened to by the mercenaries who are mechanising the habitable environment?

CAO functions

All this is well known, and yet the illusions are durable, we still want to believe in fairy stories. Everyone seems well up to date. They discuss the details, the software, its performance, its revolutionary effect (yet again ..) on the direction of architecture (as though the push button had the power to liberate forms).

It is true that from time to time images are revealed to us, breathtaking perspectives on the graphic simulator whose mysterious tools draw dangerously nearer to the architects' work and they are proposing to him some procedures which are difficult to classify; aids for drawing or conception, computer graphics, two or three dimensions, capable of modelling the object, etc.

An architecture school proposed to study, using the CAO, the perspective of a car which crashes into a wall. Yet on some small systems they are still trying to join up two points with a line.

Where is the architect situated in all this, and above all at what price? As an accessory, which part of his work can the machine best manage?

Actually 'computer graphics' seems to be used above all else in heavy industry, in the spectacular ones, for vehicles and some moving parts. Collossal budgets allow them to create fantastic drawings or incredibly accurate simulations of reality. You must go to Seattle to see the cabin of a Boeing where all the command instruments have been linked into a gigantic computer programme which simulates the flight, receives the messages from the pilot, creates geographical conditions, the climate etc, and projects in front of the windscreen a view, a little bit stylised, of the airport which the plane is approaching, (three million dollars they say it costs) or the reflections and transparencies of a vase on a chess board, or the fifty two rules which allow you to draw

fake Palladian architecture where the specialists make mistakes
.... And already to move all round a cube in perspective which
one can colour in 1,600,000 shades: it is fascinating.

Artificial intelligence

M.I.T. amongst others have really gone full tilt for one of these
approaches and they are so taken up in the game that they almost
believe they have given life to their simulation (certain
sculptors would give way to such a paternal desire; "but why don't
you talk to us"..?) They were confusing the infinitely diverse
reality with their stereotype configurations and were thus giving
a finite form to some truths created in a micro world where
everything was artificial, because they were carefully limiting
their boundaries. Making everything discrete. Even so they
called it "artificial intelligence", they have now and then asked
it to conceive some architecture .... Without roots, without
"body" (said Herbert Dreyfus 1) they would have discovered perhaps
a planning policy of "container lorries piled up the full length
of the motorway" but nevertheless beautifully coloured? The only
credulous people were certain architects and even they felt
diminished by the experience. The illusion of information dazzles
us. Those of them who believe in creating these spectacles seem
to be sucked in quickly and devote themselves to producing
quantities of them ...

Our approach to the industry

Our approach to the construction industry has been irrational and
above all moral; we say yes to the industry if it produces
architecture, and no if it destroys the image and its performance,
its social and cultural richness.   It has taken a long time to
find industrialists who are open to such ideas; they were all
occupied in confusing the religious connotations of the word
'home' with the mechanised marketing of shelter (or the
mechanisation of shelter and marketing it).

However we don't have much time for the romantics who avoid
facing these questions by escaping into a mist of ambiguities and
nostalgia, whether it be the peasant life, that of Marie
Antoinette, or classic issues of well known cartoons or
commercials (Snow White is selling well). Neither do we have time
for the mechanics who dream of long repetitive runs, where
geometry is the primary motivator, that goes so far that the
elements are constructed in an abstract-baroque style which is so
difficult to build that event the functionalist of the modern
movement never dared dream that it was possible. And then if the
rain penetrates the curtain walls where are those who worry about
function?

We have stayed very much as strangers to this whole development of
prefabricated concrete systems, their autistic method of arranging

them without cultural or historical reference.

We are again allowing ourselves to slip into the belief that industrial knowledge is able at the same time to produce the materials of an organic architecture. To be able to do that, it is first necessary for the industry to want to master the image of the constructed object, afterwards the architecture acquires a cultural neutrality in spite of the contemporary materials. That would permit a diversion away from the egoecentricity of the industry towards a more likeable expression and distinguish the format that spontaneously produces an intelligent work organisation pattern, in contrast to that which derives from a cultural laziness that brutally aligns its identical anonymous elements, or that of self satisfaction towards a Taylorist work ethic, in smithereens. However shining anodised aluminium doesn't inevitably have to be associated with luxury offices, close cropped lawns. It is possible to imagine it lost amongst other more populist materials, to imagine it take on by contrast another image than that with which it is invested. But industrial muscle has remained blind to these perspectives, so much so that it can sell almost anything. All our contacts with the industry have remained negative.

It is only the opportunity offered us by the commission to build the medical faculty sector at Woluwe, Brussels, that allowed us to explore modular coordination, openly appealing to the industry after having made some 'clandestine' prototypes. But not one genuine manufacturer would have followed us. And it is the only building to our knowledge which has been strictly drawn to a grid of 10cm with a preference towards 30cm. That above all was a good way to organise the construction for craftsmen, and to manage comfortably an enormous amount of diversity of forms. It was ahead of its time. An industrialised architecture without industrial manufacturers. For the moment the metal workers produce standard panels of 1.00m and simply mulitiply them all over the place; the concrete manufacturers fabricate boxes or walls with very little choice, take it or leave it; they are all the same. It is only later that the architecture has to be envisaged, made only out of components. But prefabrication is again halted at an intermediary stage of half open, half closed, construction systems.

The C.A.O, D.A.O, F.A.O, or A.A.O.
(Conception, design, fabrication or architecture assisted by the computer)

As long as they were limiting themselves to promoting the construction of an enormous range of inauspicious objects, the potential performance of tasks offered by the computer when allied to those ends seems to us to be extremely unhealthy. We would have preferred to discourage them.

This development is fascinating to observe in detail: a technique, a tool, it changes the object produced, and the social relationships of those who were part of the assembly line.

One must remember that the computer was first applied to motorway design in calculating their sections and the results of the surveys and presenting a view of them in perspective: miraculous but not exactly very complex. Then computer was used for extremely complicated calculations, structural resistance, soil mechanics, the performance of fluids, of buildings, and organising the functions which had to be closest to each other. It was never touching architecture except in the case of a few isolated players.

Certain building system entrepeneurs actually have employed people for computer work, but they refuse to recognise the diverse possibilities and the potential for creativity which the machine actually offers. They use it simply for repetitive activities and those of limited potential. All that is produced is simply more degrading objects. For what they require, a photocopier would do.

Closed information

Technically this narrowing of outlook is denoted by two particular aspects. The language becomes hermetic and quite deliberately incompatible with other languages. Already the amount of exchange between several makes and models of computer is restricted, but also even within the one system produced by one computer company and the logic language they all use, there isn't any intention of bringing about an exchange. Of course translating languages exist, but they are not very accurate. Also the main software systems are so obtuse, they are only capable of drawing one simple brute object. A few variables are possible with an uncommensurate amount of effort. They draw in one style of brickwork for example, often an absolutely frightful one which of course repeated immaculately every single time. We have seen measuring programmes which are so specialised that they would not be able to measure a crooked line, a curve or even different heights....

Anthromorphisms

The engineers and the companies being both powerful and methodical transform the tool so that it exactly fits that image, to the point that one can't imagine any other alternative: the odd exceptional model, a few variations in appearance, "somehow the architect manages". They reproduce in their programmes the same hierarchies, the same sense of imperviousness: one has seen procedures where there is no ripple in the sequence of actions, from the idea of the chief conceiver the orders are carried to the producer, the draughtsperson and the worker are obliged to be idiots. Without doubt industrial design tools will always escape from the architects' control. However simply the fact that the construction is done by elements, does allow this architecture to adopt a little variation across the range. The architect or even the inhabitants will be able to vary or multiply the models. This diversity is only possible within very restricted limits; the micro chip in the hands of the architect would permit that limit to be broken.....But that tactic (practically the only force for diversity) perceives quickly that the sole policy of "architecture by components" is going to suffocate itself by delay and the extra costs of that diversity.

The power of the tool on the product

The computer contains within itself (but who actually put it there?) a cunning tendency to dominate everything, to transform everything into its own image. In effect it accepts only those things which it is capable of digesting, and it can only render things absolutely precisely to a certain level, after which the imprecise is often more efficient. That's logical... but if it was the implied, the approximate, the irrational which was essential?

An opportunity : the oak trees of Emerainville

The New Town of Marne La Vallee called us in to work on an operation which is exploring two linked areas of research: the participation of the inhabitants and building systems. In a scheme of 80 terraced houses with balconies and 30 individual houses for those who sought to buy their properties, the latter group ought to be designed with the participation of the prospective owners (all or some of them).

A building system, by definition, is composed of a limited number of elements and well defined construction sequences. This was a chance to have the schemes design assisted by computer. We have launched ourselves into it.

The programme attached to our machine was only capable of churning out "shoe-box huts" destined for Africa. We are having to unscramble it and rewire it all up in another way. It is now a lot more automatic and a lot more civilised. We must above all avoid the architecture of the micro chip being reduced to that which can only be processed by the machine.

Later surely we will be spared the use of the barbaric languages (BASIC and others) and schizoid manipulations. The micro chip tool will feel comfortable with varied and simple commands (user-friendly). We are coming to it (we are actually applying it) with another generation of programmes (STAR). One doesn't need to know how to regulate the starter motor of a car to be able to drive.

Building systems

We have chosen a system agreed by the Ministry, simply for the fact that its technicians seemed open minded (more than the system itself) and that they were living on the east of Paris, the side where the site was. We haven't succeeded in improving much of its details, but in order to avoid causing troubles we have superimposed another set, a framework in wood: it permits a little suppleness and different clothing. All this, inside the limits set by the budget. We did not wish to remain within the comfortable confines of the system, but have pushed it to its outer limits with the help of the technicians, often after heated negotiations. Maybe it's enough?

The 80 terraced houses have been designed in this way; they are responding more to the particular circumstances of time and place rather than the logic of our objectives. We have broken into the process with the 30 individual houses, participating with the inhabitants as was agreed. We are only describing those parts of the scheme affected by the use of the computer. As for the 80 dwellings we will explain the rest of the story elsewhere.

Participation

After the ups and downs of approximately twenty meetings on the site we have met more than thirty families who are in different degrees interested in buying their dwelling and we have interpreted their plans for the architecture of the dwelling and for the site layout. Our experience of participation has allowed us to translate reasonably quickly the inhabitants inventions into three dimensional forms, actual construction details , approximate prices and building times, and to verify and negotiate all these with the authors of each individual project. But the precise prices were calculated for us by the building company very quickly. We asked him how much time it would take. He replied "I must draw the concrete elements first and then define the fitting out; it would need one day per plan". For thirty plans that would mean one month and a half. This was unacceptable, the occupiers did not have the patience to wait that long. Therefore a computer programme was necessary which could deal with drawing and taking off. The building company (the contractor) was thinking that with our help he could just get on with building without having to decide this himself.

It is above all the developer (the anonymous HLM companies carry out their social function with the money of the State, bound by very strict rules but in fact they do it in their own particular fashion). With precise mechanisation but knowing absolutely nothing about participation, they didn't want to know and having chosen all the modern conveniences. They just left all the inhabitants in the lurch. So here we were with 30 houses

personalised by the deceased (as it were) (like all the dwellings
in an old town which have been designed by people who no longer
exist). If on his side the developer had not ratted on his side
of the participation with the inhabitants, we would have
succeeded: the houses are all different in a very lively way but
they are empty (it's not our problem even if we find the behaviour
unpardonnable).

Without the CAO I doubt whether we would have been able to draw
and modify such a number of very different houses. Given the
opportunity of another site of thirty houses and a more efficient
organisation, we reckon we could even produce 300 (or 3000)
sharing out the work across the meetings of the inhabitants and
by proposing the designs of one inhabitant to several others.
Using this process we no longer need have any fears of
industrialised building whose potential has been increased by the
micro chip. But then again is it necessary to try it out at this
scale?

Domesticating the beast

The automation of everyday apparatus does permit a little more
diversity and exceptions. But if we just let the whole thing just
take its own course, we will soon not be able to do any more than
the machine is prepared to tolerate, the rest will be confined to
the margins into some "parking areas for the marginals". In the
same way that it was several years ago, it wasn't possible to
construct anything that wasn't defined on the drawing or in the
specification or in the estimates. Instruction by word of mouth
or in simple dialogue was sadly rather exceptional. Rendering the
object artificial had already begun.

And everyone will believe in good faith that the future of
architecture depends on the computer (?) and that this does not
allow variety or adaption. Then we will pine for the time when
nuances were permitted: That moment will soon have passed us by
just like that of the stone and the craftsman.

Or all that could be false and we could prove it by obliging the
computer to design itself a varied architecture just before the
producers and the mechanics decide that it is truly impossible.
It is a lot more complicated to programme in numerous variables,
simple yet capable of variation than to automate a few complicated
instructions which are then simply repeated ad nauseam. It's the
difference between construction and architecture, between the
complicated and the complex, between the parking lot and the
countryside.

References

1. Herbert Dreyfus 'What computers can't do!' New York.
    Harper Colophon Books

HUMAN & MANAGEMENT PROBLEMS OF DRAUGHTING SYSTEMS

David Campion
Associate
Cusdin Burden & Howitt
UK

There have been many Papers at various conferences over the last five years about the application and use of computer-aided draughting systems; however, very few papers have dealt specifically with the experience of every day human, management and staffing problems that may arise as a result of the use of such systems for preparing and updating design and production drawings in an architect's office.

David Campion is an Associate of Cusdin Burden and Howitt, Chartered Architects, and is the Director of Computer Services for the practice. He was one of the few early pioneers of the use of computer techniques in architectural practice when he developed and implemented a range of applications back in 1964 covering design calculations, simulation, perspective drawing, scheduling, management and costing. The practice acquired its first graphics computer for draughting purposes in 1978.

BACKGROUND.

The aim of this Paper is to set out some of the human, management and staffing problems that Cusdin Burden and Howitt, a medium sized private architectural practice, has experienced since installing its first graphics computer system at the beginning of 1978.

There may well be firms which are about to acquire computer equipment for draughting purposes, in order to be seen to be keeping up with the times, without appreciating some of the problems that can arise when attempting to integrate computer-aided draughting techniques into a traditional design office environment.

Few architectural practices seem prepared to admit, atleast not publicly, that there are any problems involved in applying CAD techniques; there appears to be a not unnatural fear that such an admission may reflect adversely on a firm's public image and competence in implementing and applying such techniques.

SOME POTENTIAL PROBLEM AREAS.

In general, in the context of computer-aided draughting, it is possible to consider potential problem areas under the following inter-related headings:

a. Human problems,
b. Staffing problems,
c. Management problems.

HUMAN PROBLEMS.

Some or all of the following human problems that may manifest themselves are:

a. Age,
b. Eye Strain,
c. Stress.

Age.

There is something in the traditional saying that "you can't teach an old dog new tricks".

It appears to be a fact that many people over the age of about forty five, who have had no previous involvement with computers, tend to have considerable difficulty in getting to grips with the use of computer techniques, especially where they are expected to operate the computer themselves.

There is undoubtedly a problem in that as a person gets older his brain finds it more difficult to absorb and to remember new things. This is not to suggest that anything to do with computers must of necessity introduce difficulty - many of the newer computer systems have been designed with the aim of making them much easier to understand and use - but rather that many more-elderly people just are not prepared to put in the extra effort needed to learn new ways of working.

There are undoubtedly a large number of middle aged and elderly architects, many of whom have years of experience and competence in architectural practice, who are quite happy to carry on in the ways that they have been during their whole working life, and do not wish or feel the need to become involved with the use of computers. Many types of architectural project can be easily and almost certainly more efficiently handled by an experienced person without the need to use a computer, e.g: individual houses and small scale conversion works. However, considerable problems can arise if an unwilling person is asked or expected to become a member of a team utilising computer-aided draughting techniques on a medium to large scale project.

There is no question but that younger, and particularly recently qualified architects, tend to have little difficulty in getting to grips with computer-aided draughting techniques. Their minds are agile and receptive to new ideas since they tend to be of an age that expects to pick up new things as part of the process of gaining experience. In any case, most students these days have been exposed to the use of computers as part of their education at school and at college so they tend to take the use of computers in their stride.

There are, nevertheless, even young architects who feel that computer-aided draughting facilities will limit their freedom of design.

Eye Strain.

Many studies have been already been carried out concerning the problems likely to be encountered when working in front of a computer display screen for hours on end. Apart from the possible effects of radiation, which have yet to be proved in practice, one of the main problems can be one of eye strain.

There can be a problem with some vector graphics displays where the computer is unable to refresh the complete screen fast enough to prevent flicker; this can be extremely tiring and mentally debilitating such that it is undesirable to work for more than a few hours at a time without a break. There can also be a flicker problem with raster-scan t.v. type display screens, particularly where unsuitable adjacent fluorescent lighting is in use.

Undoubtedly the most pleasant form of screen to work with is the high resolution Tektronix-type storage display; CBH experience shows that it is possible to work with such a screen for a whole day without any problem.

Stress.

The first form of stress is induced by the relatively intensive way that interaction takes place between the computer and the user during a work session; the user is not really aware of the stress while he is working but it tends to tell after several hours work where there is an unconscious slowing down of the rate at which work is carried out.

It is possible for some people to become addicted to the use of a computer-aided draughting system and not realise the effect that it is having on them; if someone works on a computer day after day for some weeks it is very easy for him to become run down both mentally and physically.

The second form of stress can be management-induced as a result of a desire to maximise the number of hours each day that the computer is put to productive use. This can lead to shift working and involve working what have come to be called "unsocial hours". Alternatively, there can be pressure on staff to work a greater than normal number of hours each day.

Therefore, whether the longer hours on the computer are due to addiction or management pressure the end result will almost certainly result in additional stress which must in the long term act against the interest of both the employer and the employee.

STAFFING PROBLEMS.

Staffing problems can be considered under the following inter-related headings:

a. Training,
b. Qualifications,
c. Turn-over,
d. Career prospects.

Training.

The problem of training and retraining existing and new staff in the use of computer-aided draughting techniques should not be underestimated.

In general, while a computer workstation is being used for training it can not be in productive use on a live project. One person being trained in-house usually means that a second computer-skilled person is also tied up teaching him and the latter is therefore unavailable for productive purposes himself. This problem can become quite acute if there are very few computer-trained technical staff in an office relative to its size and workload at a given time.

CBH have found from experience that they need atleast about five out of a total of about fifteen technical staff to be computer-skilled to provide adequate flexibility in terms of in-house training and operational requirements. However, this should not necessarily be taken to mean that up to 30% of technical staff in an office should be computer-skilled since the figure is likely to depend more on a minimum in a small to medium sized office.

It may sometimes be possible to arrange for initial training on a specific computer-aided draughting system to be carried out by an outside organisation; although this can be expensive it can also take the pressure off the computer-skilled staff in an office during peak workload conditions.

CBH have found from experience that it is useful to start a trainee off with fairly simple operations, e.g: adding room numbers and room names to a plan previously prepared by someone else; once this has been mastered then the trainee progresses by stages, at his or her own learning speed, to handle furniture layouts, internal wall elements and then external wall elements, typically in that order.

One advantage of this approach to training, particularly relative to a team of staff working on a medium to large size of project, is that a trainee can more easily be left on his own to handle production work, after only the minimum of instruction at each stage of training, without the need for skilled staff to be other than available in case of difficulties.

Another advantage of this approach is that staff can be used within the limits of their capabilities; it has been found that not all staff are capable of becoming, or want to go on to become, highly skilled at computer draughting.

There can be a considerable problem if an office relies **too heavily** on too limited a number of computer-skilled staff; if such staff leave, are away sick or are otherwise unavailable at short notice then the draughting work on a project can easily grind to a halt at a critical stage in a programme, may be with **disastrous**< consequences.

Ideally the more staff in an office that can be trained the better since this gives greater flexibility in terms of allocation of staff to specific projects. However, since the number of computer workstations available will limit the number of projects and the number of staff who can use the computer at any one time, this can mean that some staff do not have a chance to use the computer for weeks or months on end and will then need either refresher training or time to work up their speed again.

It has been said that the best way to decide whether a person has the aptitude to use a computer-aided draughting system is to test this by the score that he achieves at one of the popular home-computer games that involves quick reaction and good co-ordination!

Staff Qualifications.

A matter which needs to be considered is the question of the type of staff to use the computer; it is open to question as to whether they should be technicians, technical draughtsmen, architectural students or qualified architects.

If technical draughtmen are used then there can be the same problem of communication, supervision and checking as with manual draughting procedures; the experience of CBH is that such staff do not enable the full benefits of computer-aided draughting to be achieved and the firm no longer employs such staff.

Technicians, being a rare breed, may be considered better employed in dealing with design and detailing matters on a project, particularly when detailed drawings are not prepared on the computer; since CBH do not undertake the preparation of detail drawings on the computer they have not felt it right to involve their only technician in this role.

CBH believe that the use of qualified architects for computer-aided draughting enables them as designer to take decisions which speed up the design process. Since installing its first computer-aided draughting system CBH have not had to employ additional staff nor draughtsmen to deal with the peak workloads on new large projects.

CBH experience suggests that so long as an architect who uses the computer is actually part of the design team on a project, and is encouraged to contribute to the design process as part of his work, then he usually experiences enough job satisfaction to overcome the feeling that he is merely acting as a draughtsman and getting away from the main stream of architectural design activity.

On larger projects CBH tend to make individual architects responsible for a specific element of the design; they will then use the computer for drawing up just those parts for which they are responsible. One of the advantages of this approach is that no one person spends full time on the computer and this tends to reduce the problems of stress etc mentioned above.

Turn-over of Staff.

Considerable problems can result where there is a relatively high turnover of staff; this tends to happen more with practices situated within urban areas because of the greater ease in obtaining alternative employment.

Every time that a member of staff leaves and is replaced there is a problem in training his replacement. It may be significant that advertisements for staff often specify the type of computer-aided draughting system for which experience is required. One of the results of this can be that an office will train staff for their system only to find that they leave as soon as they are trained to take on a better paid job.

Considerable problems can be caused to team working on major projects where key staff leave and there is lack of continuity as a result of new staff taking over; this can be much worse when a computer-aided draughting system is in use.

Staff Career Prospects.

Consideration needs to be given to the genuine fear that younger and often newly qualified architectural staff have that if they become an expert computer user then they may get side-tracked and endanger their career prospects as an architect.

It is all too easy for a young architect, who has become an expert at computer-aided draughting, to be put in the position of working on project after project because there is pressure to meet dealines and he is faster at it than other staff in the office.

MANAGEMENT PROBLEMS.

The generally accepted meaning of management within an architect's office clearly takes into account the previously mentioned human and staffing problems; however, in the present context "management" is intended to refer more specifically to the problems of organising the work on an architectural project that is being handled with the use of computer-aided draughting procedures.

Management problems can be considered as a number of inter-related topics which can affect each other:

a. Type of project,
b. Size of project,
c. Multiple projects,
d. Stage of project,

e. Use of graphic standards,
f. 2-dimensional to 3-dimensional representations,
g. Plotting.

Type of Project.

It is of course possible to handle virtually any type of project on
the computer, whatever its size and complexity; where there are
several jobs competing for computer resources the problem is to
decide which job is best handled on the computer.

It should be fairly obvious that some repetition of drawing elements
is highly desirable in order to make optimum use of computer-aided
draughting facilities.

One such example is a multi-storey building where there is
repetition of the external envelope on a number of floors and the
graphic data for one can be copied to form another without having to
start each one from scratch.

Another example is where there is much repetition of complete bays
even though the building may only be on one level.

A further example is where a fairly complex plan form is handed or
mirrored so that it is only necessary to draw half of it and then
get the computer to undertake the handing or mirroring to form the
other half.

A skilled user will develop an instinct for seeing where he can copy
and slightly modify one part of a drawing to form another part
thereby saving himself time.

Size of Project.

The computer tends in general to offer more benefits, in relation
to computer-aided draughting, as the size of the project increases;
however, this can in itself lead to problems in terms of the
capability of the computer to handle the amount of graphic data
involved and the number of workstations available for concurrent
working.

There is always a danger that if the computer facilities are
inadequate for the size or complexity of a project then this can
actually impede the work and involve a higher proportion of work
having to be undertaken manually in order to maintain a tight work
programme. This need not necessarily be disasterous but it can
certainly considerably reduce the benefits of using the computer.

It is of course always possible to spend ones way out of this problem by upgrading the computer, if this can be done, or buying another computer.

Multiple Projects.

Whereas many offices have initially installed computer-aided draughting facilities to deal with a specific large project, it is usually necessary to consider how the computer is to be used at the end of such a project when it is not followed by one of similar size.

The situation is likely to arise where it is desirable to handle several smaller projects on the computer concurrently; with a bit of luck the peak computer draughting workloads will not coincide, but this can not be guaranteed. There can therefore be a problem of scheduling the use of the available workstations so as to satisfy the requirements of the architects involved with the individual projects; this can often lead to considerable dissatisfaction and complaints that the work on a particular project is being impeded by the computer. The situation may have to be faced that one of the project may have to be taken off the computer at some stage and dealt with thereafter manually.

In the experience of CBH it is quite satisfactory to deal only with specific parts of a project on the computer, e.g: location plans, where the computer offers most benefit, and to undertake the remained of the drawings manually.

Stage of Project.

A distinction needs to be made between transfering an existing set of manually produced design drawings into the computer, as a preliminary to the preparation of a set of working drawings, and the use of the computer for the preparation of design drawings during the design process itself. It may be useful, here, to make an analogy between trying to use the computer for "soft-pencil" work, where considerable change may take place during the design process, and use of the computer for "hard-pencil" work, where very specific information is already available.
In general, the approach that is usually adopted, when using a computer-aided draughting system, is to represent a building with the amount of detail that corresponds to a working drawing; there is therefore normally an assumption that the design has been worked out in a fair amount of detail before such drawings can be prepared on the computer.

There can be a problem if an attempt is made to use the computer for the preparation of small scale sketch design drawings during the early design stages of a project with the intention of converting these to larger scale working drawings at a later stage. This approach can only really work if the sketch drawings can be accurately represented in the computer from the start, but this is rather alien to the traditional way that small scale sketch design drawings are prepared manually without the need for a high degree of dimensional accuracy, i.e: with a "soft-pencil" approach.

One of the important problems to be overcome, in this context, is the amount of detail that is available at the stage that sketch designs are prepared. Is it really realistic to have to decide the detailed form of construction, including the dimensional implications of specific forms of construction, at an early sketch design stage; this has not been the case with traditional manually produced sketch drawings. Sketch design drawings tend to be symbolic rather than an accurate model of the final design.

This leads to the conclusion that while it is possible to produce sketch design drawings on a computer, with walls represented by single thick lines, it will usually be quicker to start again from scratch when commencing the later working drawings.

Use of Graphic Standards.

Consideration needs to be given to the problem of whether it is worthwhile to build up and maintain in the computer an office standard library of graphic information or whether it is better to deal with the matter on a one-off basis for each project.

Clearly this will be influenced by the range and types of project in a particular office, but it can be expensive in staff resources to maintain graphic standards because of the need to train staff not only to use the computer but also to learn about the standards available for use.

Contrary to what might be thought of as the obvious answer it has been the experience of CBH that, with the variations that take place between different projects in a private practice, it is better to deal with each project on a one-off basis.

Experience over the last five years suggests that, since a different combination of staff in the office tends to be used on each new project, the staff concerned find it easier and quicker to build up their own standards, related to the design requirements for the specific project, than to modify standards developed by a different team for a previous project.

Clearly the same situation may well not pertain where an office undertakes a repetitive building programme using a fairly rigid set of standards, e.g: a limited number of house types on an series of similar estates.

It may be as well to consider, at this stage, what can be meant by a set of graphic standards; it may consist of one or all of the following:

a. A set of office standard component drawings,
b. A set of office standard assembly drawings,
c. A set of office standard building type plans,
d. A set of office standard graphic elements,
e. A set of project-specific graphic elements.

There are a number of architectural practices who originally introduced the use of computer draughting with the intention of handling their office standard component and assembly drawings that had previously been produced manually; experience suggests that as a result of introducing computer draughting techniques some of these practices then found that they were concentrating on the use of the computer to produce the plans for new projects in the office and the idea of transfering the office standard drawings was forgotten.

There may be several reasons for this situation. Firstly, if a set of standard component and assembly drawings are generally utilised on new projects, without being amended, then there is unlikely to be much economic justification for utilising staff and computer resources for such purposes. Secondly, it often quickly becomes clear that better use of staff and computer resources occurs where draughting techniques are oriented towards the use of project-specific elemental plans and, perhaps also, elevational drawings rather than standard drawings.

It is possible to keep in the computer a set of building type plans that can be used as the starting point for new projects, e.g: house plans. CBH experience of such an approach is that it is so rarely possible to use a previous plan without much alteration that it is usually quicker to set the new one up again from scratch to meet the requirements of a specific site and a specific brief.

CBH experience indicates that the main area where some form of standardisation and reuse from one project to another is possible, in computer graphic terms, is that of symbols, e.g: British Standard lines etc., and items such as cars, trees and plants etc.

While it is possible to have standards for graphic elements such as doors, basins and furniture these invariably need to be changed during the development of a specific design if it is intended to reflect the desired dimensional and shape requirements. It is possible to have a large base of data in the computer containing a wide range of commercially available products but CBH experience indicates that the effort is not worthwhile; it is much easier to set up just that range of elements required for each new project. Is it really realistic to have to chose a specific manufacturers product at an early sketch design stage; if the office policy is to

try to make such graphic elements accurately represent the state of
design information on location drawings this can result in a large
overhead of staff and computer resources on a large project if all
such elements have to be altered during the development of the
design.

CBH experience suggests that many building elements are best treated
symbolically on location drawings with their detailed specification
covered on separate schedules in the traditional way; this involves
the minimum of changes and the need to replot completed drawings.

CBH experience suggests that the greatest scope for use of graphic
elements relates to shapes generated specifically for each project.
It is possible, for example, to see situations where particular
combinations of lines and/or text are repeatedly used and can
therefore be stored as subpictures which can be called-up and reused
again and again without the need to redraw each situation from
scratch; this can provide a major increase in the productivity of a
computer-aided draughting system. Few draughting software systems
allow other than a single level of subpicture "nesting" whereas CBH
have found from experience that up to four levels of "nesting" can
be very valuable in minimising the number of basic graphic elements
required; in addition this facility allows the stored subpictures to
be altered at a later stage without the need to change individual
location plans, which call up these subpictures, since the drawings
only then need to be replotted.

One of the major reasons for an increase in productivity that is
possible when using a computer-aided draughting system tends to come
from minimising the amount of one-off drawing that is needed.

2-Dimensional to 3-Dimensional Representations.

It would appear that of those architectural practices having
draughting systems with 2-D to 3-D capabilities the majority of the
projects handled may use only the more simple 2-D facilities; it
could be that as much as 80%-90% of all computer-aided draughting
work handled is only dealt with in two dimensions.
Clearly it is a selling point for a computer system vendor to offer
more than just a 2-D draughting system; an office will clearly be
attracted by the idea of being able to work in more than two
dimensions if the need arises.

However, based on the types and sizes of project undertaken by CBH,
experience suggests that where there is pressure to undertake a
project in the minimum of time it is quite enough to cope with
2-dimensional drawings with traditional building construction.

It is perhaps ironic that in the 60's when system building was at
its peak current 3-dimensional computer   facilities   were not

available; there is no doubt that closed systems of construction lend themselves very well to handling on a computer and can provide very much greater benefits in terms of the ratio of input effort to output drawings.

Plotting.

There can be a logistics problem related to the speed at which plotting can be undertaken depending on the type of plotter in use.

It can typically take up to about an hour and a half to plot an AO sized location working drawing, depending on the amount of information contained on it. This means that only about 5 drawings can be plotted during a normal working day, and about 35 in a normal working week. Where there are many drawings to be plotted or replotted at short notice the plotter can cause a bottleneck in a production programme.

There can be problems in keeping a number of different thickness ink pens working properly during a plot although ways have now been devised on the latest plotters to cap each pen except that in use.

CBH prefer to use a pentel or pressure biro on detail paper for all but the final drawing negatives. The plotter hardware can handle different thicknesses by going over relevant lines several times slightly off-set until the correct thickness is obtained; although plotting takes longer than with different thickness pens it has been found that less unproductive staff time is spent supervising plotting than was necessary with ink pens.

CONCLUSION.

Although this Paper has covered many of the matters which can cause problems when using a computer-aided draughting system it does not claim to have exhaustively covered all the potential problems that may be encountered.

No reference has been made to specific hardware and software systems, nor to inter-professional working, since these topics are major ones with their own range of problems.

Many of the matters covered may well be startlingly obvious to those with experience but not so obvious to those starting from scratch.

The experience gained by CBH is not necessary typical since there will inevitably be differences from one office to another depending on its size, types of project undertaken, staff composition, computer system in use and approach to handling architectural projects.

COMPUTER ASSISTED GENERATION OF HOUSES

T Oksala
Docent
Tampere Technical University
Finland

The logical basis in a generative approach to housing
planning is characterized in connection with historical
and actual examples. A raw row-house grammar is presented
and its extensions to other types of houses are critical-
ly considered. Finally complete computer generation of
small apartments covering the municipal housing production
of Helsinki town is discussed.

Tarkko Oksala is docent of the theory
of architecture in Tampere Technical
University. His research work at the
State Technical committee of the Academy of Finland since 1973 has covered
logical methods and computer applications in architecture. From 1977 he
has taught housing and urban planning
at Helsinki University of Technology.
He is a partner in architectural office Niukkanen-Oksala in Helsinki
since 1978.

A generative approach to housing planning

The idea of automatically generating plans of architectural objects develops rapidly today. This way of thinking
has its roots in the history of rationalism. Modern
computer aided design (CAD) and drafting techniques
offer new possibilities. Pioneering theoretical work in
the sense of architectural generation has been made in
the seventies by several authors including e. g. Mitchell
(1979), Stiny (1979) and Oksala (1979). The approach
discussed in this paper is based on formal grammars as
used in language theory and computer science. The method
has been implemented and tested first with simple
examples. Later the scope was extended to cover methods
offered by a variety of logical calculi. Finally the
techniques have been adapted so as to be applicable in
situations near to a practicing architect's work.

Logical extensions

From a logical point of view the set of alternative architectural realizations and its subsets may be considered
as solutions to an architectural planning problem. Between
realizations of solutions and expressions or desirable
features, hopes, specifications, requirements etc. there
exists a well-known many to one correspondence in both
directions. The know-how in architecture partially consists of knowledge concerning this relationship and
partially the knowledge about processes involved in plan
generation. This relationship between realizations and
expressions may be investigated on three logical levels
namely by investigating 1.) architectural individuals,
2.) predicates of individuals and 3.) expressions in
general. In every case the solution set is large. In
order to master it one might try to measure the width of
expressions and to introduce their probabilities and
information measures. This will be pointed out in greater
detail in connection of the following examples.

Historical examples

The generative approach was first illustrated by quite
formal examples. Especially the generation of plan layout
graphs has been studied extensively (see e.g. Steadman,
1973, Seppänen, Moore, 1975 and Earl, March, 1979).
The need of semantically more relevant applications has
been pointed out e. g. by Gibs, Mitchell and Stiny in
their "Palladian studies" (see Stiny 1979). In their work
one Palladian villa was generated in detail and an exhaustive generation and evaluation of the alternatives

was investigated. Inspired by the above enterprises and by
Wittkower (1973) and by the Palladian jubileum the author
has undertaken testing of logical methods to Palladian
villas. An exhaustive generation of the typology of a
family of Palladian villas was made by application of
logical product of three grammars generating main shapes,
locations of walls and traffic systems. In this system
it was possible uniquely to define various information
measures according to the semantic theory of information
(see Oksala 1981). The system was implemented with the
aid of a CAD system that allowed, by selection of sub-
requirements, to plan automatically a Palladian-like
villa scheme corresponding to hopes presented and acting
as a basis for further work. The variation of the Pisani
type in wall selection is illustrated in figure 1. This
also exemplifies the partial but exhaustive generation
principle (compare e.g. Avdot´in, 1980 and Galle, 1981).
The standard information measure gives 7 bits of information to select one plan of those possibilities given.

Similarly by analyzing statistically the features of a
family of architectural expressions one might develop
more ambitious systems simulating phases of architectural
style of great masters. Such analyses have been made
especially with the villas of le Corbusier and with the
prairie-houses of Frank Lloyd Wright (Koning, Eizenberg,
1981). The grammar of vernacular houses has been studied
as well (Flemming, 1981). Because the work is quite
tedious and its main value lies in historical aspects
I have, as a practicing architect, also made an effort
to do the same in the case of present day and future
projects discussed in the sequel.

Examples of grammars and Linnéan systems

Although modern generative devices used in mathematics are
quite abstract and formal, similar mechanisms can also be
found e.g. in traditional Linnéan classification systems
or statistical observation systems. They work, however,
in the opposite direction. The selection guides of house
types are also well-known from periods of industrial
housing production. Inspired by the above examples a study
called "The automatic generation of a housing group" was
realized in Helsinki University of Technology. In one
experiment we tried to form guidelines of Finnish housing
production by using housing material published in the
exhibition series "Finland builds" as a reference. The
guideline grammar was succesful in the sense that it might
function as a basis, when developing other more realistic
ones. Systems, which function in practice might contain

114

VARIATIONS OF PALLADIAN VILLAS ACCORDING TO T. OKSALA 1982
PISANI ★

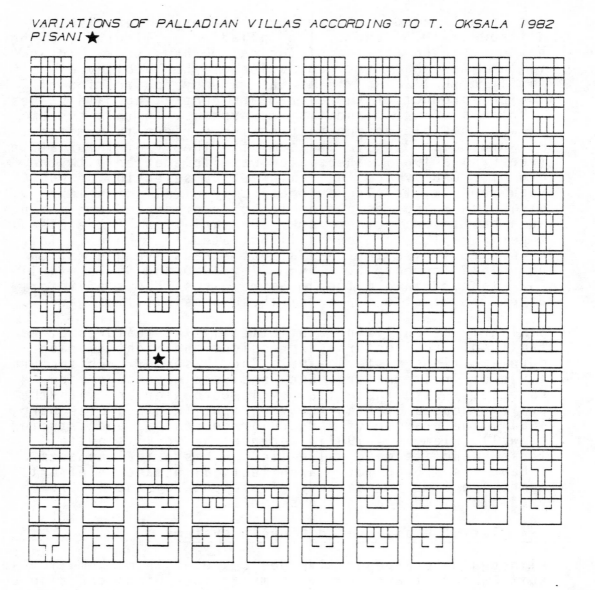

Figure 1

The variation of inside walls of the Pisani type of
Palladian villas.

sets like e. g. all houses in the Tapiola district or all
row-houses of some epoch. That is why the author has
developed a grammar called "a raw gründer row-house
grammar" in which the main interest lies in the division
of subgrammars. The entire grammar includes sketches of
grammars of how to assign houses to the site, how to
locate apartments in row-houses, how to select the section
principle, how to select constructions etc. At the same
time a summary of the housing production of Helsinki town
during the last decade was published. Using the above
experience a typology grammar covering the production
of small plans was developed. This might further be
refined with the aid of suitable construction grammars
corresponding to the ways of building.

A grammar for housing typology

In order to master the alternative realizations of house
plans in the production of Helsinki town a careful
statistical analysis was carried out. The study was based
on material representing the total production during the
seventies. The essential features were extracted in the
following categories of houses: The total number of rooms
for living was restricted to three, because a complete
analysis of apartments containing four or five rooms is
very expensive. Such large types might be understood as
transformations of smaller ones and mastered by transformation grammars. In the case of two storey solutions
of apartments only three room apartments were studied.
Secondly the main shape was restricted to be near
rectangular or L-shaped in the case of one storey plans
and nearly rectangular in the case of two storey plans
corresponding to the dominating style in the seventies.

For every main type of plans the product field of essential features were studied carefully. Impossible combinations for architectural or economical reasons were
rejected. So the above mentioned restriction of Helsinki
town production was covered nearly completely. On the
other hand many "realizable" new types were found.
Those relatively new are also new in the Finnish production in general. The derivation trees of housing plans
covering thousands of variations in type were drawn out
as illustrated in figure 2 a and b. The variation field
of single room apartments and a subfamily of two storey
rectangular three room apartments are represented in the
figure. Each pattern is labelled with a probability
measure and the codes of realizations are given under
the circles symbolizing the 'terminals'.

116

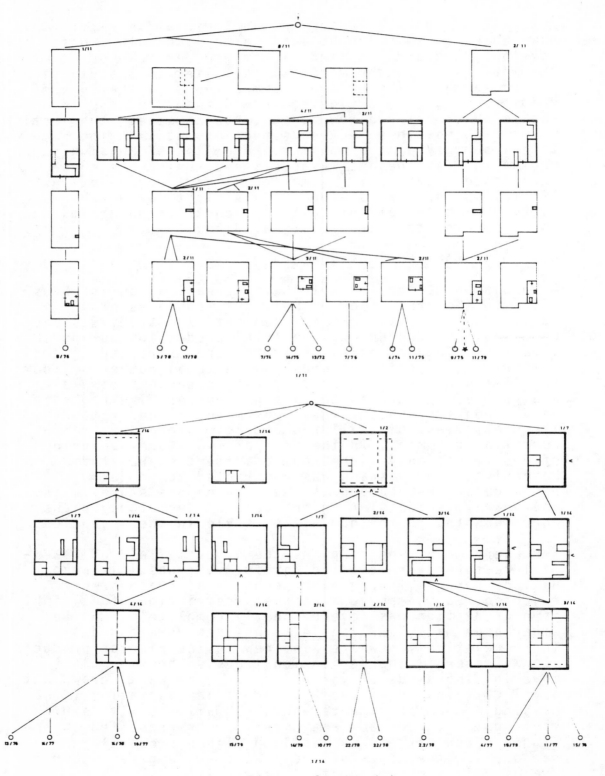

Figure 2 a and b
Generation systems for one room and three room apartments

Grammars and general optimization and decision techniques

If one has the possibility to enumerate all relevant
solutions, it is useful to develop a filtering system,
which selects subfamilies according to certain requirements. A similar way of thinking might be used on the
second abstraction level. One then filters solutions in
a quite abstract solution space, which is at hand in an
earlier stage of housing planning. In the search of
solutions elementary optimization techniques are
applicable. One might try to find optimal distributions
of apartments in an area or optimal forms of room configurations etc. (see e. g. Gero, 1979). This is easily
achieved in a computer assisted planning system by using
standard elementary optimization program packages. In
figure 3. a linear optimization problem is exemplified.
Its solution gives the optimal number of one-family
houses and row-house apartments in an area consisting of
building area and green-zone area under certain norms
(compare Seppälä, 1973). On the basis of the data given
by optimization it is easy to continue planning with the
aid of the typology grammar illustrated above. In this
process of planning action the final decision might be
reconstructed as well. The possibility to calculate
probability measures and different indices of optimality
allows us to use exact decision theoretic framework in
the description of an architect's work.

Construction grammars based on typology grammars

By using typology grammars in a planning situation one
might select a given type for further work by listing
known requirements. A central problem in the design is
to develop such a type into an acceptable real plan.
For example Helsinki town and most entrepreneurs have
quite accurate norms concerning constructions used in
housing production. Based on this it is possible to
develop transformation rules underlying the process
when one extends the 1:200 scale schemes to 1:100 or
1:50 scale drawings and analogously to realizations.
A plan might be considered as a composition of acceptable
symbols of building components, furniture etc. One
realization is always easy to produce. In real planning
work the situations, however, change in many phases
although under the guidance of the main idea. In one plan
type the measures of distance should be understood as
parameters as well as certain objects should be considered as variables.

In order to find the articulation and tolerance of

Land use	building area	green area
small houses = x	800	200
row-house apartments = y	200	400
supply	60000	40000

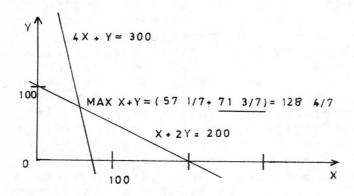

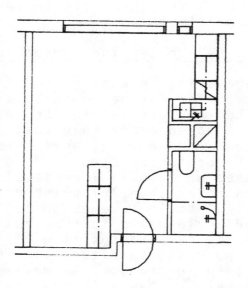

Y

$4X + Y = 300$

100

MAX $X+Y = (57 \ 1/7 + \underline{71 \ 3/7}) = 128 \ 4/7$

$X + 2Y = 200$

0

100

X

Figure 3.
A linear optimization problem giving the number of row-house apartments in an area.

Figure 4.
A plan of a single-room apartment in scale 1:100. The plan is denoted by an asterix in figure 2 a. It is generated by an elastic construction grammar from a product of a typology grammar.

variation of a plan covering the reasonable changes
depending of clients needs, one might apply the old idea
of elastic standardization. This has been emphasized in
modern architecture e. g. by the Finnish school, first
of all by Alvar Aalto in the fourties. In the production
of near variants of a type computers may also offer new
and effective design aids. The idea of elastic design is
exemplified in the connection of a single room apartment
type, which was accepted as a basis for further work by
a pensionate. The plan satisfies the area norms as well
as certain dimension and furniture norms of the Finnish
housing administration. All measures relevant to its (fig.4)
construction under the rectangularity condition are,
however, given as parameters when the plan type is used
as a part of a larger plan in drafting work. So if one
part changes in some dimension the corrections are automatic in drafting. The plan is drawn using a PASCAL based
design language called COMPOSITA. I hope this simple
example shows the possibilities, which we might generalize
to cover housing production in a district, a town etc.

Complete generation as a skeleton aiding mastering

The solution sets in architectural planning are enormous.
Consequently a complete generation is possible only in
restricted situations or in theoretical treatment.
Such derivations show, however, the main lines also in
practical planning work. When the designer has a control
over the principles he can also master continuous changes
in design possibilities. A grammatical approach in
architecture has deep meaning not only in computer
techniques but also in architectural theory as was stated
by Alvar Aalto when he proposed the idea of combinatory
systems as a basis for elastic standardization in 1941:

"It is obvious, that the standardization in architecture should not be applied to ready houses or to un-
elastic entities, but rather to its internal organs:
i. e. to building parts and elements, but in such an
order, that the main stress should be given to such
features that the parts may form an uncountable set of
different combinations. This is to say a system in
which from similar parts one may form an unlimited
amount of varying wholes with respect to their function and form."

In those days the main concern was in building standardization. Today we are working with the standardization of
planning routines. The basic problem of variation remains
the same but the problem is none the less not smaller.

References

Aalto A, 1972 Luonnoksia (Otava).

Avdot in L N, 1980 "The use of computing techniques in the design of residential buildings", Environment and Planning B 7 47-86.

Earl C F and March L J, 1979 "Architectural Applications of Graph Theory" in Applications of Graph Theory, Eds. Wilson R J and Beineke L W (New York) pp. 327-355.

Flemming U, 1981 "Structure in bungalow plans", Environment and Planning B 8 393-404.

Galle P, 1981 "An Algorithm for Exhaustive Generation of Building Floor Plans", Communications of the ACM vol. 24 pp. 813-825.

Gero J S, 1979 "Design by optimization and beyond" in Proceedings of the International Conference on the Application of Computers in Architecture, Building Design and Urban Planning (Berlin) pp. 393-401.

Koning H, Eizenberg J, 1981 "The language of the prairie: Frank Lloyd Wright's prairie houses", Environment and Planning B 8 295-323.

Mitchell W J, 1979 "Synthesis with style" in Proceedings of the International Conference on the Application of Computers in Architecture, Building Design and Urban Planning (Berlin) pp. 119-134.

Oksala T, 1979 "The language of formal architecture", Environment and Planning B 6 269-278.

Oksala T, 1981 "Logical Aspects of Architectural Experience and Planning", Helsinki University of Technology Research Papers 66 (Otaniemi).

Seppälä Y, 1973 Matemaattinen yhdyskuntasuunnittelu (Helsinki).

Seppänen J, Moore J M, 1979 "String processing algorithms for plant layout problems" in INT. J. PROD:RES, vol. 13 pp. 239-254.

Steadman P, 1973 "Graph theoretic representation of architectural arrangement", Architectural Research and Teaching vol. 2 pp. 161-172.

Stiny G, 1979 "A generative approach to composition and style in architecture" in Proceedings of the International Conference on the Application of Computers in Architecture, Building Design and Urban Planning (Berlin) pp. 119-134.

Wittkower R, 1973 Architectural Principles in the Age of Humanism (London).

DIS-INTEGRATED MODELS FOR BUILDING DESIGN

Paul Richens
Technical Director
Applied Research of Cambridge (ARC) Ltd
UK

An integrated design system is based on a central database for the storage of all sorts of design data: it is intended to aid coordination and enforce consistency while enabling all members of the design team to work with the most recent information.   In fact there are problems in allowing several people to update the data concurrently, while also enforcing consistency. The dis-integrated model is proposed as an alternative which offers very good concurrency at the expense of some kinds of consistency. It is particularly suited to multi-disciplinary design using distributed or even separate computers.

Paul Richens is Technical Director of ARC, responsible for software development.   From 1972-5 he developed the OXSYS system for building design, subsequently adapted to become BDS.   From 1978 he lead the development of GDS, now widely used for drafting in the construction (and many other) industries.

Integrated Design Systems

An integrated computer-aided design system consists of three components:

(i)   The design database

(ii)   Procedures for manipulating and interrogating the database

(iii)   The hardware and software implementation.

The design database itself describes the project in terms of (a) "entities", (b) associated "attributes" and (c) "relationships" between the entities. As an example, Table 1 identifies the entities and attributes used in our BDS system, and Table 2 the relationships it maintains.

The principle aims in designing such a database are:

a) Comprehensiveness - it should describe all relevant aspects of the design.

b) Non-redundancy - information should be stored once only. This distinguishes the integrated system from a set of drawings where information is duplicated many times, and the possibilities for incompatibility are manifold.

c) Consistency - the data should represent a feasible building, not a jumble of nonsense.

d) Availability - the design database should be available to all disciplines all the time, so that everyone is working with the most up-to-date information.

Of these aims, consistency is probably the hardest to pin down and achieve. It is a semantic requirement which can only be defined in terms of the meaning of the data (unlike non-redundancy which is much more a logical property of the data structure).

Name	Typical Attributes	Describes
PLANE	Position, label	Grid lines, floor and ceiling planes
ZONE	Shape, Name, Use	Rooms, depts, floors, etc.
PART	Position, special properties (e.g. Door Number)	An instance of a component in the building.
COMPONENT	General properties e.g. Shape, description, Cost.	An item in a catalogue of "things" and "specifications".

Table 1. Entities and attributes used by BDS

Entities	Relationships
ZONE-ZONE	Functional heirarchy, spatial enclosure, overlap etc.
ZONE-PART	Things located in a room etc.
ZONE-COMP	Specifications associated with a room etc.
PART-PART	Connectivity (especially in services).
PART-COMP	Type of component instanced as a part.
COMP-COMP	Assembly/subassembly relationship.

Table 2. Relationships used by BDS. Note that all
entities except COMPONENT are spatially
related by their position coordinates.

There are three approaches to maintaining consistency:

a) Define manipulation procedures that are only capable of converting one consistent state into another.

b) All changes are validated by the system, which checks against a set of consistency "constraints".

c) Inconsistencies are allowed, but occasionally the database is checked by a special consistency check procedure. Rectification is carried out by the designers.

The most important aspect of consistency in building design is the coordination of structure and services; the most important rule is that spatial clashes are not allowed.

The argument of this paper is that the aims of availability and consistency are not compatible, and that some reasonable compromise between them must be made if a system is to be successful.

The Bankers Problem and Serialisability

The problems of maintaining consistency in a database subject to multiple concurrent updates are well known, and can be easily illustrated by the "Bankers Problem":

You and your wife operate a joint account with £50 in it. You each have a cash-card allowing you to withdraw cash from a dispenser. The dispenser operates the following protocol designed to stop you overdrawing your account:

a) Read current balance B from the database.

b) Enquire amount A to be withdrawn.

c) If B greater than A then
        updates balance to B-A
        issue cash A
    otherwise confiscate card.

Suppose now you try to withdraw £30 at the same time as your wife at another dispenser tries to withdraw £40. Each machine finds that B is greater than A. One will update it to £20, the other to £10. As both issue the cash, both possible final states of your account are wrong.

A fundamental theorem in the science of databases states that the outcome of a set of interleaved transactions (such as I have described) is correct if it is the same as doing them serially (one after another). In the example one drawer should get the cash, the other lose the card (the outcome is correct whichever way round it happens). The problem of concurrent access is to ensure that transactions are serialisable while allowing them to overlap as much as possible.

It is not hard to envisage similar problems in a design database. Consider for example an engineer locating a radiator on a partition, while simultaneously a layout planner is locating a cupboard, and an architect is moving the partition. Even if consistency rules state that cupboards and radiators must be fixed to partitions, and that spatial clashes are not allowed, the outcome could easily be a radiator and a cupboard occupying the same space, and the wall somewhere else altogether.

Locking

The classical answer to the Bankers Problem is to "lock" the record describing your balance so that no-one else can see it until the transaction is complete. This allows no overlap. Alternatives are to allow the second to look at the record, but forbid it to update it; or conversely to forbid the first to update if a second is looking at it.

The first approach allows no concurrency; the others allow some but with a risk that one or other transaction will fail and have to be restarted. (The first protocol can also need restarting if a "deadlock" occurs.)

Restarting a transaction is acceptable for simple cases such as the bank dispenser. It is very doubtful that it would do in a design database.

A design "transaction" is rarely as simple as drawing cash from a bank. The designer looks at a lot of records (everything drawn on his screen). He may think about it and modify things for a considerable period (hours or days) before he is ready to "commit" the transaction to the database. He must be given the opportunity to "rollback", that is to withdraw his updates if he changes his mind and thinks of a better approach.

Lock Granularity

When considering database locking schemes, there are two dimensions of interest. One is the "granularity" of the lock, which can vary between a single record and the whole database; the other is its duration.

The duration in transaction processing systems is usually a few seconds. This is too short for most design problems, and makes the designer "commit" himself too soon. More reasonable durations would match the time between repaints of his screen (a few minutes), or a working session (a few hours), or a complete design excercise (a few days). It is undesirable to combine the locking of a large number of records with long duration, because it gives a high probability of a deadlock developing late in the period, necessitating someone retrying a lot of work.

My recommendation is that the unit of locking should be more than a record, less than the entire database, and should normally last for a workstation session. The unit of locking I will call a "dataset". One or more datasets are locked during a session. Occasionally the locks are freed early, without ending a session, and sometimes held longer, over several sessions.

Subdividing the Database

The basic notion of "dis-integrated" modelling is to subdivide the database into independently lockable datasets.

Four ways of dis-integrating a model suggest themselves:

a) Geographical - split into spatially separate parts e.g. wings and floors of a building.

b) By model type - for example the BDS Zone model and located part model might be separable.

c) By discipline - architecture, services, structure etc.

d) By trade or element - e.g. concrete, fixtures,

ducting, piping.

These subdivisions are in practice combined, so that you could have "Floor 2 heating zone model", or a "Floor 3 fixture part model".

This kind of dis-integration is equally applicable to drafting systems. Here the drawings are split into separate overlays which can be viewed together or separately as necessary, and are independently lockable for update purposes. Similarly it is envisaged that the dis-integrated models can be superimposed on the screen when desired. It is even possible to envisage a mixture of drafting and model overlays combined on the screen.

Successful dis-integration demands the absence of relationships between the sub-models, though not necessarily of those between entities within a model. The BDS schema has one problematical relationship, that between zones and parts. This is a problem because anyone updating zones or updating parts would need access to it, and so independent locking of zones or parts is of no benefit. One would try hard to eliminate such relationships, though some are sure to persist.

Multi-access Protocols

Given that the design database has been split into separately lockable datasets, it is worth re-examining locking protocols to see what trade-offs between consistency and concurrency are possible. There are three basic protocols to be considered:

a) Many readers or one writer. If you are reading a dataset no-one can write to it. If you are updating no-one can read until you've finished by committing or rolling-back your changes.

   This is the usual protocol enforced by computer filing systems as it avoids the worst confusions. If the protocol is strengthened so that you hold all your locks until the end of a session when you release them all, serialisability is guaranteed. This means that consistency between sub-models can be enforced. The cost is in low concurrency. You cannot look at any part of a model someone else is updating.

b)   Many readers <u>and</u> one writer. If you are reading
     someone else <u>can</u> update. You don't see his updates
     until they are committed and you ask for them. If
     you are updating, others can see the state of the
     model before you started.

     This protocol loses serialisability insofar as
     transactions affect multiple models. So consistency
     <u>between</u> models is not enforceable, though it can
     be <u>within</u> a model.

     On the other hand concurrency is markedly improved.
     The architect can work on his model while seeing
     overlayed the most recent services model. The
     services engineer can do the reverse. This of course
     does not guarantee consistency, but is near-perfect
     concurrency.

c)   Many readers and many writers. This is a slight
     elaboration of the previous protocol, with some
     advantages. Several people can simultaneously
     modify the model. However only one can commit his
     changes permanently and make them visible to others.
     Some method of arbitration is necessary. The most
     obvious application of this protocol is in the
     development of design alternatives. Several schemes
     are worked out, only one of which is finally
     committed. Or perhaps both are retained, leading
     to divergent design variants .. ?

Our preferred protocol is the middle one, permitting
"many readers and one writer" to access each sub-model
simultaneously. Users are able to access any part of
the database at any time, even if someone is updating
it. They are of course warned that this is going on,
as it means they cannot update it, and what they are
looking at <u>may</u> shortly be out of date (on the other
hand the updates may never be committed). They are able
to update any sub-model that no-one else is already
updating. Their access commands have some unusual
possibilities:

ROLLBACK - cancel all updates I've made but not released.

RELEASE - commit my updates so that others can see them.

REFRESH - re-open models I am reading so that I can see
           any recently released updates.

Conclusions

Concurrency and consistency are mutually inconsistent
aims. For design databases I would recommend going
for high concurrency and accepting that consistency
between sub-models cannot be enforced. It can still
be checked when required. This is perhaps disappointing
to those who had hoped that certain intractable problems
(such as coordination of structure and services) would
be handled automatically by CAD. My conclusion is
that coordination can be enforced "as you go" if

a) you allow only one designer to work at a time, or

b) you use a transaction approach where decisions are
    rapidly made and committed piecemeal.

The first of these conditions makes a nonsense of
multi-disciplinary design, and is impractical on any
reasonable size project. The second denies the designer
time to take thought, experiment and discard ideas.
If a system enforces either restrictions, the result
is that the designers work at their desks in pencil on
hard-copy, and input when they get a chance. This is
in fact what the dis-integrated system does on the
computer. Each designer works on his own part of the
database, in private and without interference. He can
check consistency with previous states of other models.
Total consistency can only be checked during a quiet
period when no-one is updating.

Besides the high availability of (not quite up-to-date)
data, the dis-integrated model has advantages in giving
each discipline control of its own data, and in working
in just the same way when they are using separate
computers. The restriction on relationships between
entities in different sub-models may curtail some of
the more elaborate fancies of system designers, but will
pay-off in a cleaner, more modular structure in the
overall system. We envisage a series of model types,
and drafting, which can be mixed in whatever way the
project demands. The separation of the various
techniques means that an operator has to understand no
more of the total system than is relevant to his task.

STYLE FOR 1984: COMPUTERS AND BUILDING FORM

Antony D Radford
Garry Stevens
Computer Applications Research Unit
Department of Architectural Science
University of Sydney
Australia

The relationship between computers, building form and
building style is examined. Speculations on future
influences of the use of computers in the design process,
in the construction process and in the control of
buildings are based on some existing examples.

Tony Radford, Ph.D., is an
architect and planner and
Associate Director of the
Computer Applications Research
Unit, Department of
Architectural Science,
University of Sydney.

Garry Stevens, Dip.Arch.Comp.,
specializes in computer-aided
architectural design and is
currently working with the
Computer Applications Research
Unit.

1. Introduction

"The Ministry of Truth - Minitrue, in Newspeak - was
startlingly different from any other object in sight.
It was an enormous pyramidal structure of glittering
white concrete, soaring up, terrace after terrace, 300
metres into the air..... The Ministry of Truth
contained, it was said, three thousand rooms above
ground level, and corresponding ramifications below."
(George Orwell, 'Nineteen Eighty-Four',1949)

Style in architecture results from a combination of
social, economic, historical and technological influences.
In George Orwell's Oceania, technology, despite the
telescreen by which Big Brother can watch you, is really
rather low level. The Ministry of Truth manages to work
remarkably efficiently without a computerized database. A
Minitrue Building designed in 1983 instead of 1948 (Orwell
did, in fact, seriously consider calling his novel
Nineteen Forty-Eight, and the technology, if not the
society, reflects that age) would be more distinguishable
by its electronic communications networks and computer
halls than by its three thousand rooms. This is a paper
about the relationship between building form and the
electronic microprocessor-based technology of computers
and computer-controlled systems. Our theme is that a
discernable relationship does exist, and that it arises
both through a generalized diffusion of a particular
technological imagery and through three quite specific
meeting points of this technology with architecture:
computers in the design process, computers in construction, and computer control of buildings. Although it
is difficult to isolate these influences from a myriad of
other determinants of building style, we want here to
discuss some case studies and arguments which point a
direction.

2. Technological Icons

Oceania's Minitrue Building displays the traditional
symbolism of power: strength (the pyramidal shape), size
(300 metres into the air), conspicuousness (glittering
white concrete), and an army of people (3000 rooms).
Computers are physically weak, small, come in muted tones,
and require few people: yet still we call them powerful.

I have in front of me an ad for the latest Buick, an American car made by General Motors. The centrepiece of the ad is, of course, a photograph of a Buick. The photograph is enclosed in a black screen-surround. The car is silver-grey. Around the photograph of the car, peeking out from the margins, are various bits of modern electronic consumer goods. Just in front of the Buick, right in the centre of the ad, is a floppy disk drive and a keyboard. All these are silver-grey and dark grey, with black trim.

Here is the microchip aesthetic with a vengeance: matt, muted greys, blacks and whites; smooth, sleek lines, just slightly rounded at the edges. Rectilinear forms or elegant wedges you could fondle without feeling a sharp edge. The elements are composed so that nothing looks misplaced or otiose. Utility without decoration, functionality without distraction: both keyboard and car. This imagery is common for modern electronics goods, and can be seen in radios, irons, and hairdryers, though few of these contain microprocessors.

The tall blue cabinets of mainframe central processors and tape drives had little influence on popular industrial design, no doubt because few people actually ever saw them. In the 1960's and 1970's the conventional image of a computer, replete with blinking lights and overworked tape-drives, bore little resemblance to the actuality. This image is fast disappearing from the public mind. Edward de Bono can be seen in prime time television laterally selling stylish Olivetti equipment, the paragon of microchip aesthetic. A large exhibition of micro-computers was held earlier this year in a Sydney shopping mall at which several thousand members of the public inspected the very latest products. Apart from the usual gaggle of confused businessmen and computer-wise teenage boys, the largest group consisted of families making an outing of the event. Not one of the computers at the exhibition had flashing lights or wildly whirring tape drives. But downstairs, in the shopping mall, an astrologer was advertising computerised horoscopes. Dominating the little Apple he actually used to produce these wonders were boxes of gratuitous electronics - with rows of flashing lights.

Following sociological usage, culture in its widest sense may be divided into a Great Tradition and a Little Tradition. The Great Tradition is characterised by literacy, formal, written traditions and norms, and selfconscious articulation. The Little Tradition encompasses in part what we would call folk traditions,

and is typically passed down from person to person.
Architect's architecture - the sort of building that
appears in national architectural journals - is clearly
part of the Great Tradition. Most private housing
continues to be built without architects and buildings of
the Little Tradition fill the world's dormitory suburbs
and industrial parks.

The Futurist architects used the symbols of early
industrial power, heroic in scale and form. The pioneers
of the Modern Movement used the symbols of mass-production
and engineering precision, although Le Corbusier was
obliged to imitate the image of manufactured precision in
the Villa Savoye with handcrafted components and Mies van
der Rohe demanded tolerances which could only be achieved
at enormous expense. The studio work of Archigram,
Superstudio and Tange takes images from developed
production technology and applies them to cities and
dwellings. All of this work concerns style, in the sense
that it operates predominantly on images to evoke certain
emotional and aesthetic feelings (as does the Buick
Century and the astrologer's computer) rather than
originating as necessary responses to the technology of
the time. Indeed, architecture schools, with a curriculum
concentrating on design, style and aesthetics (if not in
intention, at least in the status associated with these
subjects in students' minds), have produced graduates who
have been ill-equiped to genuinely understand and exploit
technology. For the best response of the Great Tradition
to computers we should look first at the buildings of the
computer industry, buildings like those for Inmos in Wales
or for Digital in California. These two buildings are
different in many ways (Digital conceals everything inside
its crisp and anonymous black box, whereas Inmos holds its
structure and services out to view) but together they
display some characteristics of the technology within
them: they look fragile rather than strong (glass at
Digital, delicate structure at Inmos), relatively small
and low, and make no attemp to dominate their surroundings
(much of Silicon Valley is obscured by landscaping, and
Inmos stands out for its originality rather than
deliberate self-advertisement).

The principles of the Modern Movement passed through to
the Little Tradition in the form of an emphasis on
simplicity and rigour, and an awareness of prefabricated
and industrialised building techniques. Builders and
developers retained the economic message while discarding
the aesthetic. For a variety of reasons which are also
more to do with construction than with aesthetics - see
below - the real and lasting effects of the computer on

the built form may depend on the pragmatists of the Little
Tradition and their utilisation of its abilities.

3. Design Technology

Superimposed on this notion of the computer as a symbol of
power is any stylistic or formal design results of the use
of computers as part of a new design technology. Marshal
McLuhan has argued (1967) that the prose style of both
Henry James and Wyndham Lewis significantly altered when
they changed their means of recording their ideas from
writing down text to dictating it. Our use of a word
processor to create this work is influencing its final
form since we are very ready to make minor alterations to
the draft typescript. Our question here is whether the
medium of computers in design affects the message of
building form, and whether in the future that effect will
amount to an influence on style.

At one level we can present computer-aided architectural
design (CAAD) systems as analogous to a 'sharper pencil',
qualitatively in the same class as the old design tools,
bringing benefits of increased speed and efficiency rather
than a significantly different architecture. The initial
response to our own questions of users of computer
drafting systems as to whether their resulting
architecture has been influenced by their use of computers
has always been denial. Indeed, the question is seen as
aggressive, seeking evidence of undesirable
standardization or the reduction of a designer's creative
freedom. In the words of a drafting system vendor "no
firms have yet admitted to that". The truth of this
denial appears to be supported by the difficulty, if not
impossibility, of spotting on the ground a building which
has been designed with computer aids. To regard CAAD
systems as merely 'sharper pencils', though, is equivalent
to regarding a motor vehicle as merely a better kind of
horse. The reluctance to accept that architecture might
be influenced by the tools of its creation stems, we
think, from two factors. The first is the protective
attitude of many architects towards "this most creative of
the professions" (Manser, 1983) and their mistrust of any
externalization or formalization of the design process.
The second factor is that with computers in architecture
we are still just at the beginning of a long trail of
development. When motor cars travelled at walking speed
and had to be preceded by a man with a red flag, the
notion of their being a better kind of horse made sense.

In the same way that the early motor car influenced where
the traveller journeyed (over roads but not cross country)
we should, though, expect to see some result in the form
and detail of buidlings from the use of existing computer
tools. The first area in which to look for evidence is
not with computer graphics but with mathematical
simulation and analysis models. In environmental design,
thermal performance analysis tools such as ABACUS's ESP
(Maver and Ellis, 1982) depend for their very existence on
the supposition that use of the computer will influence
the resulting built form: if there is no connection, then
there is no point in using the tool in the first place.
Since there are now buildings which have been designed by
a process which has included such analysis tools, we can
reasonably assume that their final forms owe something to
the computer analysis.

Even with the current generation of drafting systems,
intended primarily for documentation rather than design,
there is some link between the drawing medium and the
resulting building. Consider the standard detail: all
computer drafting systems make standard details very much
easier to manage and adapt and this ease can itself
encourage their use. Since many totally non-computerised
offices also use standard details this is an extension of
aл existing link between a design methodology and built
form rather than the forging of a new link. What is new
is a benefit at the design presentation and documentation
stages from the standardization of fixtures and fittings.
The careful definition of the 2-D or 3-D form of a
building fixture, or piece of furniture is a time-
consuming operation: "it takes 15 minutes to set up a
piece of furniture simply, maybe 3 hours to do a really
good job for presentation drawings" (Blunden,1983). The
result is a tendency to standardize both within and across
jobs where a repertoire of carefully chosen elements are
selected, represented and re-used. Sanitary ware and other
manufacturers are now prepared to provide designers with
digitized descriptions of their products. We could
classify such cases as forces towards standardization,
although such a force, if the standardization is on the
whole demonstrably good, may be desirable rather than
undesirable. Standardization at this level is in a way
only the codification of the experience and preferences of
an architect or office.

What is important, moreover, is that these forces for
standardization are counter balanced by other forces for
diversification resulting from the richness of the
computer as a drafting medium compared with the
traditional drafting machine. In traditional drafting the

basic unit is the line and a drawing is an assembly of
lines. The only variation is in line thickness. In
computer drafting the basic unit can be any drawn image.
The drawing is an assembly of images with variation in
both image and transformation (scale, rotation,
translation) of that image. It implies a very different
way of drafting which allows different formal
explorations. At Sydney we developed as a student project
a 2-D drafting system for the facades of Victorian terrace
houses, with an appropriate set of images for Victorian
windows, doors, and decorative elements. By exploring
transformations and combinations which are not normal to
Victorian architecture, one student produced facades of a
style more akin to the work of Walter Burley Griffin or
Frank Lloyd Wright. At a bigger scale, it is fairly easy
to lay out and control the dimensions of, say, an
elliptical building using the drafting system to provide a
suitable grid in a way which, with manual drafting, could
only be done with a rectangular building. Sometimes the
use of a computer system suggests an entirely new approach
to design problem solving: the use of the orthogonal OXSYS
CAD system for hospitals suggested the the simplified
solution of orthogonal plumbing (Jones, 1982). In the
longer term, the incorporation of knowledge into drawing
systems (Bijl, 1982) should allow architects to start
designing at a higher level, not resolving the repetitive
problems of keeping the warmth in and the rain out (that
will be known within the system's knowledge base) but
solving the design problems which are particular to the
project.

Our present readiness to accept the limitations of our
design tools is illustrated by the difference between 2-D
and 3-D computer drafting and modelling systems. I was
recently told by a very satisfied user of a 2-D computer
drafting system that architects did not need 3-D systems:
after all, the images must finally be reduced to two-
dimensional plan and elevation form for communication to a
building contractor. My response is that the limitation
of communications to two-dimensional drawings has been a
major handicap in achieving good buildings. We all know
of cases where the real construction difficulties have
been in three-dimensional junctions of walls, roofs,
structure and services which plans and sections have
failed to adequately describe. The restriction of the
creative and documentation process to two dimensions seems
to me to be an unfortunate necessity caused by the design
and documentation medium we use rather than a desirable
abstraction. Architects do not - cannot - know what it is
like to work consistently in three dimensions because they
have never had the tools to do so, although we do know

that many of what are widely recognized as the 'best'
architects have made extensive use of physical models as
part of the creative as well as the presentation process.

Computers have made a substantial impact in the graphic
arts. The result, of course, is a 1980's style of
graphics which has been very clearly and very considerably
influenced by the medium of its creation. One has only to
look at television logos and advertisements to see the
extent of this influence. Very few architects have used
computers to explore design ideas for buildings in any
comparable way. Of his work with three-dimensional shape
modellers, Harold Borkin of the University of Michigan
reports that "only once or twice" has he "been able,
through Boolean operations (on component spaces), to
create a space which (he) couldn't visualize - but that's
exciting when it happens", (Borkin, 1983).

The 1983 reality is that using such approaches in
architecture are still quite clumsy, the effort required
to define an object in three dimensions is still onerous.
The effort of using the tool dominates the creative
process. I do not think, though, that this will always be
the case. Three-dimensional graphics tablets for data
input were mooted long ago (Sutherland, 1974) and models
now exist. For output, perhaps holography will provide a
true three-dimensional answer. It is said that the
biggest market for holography will be pornography;
perhaps architecture will come second.

4.   Construction Technology

Graphic design, where the medium of design has clearly
influenced the resulting expression, is quite different
from architecture in that the medium of design is the same
as the medium of production. A graphics designer can
create and explore images on a computer screen and, when
he is happy with the result, those same images are the
final product of his design process. In architecture,
drawn images are only a means of communication with a
separate organization which realizes the product. If we
are going to look for the influence of the design medium
on architectural style, we should also look for the
influence of the construction medium.

Compared with other production industries, building
construction is still very labour intensive and
unmechanized. Certainly, construction has problems which
other production industries do not share: the need to
work outdoors, in all weathers, and putting together
largely one-off products on sites remote from any

permanent industrial base. The result is a major change
in the balance between the cost of artifacts which can be
manufactured in fully mechanized factories and the cost of
buildings. In Sydney fifty years ago the cost of a
suburban house was about two to three times the cost of a
family car. Today a comparable house, now excluding the
land on which it stands, would be about eight times the
cost of a comparable car. The reason is that car
construction has benefited from miniaturization,
standardization and mechanization whereas methods of
domestic scale building construction have changed very
little indeed.

One of the reasons for the marked trend towards timber
framed housing in Britain, away from full brick housing,
is the transfer of construction activities from the site
to a factory. There is now a whole new industry of 'panel
bashers'. It does not sound like high-technology, but the
panels for about 20% of British timber-framed houses are
laid out by a computer program which runs on a small Apple
microcomputer (Hobin, 1983). Moreover, the transfer of
this element of construction into workshops facilitates
mechanized handling, layout jigs and fixing. Prefabricated bathrooms and plumbing units are part of the
same trend.

There is, of course, nothing new about prefabricated
buildings. What is new is the possibility of applying
computers and numeric-controlled machines to construction
processes, and such applications are (so far) much easier
to introduce in a controlled environment than out on site.
The integration of CAD/CAM (computer-aided design/computer
aided manufacturing) systems, so that a designer can use
his design medium to generate a digital tape to directly
control a numeric control machine, is already under
investigation in the metal buildings industry in the
United States: "The design software is expected to link
the drafting room electronically with the fabricating
shop" (Vonier, 1982). Interestingly, standardization of
components and processes in this industry has not led to a
uniformity in the resulting buildings, and because clients
are becoming less rather than more willing to accept pre-
set solutions manufacturers are "moving away from 'hard-
tooling' and towards microprocessor-controlled
fabrication" (Vonier, 1982). CAD/CAM need not be confined
to industrialized building, though. Peter Blunden of
Jackson, Teece, Chesterman, Willis, a Sydney, Australia,
architecture firm which is using its GDS drafting system
in the restoration of the 19th century Sydney General Post
Office, reports that they have "started making discrete
enquiries both here (Australia) and overseas to see if we

can use our data to run stonemason machines - not so much
for the one-off piece of stone as for continuous egg-and-
dart mouldings" (Blunden, 1983b).

Maybe (is it a romantic hope?) this technology will not
only be applied in building restorations but also make
possible a richer and more decorative form of architecture
generally. And why not use it for the one-off piece of
stone? All we need is a different tape. In the whole
range of building products, robots and microprocessors in
the production process ought to provide more choice and
diversity of product.

I think the point we want to make in this section on
construction processes is that there is going to be an
increasing pressure to design buildings which allow for
the use of robots and mechanization in their construction,
with a significant cost penalty for buildings which do not
make those allowances. We shall probably soon find robots
on site (the University of New South Wales in Australia is
one organization researching this field, and on a much
larger scale Hitachi in Japan is working with a major
construction firm), but it does suggest dry construction
methods (high-tech electronics and water do not mix very
well). Robots may also allow the construction of building
forms which are otherwise impossible: they may soon be
shinning high up steel stanchions, or digging their way
deep underground, to find themselves in positions where no
sensible man would dare go.

5. Computer Control in Buildings

The third element of this triumvirate of computer
influences on building form is the use of computers and
microprocessors in buildings, both as a part of the
occupational processes within the building and for the
control of the building itself. The former may well be
the most significant influence on the form of our
buildings and cities of all; we have all read scenarios
of deserted city centres and impoverished developers whose
multi-storey monuments have been rendered unnecessary by a
technology which allows people to work from idyllic
country cottages without the necessity of meeting in one
place. In the second category, Design magazine in 1981
was announcing "the birth of the intelligent building" in
describing a project by Cedric Price to construct a guest
house in Florida with walls that would move under computer
control in response to its residents' moods (Sudjic,
1981). Existing computer control in buildings is more
prosaic, encompassing security systems,
heating/cooling/lighting systems and lifts. These

lighting and thermal systems should be able to react to expected conditions (using satellite or other remote data) instead of present conditions. Certainly many more items of domestic and commercial equipment will contain microprocessors, and this may effect space requirements through miniturization, but this will probably have little effect on building form, unless ...

The 'unless' refers to a different kind of living, somewhere between Archigram's living pods, the video games and imaginary world of the film Tron, and the subterranean introverted world of E.M. Forster's 'The Machine Stops' (Forster,1947). Computer imagery enables us to get out of the real world and live in a pseudo-world of the mind and simulated reality, as in the real-time flight simulator. Perhaps we could plug in a digital simulation of strolling through the streets of Venice, as Nick Negreponte has created a video simulation of strolling in and around the buildings of Aspen, Colrado. Certainly in Forster's world travel has gone right out of fashion. We don't, then, need real buldings, real architecture: a computer simulation will do.

6. A Style

We want in this final section to address the promise of the title and to speculate on a style for the future: post-post-modern, or digital-tech, or whatever else we like to call it. In it we are being frankly speculative; there are probably as many different scenarios as there are readers of this paper. We shall only assume a continuing desire and need for real buildings, rather than exclusively digital simulations for people living in a personalized cocoon.

Since we are speculating we may as well be optimistic. We are going to argue for a rich, diverse architecture of the future which has been designed much more completely than most existing buildings are designed, which is individually fitted to its local environment because of the computer analyses which have been used in its design, and that has been put together accurately and consistently with the aid of robots and numeric-controlled machines. It is an architecture which combines rational responses to performance requirements with the spark of delight and imagination which distinguishes the great from the mundane. And it is a sculptural architecture, freed from the need to be strictly rectilinear, without the pressure to give stock answers to standardized design problems. In short, we hope for a magnificently creative period of architecture spurred by new tools and techniques, in the same way that the early days of the Renaissance and the early days of he Modern Movement led to a creative period of architecture.

So where does this leave us? It leaves us with the prospect of a very different set of design tools and a very different set of construction tools, which are much more closely linked together than is now the case. It leaves us with the prospect of designing buildings for a world of industry and commerce which is dependant on computer technology and, perhaps, for a population which can choose to reject that real world and retreat into a personal land of computer imagery and computer games which responds to their actions and moods in a way that the earlier retreats of literature, radio and television could not. The style of buildings that result will be a response partly to this computer technology and partly to those other social, economic and historical influences which we listed at the beginning of this paper. The post-modernism of the early 1980's, after all, can hardly be described as a rational response to the technology of the time. And there will probably be great, mediocre and bad computer-aided designed architecture, just as we have great, mediocre and bad pencil-aided architecture now. It may even be the same architects producing the good results. Fortunately, there seems no reason whatever why our 1984 architecture should bear any resemblance to the Minitrue Building in Oceania.

8. Acknowledgemnets

We acknowledge the contribution of our colleagues in the Computer Applications Research Unit, and particularly those individuals cited in the references, to the ideas contained in this paper.

9. References

Bijl, A. (1982). 'Dumb Drawing Systems and Knowledge Engineering', CAD82, ed. A. Pipes, Butterworths, Guildford.

Blunden, P. (1983). Personal communication.

Blunden, P. (1983b). 'Experience in Practice', lecture given in the Overview of Architectural Computing series, University of Sydney.

Borkin, H. (1983). Personal communication.

Forster, E.M. (1947). 'The Machine Stops', <u>Collected Short Stories</u>, Sidgwick and Jackson, London.

Hobin, R. (1983). Personal communication.(program author)

Jones, E.M. (1982). 'The Design of a Complex Building using an Integrated CAD System', <u>CAD82</u>, ed. A. Pipes, Butterworths, Guildford.

Manser, M. (1983). Quoted in RIBA Journal, June.

Maver, T.W., and Ellis, J. (1982). Implementation of an Energy Model within a Multi-Disciplinary Practice, <u>CAD82</u>, ed. A. Pipes, Butterworths, Guildford.

McLuhan, M. (1964). <u>Understanding Media: The Extensions of Man</u>, Routledge, London.

Orwell, G. (1949). <u>Nineteen Eighty-Four</u>, Secker and Warburg, London.

Sudjic, D. (1981). 'Birth of the Intelligent Building', <u>Design</u>, January.

Sutherland, I. (1974). 'Three Dimensional Data Input by Tablet', <u>Proceedings of the IEEE</u>, 62:64 (April).

Vonier, T. (1982). 'Beyond Shade and Shelter', <u>Progressive Architecture</u>, Nr.3.

CESSOL: An expert system for the specification of site investigation

D BOISSIER
Doctor of Sciences
Laboratoire Methodes
Department Genie Civil et Urbanisme, INSA

J C MANGIN
Director
J P MOUGIN
Doctor of Engineering
Laboratoire Genie Civil et Habitat
Universite de Savoie
France

This paper presents the expert system CESSOL, whose objective is to contribute to the specification of site investigation for buildings.   We describe what an expert system is, why this technique is adopted for this problem. Second, we present the basis, the structure, of CESSOL and examples of expert rules.

D Boissier is doctor of sciences, member of the Laboratory "Methods' in the department of Genie Civil et Urbanisme in INSA at Lyon. His research relates to CAD systems and connections between soils, foundations and buildings.

J C Mangin has been director of the Laboratory 'Genie Civil et Habitat' at University of Savoie since 1980.   From 1968-1980 he was in the department 'Genie Civil et Urbanisme' in INSA at Lyon. His research relates to the development of CAD systems or expert systems for the conception of buildings.

J P Mougin is doctor of engineering and a member of the Laboratory 'Genie Civil et Habitat' at University of Savoie.   His research

Introduction

CAD systems have developed during the last ten years. They allow flexible linking of algorithmic modules in applications programs. Our research, in preliminary building design stage, leads us to build such systems. One of their limits is that they are only able to answer problems which can be solved by algorithmic methods.

Expert systems, derived from work in artificial intelligence, permit us to get over this limit. Their way of reasoning is separated from the knowledge base of the field. This knowledge, brought to the system in a declarative form, allows problems to be tackled which would be difficult to solve by algorithms.

The expert system CESSOL that we propose is a prototype whose aim is, to aid designers early in design to define a site investigation consistent with the brief. The results of this exploration are needed subsequently to define the foundations of the buildings.

1. An expert system for site investigation

1.1. Notions about expert systems

An expert system is software able to solve problems for which we don't have algorithms. It makes use of specific knowledge of the field being studied. Knowledge is integrated in a 'knowledge base' which contains facts and rules allowing non-trivial inferences to be made from these facts. The rules formalise the 'know-how' of experts.

The knowledge base is built in a declarative form. The facts and the rules are inserted in any order, which does not prejudge the way this information is utilized. A fundamental step in building any expert system is to get the experts to formalise their knowledge and reasoning. This information is frequently informal, badly structured, empirical and sometimes inconsistent.

The essential characteristic of an expert system is that there is an interaction between the knowledge base and the procedures for exploiting them. These procedures form the program named the 'inference engine'. It uses the knowledge in the base required to solve a particular problem. This distinction between knowledge base and inference engine offers great flexibility during the development of the system. It is easy to complete the knowledge base by self-education, adding facts as they become known.

The conversational aspect of an expert system is primary. An expert system must always be able to explain its reasoning, to say why it reaches this or that conclusion, why it rejects this or that hypothesis. The possibilities of dialogue in a quasi-natural language are necessary conditions for the user to accept the system as really expert.

1.2   The problem of site investigation

A site investigation traditionally begins from a preliminary inquiry which aims to collect available information about the site, the ground and the buildings.   This inquiry comprises a geological survey, an examination of the site, a study of programmes of tests previously made on this site or on surrounding sites, a study of nearby buildings and of their geotechnical context.

From this information, it is then necessary to decide on an investigation program from which it will be possible to specify:

- the composition of the ground to a sufficient depth (identification and geometry of the various layers):

- the mechanical properties of the layers:

- some possibilities for carrying out the work if necessary.

This programme of tests can be defined in many ways. The selected solutions are very often a compromise between full but expensive investigations and lesser ones involving more risk.   It is therefore necessary to build a programme of investigation that forgets none of the elements which are important for the project and answers all necessary questions.

1.3   Why an expert-system for site investigation?

Experience shows that all technical elements can't be integrated in an algorithmic way. The various kinds of investigation programmes make the procedural approach unrealizable in practice.

The experts don't all use the same strategy.   They are inclined to consider any problem as a particular one. A fixed system would require a definitive choice of some of these strategies.   The experts would not agree with this approach because it could not be proved to be able to cope with every problem.

There is a continual technological evolution of site tests.   These innovations induce new behaviour, new reasonings which can't be easily introduced into a fixed system. Such an algorithmic system is, in fact, closed and every modification of its structure is expensive.

So the two essential reasons for which we have opted for an expert system become evident:

- independance of the knowledge base and of the inference engine:

- flexibility of restatement and improvement of the knowledge base, if it is not ordered it can easily be changed.

It lastly appears of prime importance that we can explain the proposed programmes of investigation through the justification of which tests are retained or rejected. The notion of expert system allows this and we have attached a great importance to the explicative character of CESSOL. This is imperative because of the complexity of the domain and of the great number of potential test programmes. It is therefore necessary to:

- check the good fit of propositions to the problem which must be solved:

- improve the quality of the propositions by eliminating any arbitrary or biased reasonings of designers:

- make explicit new approaches by self training of the system (adding new facts and new rules).

2. The basis of CESSOL

CESSOL aims to propose geotechnical tests defined by their nature, implantation, number, depth. These tests are regrouped in one or more programmes of site investigation consistent with the case being studied as a function of user's practices or economic necessities.

Now, we describe the data for CESSOL and the functional schema which permits it to reason.

2.1. Entry point in CESSOL

CESSOL makes use of data which lie in the knowledge base which is in two parts:

- the geotechnical data interpreted by facts and rules:

- the particular data of the problem to be solved.

These latter part comprises the answers to a questionnaire about the site and the ground, the building and its foundations. The interactions between ground, foundation and building involve the designer in interrogating himself about these three elements.

- interrogations about the site and the ground

For the site, they concern the dimensions, the form, the environment, (urban, noise,....), the vegetable layer. Interrogations about the ground concern the following points: the layers (nature, homogenity, quality, slope, thickness), the

ground water (water level, circulation), the natural or man-made
anomalies (blocks, cavities, galleries, mines, embankments).

- interrogations about the buildings

We collect information about the purpose of building, the height
or the number of floors, the number of floors in basement or the
depth of the last basement, the dimensions and the form of the
building on the site, the structure (columns, inner walls, ...).
Details may also be collected of the location of the building on
the site relative to its topography.

- interrogations about the foundations

They relate to the system of foundations proposed a priori, the
foundations used in the neighborough and the location of the most
loaded foundations. The designer is not necessarily able to
answer these questions concerning the brief, the draft master
plan, the rough plan, the tehcnical choices. No answer is
obligatory. Nevertheless, the quality of the results will depend,
of course, on the precision of the information given.

2.2. General schema of CESSOL

The analysis of experts' reasoning in proposing site investigation
programmes has allowed us to elaborate the following schema.

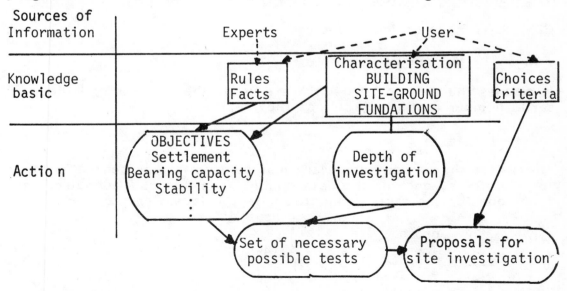

Figure 1 : General schema of CESSOL

A. Sources of information: the experts participate in the
   elaboration of facts and rules. The user of CESSOl defines
   data particular to the case, and may introduce his own rules
   and his criteria of choice.

B. Knowledge base: it is made of rules and facts, economic data, data about the case being investigated. The facts represent a state of knowledge; the rules allow inference.

C. Action: from real cases studied with experts, it appears that just a part of the action proposed is concerned with the expert system approach. The depth of investigation must be estimated, with an algorithmic program module before applying some rules.

Making proposals for site investigations taken from the set of necessary possible tests can be dealt with by operational research. This involves making a selection based on economic and user's constraints.

The inference engine identifies first, from a subset of appropriate rules, the objectives that it must meet. The five possible objectives are: bearing capacity, settlements, stability, ground water and earth pressure. It determines the set of necessary possible tests by creating, from chosen objectives, a tree AND/OR whose terminal nodes are tests (cf fig.3). Each terminal node represents a part of the solution in a given level of the tree for a given objective. Amalgamation by compatibility is then done, first on each of the levels of the tree, then on the different objectives.

3. Structure of CESSOL

CESSOL is made of four modules.

3.1. The dictionary

It defines the descriptions which are used, their nature and the serial number of the object that they represent.

3.2 The facts

The set of the objects which are manipulated is represented in the form of trees, one for the data coming from the questionnaire, the other one for the facts connected with the layers (fig.2).

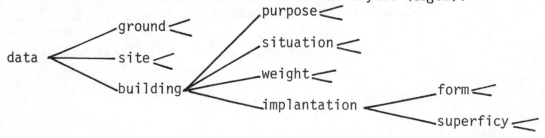

Figure 2 : Tree for the questionnaire

Some other facts are represented in the form of tables. For instance, for each type of layer (13 types are defined), lists of useful or recommended tests, and of tests able to deal with a given level are established.

3.3. The rules

They allow the inferences. A rule occurs in the following form:

if < premises >, then < conclusions >.

A rule may have many premises connected by AND. If the premises are to be connected by OR, we write several rules. This simplifies the formalism. On the other hand, the conclusions, if they are multiple can be connected by AND or OR. From the general schema of fig. 1, we are led to separate the set of rules into four parts:

- the rules completing the facts

They are applied directly to the data. They contribute by increasing the base of facts.
Example 1: if the weight of the building is 'heavy' and if the layer is 'fractured rock', then it is 'susceptible of settlement'.

- the rules which activate the objectives

From specific data, these rules activate some objective whose premises are satisfied. There is no specific instruction to take into account such an objective, its relevance is derived by rule. As a result is the list of objectives which must be active is known. Example 2: if topography is 'uniform with a steep natural slope', then the objective of 'stability' must be active.

- the rules which put tests in the place of objectives

They are used to develop the tree of solutions. Each branch ends at a possible test either with the application of a single rule or with the concatenation of some rules which take into consideration the properties of the levels.
Example 3: if 'geohydrology' must be known, then it can be set as a test 'pie-zometers' and/or it can be made 'seismic or electric geophysical survey'.
Example 4: if the objective of 'bearing capacity' is active, and if the layer is 'compressible soil', then 'cohension', 'internal friction', 'density' or 'pressuremeter modulus' must be evaluated.

- the rules excluding some tests

They prohibit tests which are impossible to realize or which give bad results.

Example 5: if the environment is 'urban', then 'seismic refraction', is impossible.

3.4. The inference engine

It builds the tree of possible necessary tests.   Each node of this tree is a node AND or a node OR. At each step, it defines a conflict set constituted by the rules whose premises are satisfied.   A strategy leads to a choice of rule, which is then applied.   Information so created is integrated into the knowledge base and a new conflict set is built.   This procedure is stopped when all the nodes of the tree have become tests.
(fig. 3).

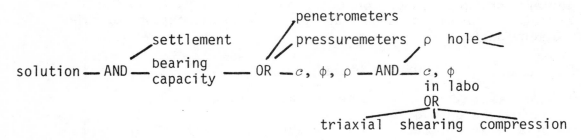

Figure 3 : Tree of solutions

4.   Conclusion

CESSOL is actually composed of 300 rules or facts. It is in a testing phase in association with experts.   It is based on a french microcomputer (16 bit, 64K) and is written in PASCAL. The first version is used in the laboratory of 'Genie Civil et Habitat' at Chambery (France). We are developing an industrial system which will be operational in 1984.

Large efforts are made to give users explanations of CESSOL's solutions: why is this test in the solution?   what are the reasons of the rejection of this test?

It is very important to note lastly the pedagogical benefit of such a system for civil engineering students.

Bibliography

1. BOISSIER D, DUFAU J, MIRAMOND M. 'Technical and economic evaluations with microcomputer for the preliminary building design stage' Second international conference and exhibition of engineering software, mars 1981, London.

2. BOISSIER D. Contribution a la prise en compte des interactions

sols-fondations-bati dans la conception des batiments -
Approche probabiliste de la securite These D E 8205, 1982,
Lyon, France.

3. CORDARY, GIROUD, OBIN Choix de la profondeur de
reconnaissance pour les fondations superficielles Revue
francaise de geotechnique, n°7, mai, 1979, pp. 57-71

4. AYEL, LAURENT, SOUTI CESSOL, un systeme expert pour definir
des campagnes de reconnaissance geotechnique au sol Congres RF-
IA, AFCET, janvier 1984, Paris

5. LAURENT J.P. La structure de controle dans les systemes
experts Techniques et sciences informatiques. A paraitre (in
preparation).

6. ANTOINE, FABRE Geologie appliequee au Genie Civil 1983, Paris,
Masson.

DESIGNING & BUILDING WITH CHIPS: NEW DEVELOPMENTS & THEIR APPLICATIONS

Nicholas D Coutts
Consultant
Nicholas Coutts Associates
UK

Major trends in the development of both low cost and large computer systems are identified and their implications for the construction process are assessed.

Particular emphasis is given to the significance of these developments to architects.

Nicholas Coutts directs a consultancy specialising in computer strategies. He is a director of a UK Group with interests in microcomputer equipment and programs and a contributor and consultant on computing to The Architects' Journal.

He was a founder member and convenor of the RIBA Computer Group, a member of the CICA Advisory Committee and of the winning team in the Philips Office of the Future competition last year.

(Photograph reproduced by permission of The Architects' Journal.)

1   INTRODUCTION

Developments in computing are not limited to the explosive growth of microcomputer systems. Continuous enhancement of larger systems is also taking place, with significant improvements to both equipment and programs.

New features in the larger systems are often good indicators of what is likely to be available as a microcomputer system in a few years' time.

Not all the advances are being made however by the larger systems. Some changes in technique and application are being originated by microcomputer systems which enable people to use computing power in different ways compared with the use of large computer systems.

The rate of change, especially in microcomputer systems, is high and shows signs of accelerating. This makes the task of forecasting the appearance and timimg of specific developments a risky business.

The emergence of developments is very dependent upon the ability of potential users to perceive the potential of a development and implement a change. This may well be strongly influenced by the media which are devoting increasing coverage to computing topics.

The rate of change in this technological revolution probably depends as much on the rate at which society chooses to accept new techniques as on the rate at which laboratories and manufacturers produce new micro electronic products.

An example of the complexity of this process is that of communication between computers and can be compared to the development of the telephone network. As the telephone became more widely available, the value of being able to use the system grew.

The first users of the telephone had either a specific need, which could be met by having a telephone, or an interest in a novel piece of equipment. This is true of many users of microcomputers. As the costs fell, more people subscribed to the telephone system, the benefits of the system grew and new uses were discovered.

Computers have the same potential. Indeed, this is one of the major trends that are identified below.

Whether this potential is fully realised depends not on the computer's ability to send and receive electronic messages, whatever the distance between the machines, since most computers, large and small, can communicate. Realisation of this potential depends on users finding ways of benefiting from communicating this way.

While making the techniques of communication between computers simpler and cheaper is vital, a major factor is the desire of users to communicate based on the benefits they will obtain by linking their computers.

The developments that are taking place in computing affect architects more than other groups. The content of the work of lawyers, engineers, doctors and other professions can be more readily accommodated by the technology without significant changes to their systems and methods. While changes to systems and methods will help these groups to gain more from the application of computer technology, the architect is faced with revolutionising systems and methods in order to take advantage of the possibilities offered by the technology.

The architect is faced with adopting and adapting to changes in the structure of the profession, methods of practice, methods and types of building and environment and clients whose society is altering rapidly, as a result of possibilities offered by the technology.

The Contruction Industry Computing Association (CICA) in its report on Micros in Construction (1980) highlighted the following reasons why the contruction industry is reluctant to adopt new techniques.

With many different sectors, each made up of many small firms, the industry is fragmented with three significant factors which affect the adoption of computing.

First, the capital expenditure involved in the purchase of computers is hard to justify for the majority of firms, which are quite small.

Secondly, the different requirements of the various sectors of the industry inhibit standardisation and the formation of a large market for specific products. This has kept the price of programs and special equipment, which the industry needs, high.

The third factor includes poor communications and the lack of coordination between the members of the building team; aspects which have been identified by various groups and bodies over the past two decades.

It therefore is not surprising, given the fragmented nature of the industry, its communications problems and the rate of technical change, that only a small proportion of those involved with construction use computing power to assist their role.

Changes are however taking place and several major trends can be identified in developments in computing which are likely to substantially affect the process of design and construction.

These developments are explained in detail with their significance for architects.

Four major trends can be identified:

INTEGRATION

POWER

PORTABILITY

COMMUNICATIONS

The last two trends, portability and communications are specifically related to development in microcomputer systems.

INTEGRATION

The size of individual programs, such as a drafting program, or energy use simulator, has often prevented programs from being logically linked together as an integrated suite of programs, sharing and exchanging data.

For example, a word processing program can easily occupy all the space available on a floppy disc in a small system, while few programs can integrate with the programs of different software houses. This obviously creates difficulties for users who will want the best program for a specific task and thus be faced with taking programs, using different operating systems and running on different machines, from several sources.

Although some degree of integration of microcomputer programs and data is given by the adoption of the de facto standard operating systems, such as CP/M, MS-DOS and UNIX, the lack of standards for disc formats, graphics and data file structures reduces the value of using a standard operating system.

Disk drive controllers are now being developed which enable systems to read discs of more than one format, automatically recognising the type of disc to be read.

This development is significant for several reasons. The ability to use the same disk on several systems, providing they have the right operating system, reduces the constraints of having the right machine to use a particular program or having the program re written to run on a specific machine.

The solution to this problem is the increasing availability of microcomputers with the ability to run more than one operating system.

By providing the computer with more than one central processing unit (CPU) which is the main chip of the computer, the user is not dependent on a single operating system. Usually, the operating system is loaded from disc; chips with operating systems permanently stored in their memory are now available, making systems faster and easier to use.

Being able to use the same disks in different microcomputers makes it much easier for the user to take advantage of technical improvements, such as upgrading from an eight bit system to a sixteen bit system, without having to convert data and dispense with an older, but perfectly useable, machine.

As the number of users of computers rises, and the amount of information captured by users grows, the need to be able to easily transfer data from one program to another will grow. If programs are to be useful and successful in the mass market, they will need to be able to use data already captured.

Software writers, especially the large, and usually american, producers of microcomputer programs for the mass markets, are creating programs that will act as an integrated suite, and have facilities to exchange files between programs from different sources.

This integration is presently limited to the most commonly used programs, including wordprocessors, databases and spreadsheets.

New language technology, such as the P system, makes programs written in P code more easily transportable between microcomputers using different operating systems.

As both large and microcomputer systems are being supplied with increasing amounts of disk storage and random access memory, often with no increase in physical size of the component, the larger capacity available is being used to integrate programs and devote more of the program to making the system easier to use.

Examples of this trend are the use of the mouse, which reduces or obviates the need for instructions through a keyboard, and the display of programs as a series of pictures and items representing the choices available to the user.

Early computer aided design (CAD) systems would fully extend the capacities of memory and disk. Little attention was paid to programming that made operation of the system easier, as response time and space for programs prevented the additional programming that this would require.

Today, manufacturers are supplying CAD systems with voice control of certain functions, enabling hands free operation, and with programs for direct survey input, energy simulation, facilities management, HVAC sizing and design and data base management as an integrated suite.

This integration makes the use of building information more efficient, by enabling data to be quickly shared between programs, without the need to rekey data from one program to another.

Increasing the ease and speed of data exchange between, for example, a daylighting program and a file containing the dimension data of a room and its windows, increases the ability to test and check alternative designs.

Through integration, information about design and performance options is made available much more rapidly, in more detail, and with greater accuracy than other approaches allow.

This ability to assess accurately through simulation, the performance of a design, or a number of alternative designs, before a single working drawing is produced, has significant implications for design and construction management.

It raises questions about how the building team should be organised to make the best use of the integrated suite of programs and how consultants are remunerated for their contribution.

One proposal is to link consultants offices to share the design and specification data. The system proposed by Ernest Nagy links the architect, by dedicated communications lines capable of transmitting voice, alphanumerics and graphics, with the structural engineer, the quantitysurveyor and the contractor on site together with a central master data base.

The information stored on the data base will include specification details, with graphic images of the components in vector form, enabling the designer to incorporate the image onto the drawing.

The trend of integration will continue, with the application and use of programs determining the specification of the computer system on which its runs, rather than the other way round at present.

In the medium term, this means the integration of software with some of the equipment components of the system. Examples include communications software for use with a modem card and programs for plotting embodied in plotters.

In the long term, integration will include linking computers to other systems, such as home control equipment and robots. A host of machines will be classed as peripherals, including central heating systems, ovens, refrigerators and television sets.

The major implications for architects from the trend in integration relate to ease of use. Systems that are easier to use will encourage the growth of the use of computing in many areas, particularly in industry, which will find the newer systems require less training and provide greater productivity.

Significant growth in the use of computing will affect the number, location, design and use of individual and corporate workplaces.

The recent Orbit study highlighted the criteria to be considered when incorporating information technology systems in workplace design and came to the conclusion that it seems likely that people will eventually only need to go to work for meetings and to use equipment that otherwise is not available to them.

Ease of use will also extend computing into the home, into education and into professional practice. As a result, most projects will require computers to be accommodated in the design. A good argument why architects should use the technology is to gain personal experience which will help in integrating the machines into homes and industrial workplaces.

In architecture, the potential benefits of using the technology are significant. For example, the ability to easily simulate the performance of a design would enable new materials and techniques to be employed with significantly reduced risk of failure.

Powerful computers are needed for the development of fully integrated architectural modelling systems and developments in making systems more powerful is the next major trend to be assessed.

POWER

Much of the progress towards integration has been as a result of increasingly powerful systems. Power is defined as the speed of response and the ability to run increasingly sophisticated programs. It is closely linked to developments in chip and memory storage technology.

Generally the trend is towards better and cheaper equipment. A powerful computer, which was formerly large and comprised several printed circuit boards, can now be accommodated on a single board. As a result, it uses less power and does not require a special environment.

The trend in power, a combination of major advances in chip design and production and inexpensive memory, offers system designers new ways to design increasingly sophisticated programs which are computationally more powerful, easier to use, or a mixture of both.

It is interesting to note how the microelectronics industry has been applying the technology, such as computer aided design and automated production to develop increasingly complex products, while reducing the cost of computing power significantly.

As a result, complex and expensive systems, such as draughting and simulation of energy use, which can be afforded by only a few practices will be affordable, and easily useable, by the majority without specialist help.

This should result in the smaller practice being able to compete effectively with the large practice, the emphasis being placed on creativity, analysis and design performance with the partners using the computing tools themselves while spending significantly less time on managing the practice and producing information.

As a result of increasingly powerful systems, major introductions can be expected in:

> computer controlled video, with implications for specification libraries and education and training of architects

> expert systems to support design selection and testing

> integrated voice and data networks within and between buildings.

The biggest impact of cheap computer power will derive from the extensive use of computer based modelling systems, which require substantial amounts of computing power to store, manipulate and display data quickly.

A comprehensive, integrated building model would include the following programs:

> a design tool for sketching in colour, with shape and pattern generation programs

> a group of expert systems to assist in the selection of components, elements and systems and in the testing of alternatives

> a data base which permits users to change graphic and specification data

a visual simulator to represent, with
photographic quality in full colour, aspects
of the model

a sensory simulator linked to a computerised
chamber to simulate the physical environment

a draughting program to provide perspective
and working drawings

cost and management programming to monitor
and assess changes in design, components
and build time.

To develop these complex systems, new languages and
programming techniques are being developed. Ways of
conversing with computers in plain english are being
tested and will be of increasing importance if computers
are to be used more easily by non-experts. These natural
language techniques assist in activities such as
translation by computer from one language to another
and translation from speech to writing and vice versa.

Many existing languages were designed to enable
computers to carry out mainly numerical computation and
lack facilities that would make programming
architectural design work more feasible, where logical
relationships are more important than computational
efficiency.

PORTABILITY

The concept of portability covers two significantly
different issues: portable computers and portable
computer programs. Aspects of the portability of
programs have been covered above under integration.

The ability to easily carry substantial amounts of
computing power offers new ways of using computers and
has significant implications for the use of space. More
freedom in choosing where to work and when to work has
implications for the capacity of buildings, especially
if people choose to avoid rush hours.

Designs to ammodate these changes are more likely to
provide successful solutions if the technology is in the
assimilation of complex requirements and in testing
alternative solutions.
These techniques could lead to the multiple use of space
in a building at different times by several users.

Portability is a major factor in the gradual shift in computing power to individuals that is taking place. This shift will affect methods and places of work, education, shopping and leisure. Previously, only major banks and financial institutions transferred funds electronically. Today individuals can make electronic transfers to pay bills and obtain balances of their accounts twentyfour hours a day.

Portability offers architects new methods of fulfilling their job roles, linking visits to sites to the building model to provide control through access to the cost and management program and to the data base for correspondence.

The power and performance of portables is increasing, while their weight is reducing. Portables will have all the features found on desk top systems and will probably use bubble or static memory to increase the amount of data and programs that can be carried with the machine.

This will enable a personal data base, both graphic and alphanumeric to be carried within the portable microcomputer. The advantages of portables will grow as communications improve, making it more worthwhile to carry computing power.

COMMUNICATIONS

To enable users of computers to send the results of their work, as soon as it has been completed, to someone else, or to a store, several developments are necessary.

These developments include standards for data formats and data interchange; multi chip devices capable of recognising and running one of the several current different protocols and the integration of modems within computers.

The lack of standards for networks has probably slowed down their introduction, although the benefits of linking computers to share data, programs and expensive peripheral equipment, such as plotters and high quality printers, within buildings and between buildings, are obviously attractive.

Easy communication between computers will allow architects access to a wider body of knowledge and to monitor design and building performance more easily.

Several data bases are already available, while trial
information services are being run, providing cost data
and practice data.

Easy and cheap communication between computers is
necessary if users are to be able to work remotely
and still send the results of their work to those who
need them.

The increasing use of satellites and optic fibres by
telephone companies, and deregulation of the
telecommunications industry leading to independent
carriers such as the Mercury project will make
communication between computers cheaper and easier.

With telephone networks changing from audio frequency to
digital transmission, computing and telecommunications
will integrate further, encouraged by the break up of the
US and UK telecommunications monopolies.

Deregulation of the industry is likely to increase the
rate of development of computer communications, as
designers of computers will be more readily able to
incorporate communications facilities within their
designs for equipment and programs.

CONCLUSIONS

The four major trends integration, power, portability
and communications are interelated. Increases in
power enable new approaches to be taken with regard
to integration and portability. Increasing use of
portable computers will affect the rate of development
of communications.

Not all these developments are included in any one
computer system. Together, the major trends will
have significant impacts on society. They offer
opportunities to architects to change the practice
of architecture, the design and control of buildings
and spaces and to use new materials and methods.

For example, improved systems and communications
could lead to the formation of buying groups,
enabling architects to develop specific components
for new designs.

Design simulation could enable choices to be made, reducing, for example, technological obsolescence in buildings, with realistic cost and performance comparisons between a low cost building to be replaced in ten years and a more expensive structure lasting fifty years.

To predict what offices and industrial workplaces will be like in five, ten, and fifty years time is an exciting challenge.

Architects should be receptive to the possibilities of the technology and the changes that can result from its adoption by clients and in practice.

CAN COMPUTERS UNDERSTAND DESIGNERS?

A Bijl
Reader
University of Edinburgh
UK

Any great expansion of the population of computer users, embracing architects and other ordinary people, will happen only if we change from current computing technology to radically new software technology.

Criteria for new technology are discussed, with reference to inadequacies of current technology; we should strive for computers that can understand people. Logic programming is described as one development towards this goal, illustrated by the example of Prolog serving as interpreter of user demands and supporting partial and changing local models of user activity.

Architects can choose computing options now that will put them on a path leading to future new technology. Choice is explained, favouring a software environment that is used by researchers and also supports immediate and practical computer applications.

Aart Bijl, Reader in charge of the Edinburgh Computer Aided Architectural Design research unit at the University of Edinburgh. His responsibilities include externally funded, speculative research projects, development of practical computer applications for architects' offices and government departments, and teaching courses for undergraduate and postgraduate architecture students. From 1965-67 he was engaged in research on design methodology at the University. Prior to 1965, he practised as an architect in London, Rotterdam (Netherlands) and Cape Town (South Africa).

The world of computer users

When a designer is invited to use a computer, some part of the designer's normal activity will need to have been encapsulated in the computer. The visible manifestation of that encapsulation must then be capable of being understood and assimilated by the designer into the rest of his or her activity outside the computer. Here we have the essential goal of computer aided architectural design, and we also have the clues to problems which still stand in the way of successful CAAD systems.

We know that designers have to be responsive to the volatile world of all people who make demands on buildings, and that designers in turn present a volatile world of procedures to computer systems (Bijl 1982). The argument that design procedures are necessarily idiosyncratic to individual designers, design offices and design projects is illustrated in figure 1. The idiosyncratic nature of design procedures is a consequence of the world of all people to whom designers are answerable, to the world of butchers, bakers and candlestick makers.

On the other hand, we have a body of computer programs that represent a considerable investment in research and development and which is intended to be used by designers. What prevents designers using these programs? Generally, these programs have grown out of the tradition of computer applications in disciplined scientific and technological fields, in academia and industry, and in commercial fields such as accounting and banking. This tradition aims computer applications at fields in which demands on computers can be explicitly identified and where demands stay constant for long enough to allow system analysts and program implementers to do their work. There can be a reasonable expectation that finished programs will perform tasks which users will recognise as being valid.

In the volatile world of designers, this expectation is not reasonable. Users will argue with the view they are given of computer resources through the programs that are offered to them. The programs will not do what they want. The arguments become louder the more nearly programs are successful; programs that are good enough to be used will attract the most criticism and thus we get the third law of computer programming (Dickson 1978); if a program is useful, it will have to be changed.

Need for new technology

Broadly, there have been two responses to this conflict between designers and computers. The first is to say that existing computer programs represent substantial achievements and that users have to be changed, educated, so that their work-practices will present the necessary uniform and stable context for existing programs. Thus we get the attempts to coordinate, harmonise and standardise design practices nationally and internationally across Europe (CIAD et al 1979).

The second response is to say that the volatile world presented by designers has to be accepted as given, and that any conflicts between designers and computers point to inadequacies in computing technology. This argument recognises that the technology is still at an early stage of development and is going to change. The demands made by designers are then accepted as a welcome influence on the further development of new technology.

This latter response fits into the new national and international programmes for Advanced Information Technology (AIT) and Intelligent Knowledge Based Systems (IKBS) following the Alvey Report (1982), and the Japanese Fifth Generation Computers project (JIPDEC 1981). These efforts, and particularly the Japanese project, take a long term view that foresees a vast expansion of the population of computer users, beyond the present relatively small groups of specialist computer users and including ordinary people; we may choose to see the latter as being represented by non-specialist designers. The Japanese see this expansion as essential, to provide the economic base for production of new hardware that we already know how to make.

This link between commercial interests and the variable needs of ordinary people will ensure that future computers will look very different to Pets and Apples, or even the most upmarket minis. We can have a fair idea of what future computing systems will look like, but architects who wish to get into computers now will, quite reasonably, be wary of jam tomorrow. The promise of new technology can be important in helping architects to make practical choices now that will put them on a path leading to future better systems.

Criteria for new technology

What are the criteria by which we will recognise the emergence of new computing technology that can serve the varying demands of ordinary people? How can we judge whether some new development is significant?

The single most important criterion is the ease with which something can be undone and reconstructed, to allow you to change your mind. Design, like many ordinary human activities, has to be responsive to unforeseen situations presented by any other people. It is not practical to devise a single and complete design system that will operate consistently in different design contexts. Nor can we be confident about fragmenting design into sub-systems that will be recognised as equally valid among different designers (Bijl et al 1979). Whatever system is implemented in a computer for use by designers, and however enthusiastic the system authors and system sponsors are, if the system is used on live design projects we can be sure that the system will need to undergo change. So we need a computing environment in which it is easy to make changes to systems that are offered to people.

What has to be capable of being changed? What are the elements of a computing system that we need to be conscious of, which inhibit change?

To answer this question, we need to establish a view of computing systems. These systems may be described in terms of three main elements.

1 Logical model; this represents how you think about the task that the computer is going to help you do, an abstract representation of the tasks of designing and analysing things.

2 Software system; a means of implementing a logical model in terms of descriptions and instructions that can be "understood" by computers.

3 Hardware system; the electronic and mechanical devices that constitute the physical objects we recognise as computers, whose operations are invoked by software.

The logical model, encapsulated in software which in turn governs the operations of the hardware, has to match your expectations of the tasks you want to see a computer perform. It is the abstract logical model that needs to be capable of being easily changed.

Developments in software and hardware technology should be judged by how they improve the ease with which logical models may be changed. The need for improvement should be apparent if we consider how people currently gain access to computer resources.

Figure 2 shows potential computer users, architects, on the one hand, and computer resources that are potentially able to assist users on the other, with programmers serving as intermediaries. The programmer offers his knowledge of the internal workings of computers, and interprets what he can see of a user's world in terms of operations that he knows he can get a computer to perform.

Note that the user cannot normally expect to exploit the full potential of the computer, but only the potential of the programmer's knowledge of the computer. The need for the programmer as interpreter is a symptom of the sheer difficulty of getting computers to do things, of the current primitive state of software technology. How much better if computers could be made to interpret for themselves and understand people who want to use them, without programmers.

Problems with current technology

What is wrong with current software technology? Essentially, software consists of instructions telling computers how to execute machine

operations. Sets of instructions have to be complete before a
computer can do anything for you. This pattern occurs at all levels
of software, from basic machine operating systems up to a user's
application program. You cannot discuss with a computer what you want
it to do, unless the detail content of your discussion has been
anticipated and programmed into the computer, and that is no discussion.

This almost universal limitation arises from the need, at present, to
achieve a one-to-one mapping between a logical model and its
implementation in software. Software, in the form of written code
transmitted to a computer, has to match the abstract logical representation of a user's world. The logical model has to anticipate the
content of information used by people. Before a computer can respond
to any change in the user's world, it is necessary first to return to
the program code and change it - a costly process that inhibits users
changing their mind.

As an illustration of this tight relationship between a logical model
and its software implementation we can consider the familiar (among
programmers) records and pointers data structure. Essentially, this
requires a decomposition of the subject matter seen in the user's
world into its constituent parts. The parts then form records stored
in computer memory. The records contain pointers to memory locations
of other records. By means of the pointers, assemblies of records can
be recreated corresponding to assembled information that is required
at different stages of some process, such as a design or analysis
process (figure 3).

The crucial issue here is that the structure of pointers and memory
locations refers to the physical organisation of computer memory, and
this has to be represented explicitly in software. This is why these
data structures are commonly described as physical implementations of
logical models. Pointers then are the access paths to data stored
in memory locations; in any hierarchical arrangement of pointers,
only those data that lie on access paths can be accessed and, for any
computing application, the appropriate arrangement of pointers has to
be complete. The view that a user can get of the stored information
and the operations that can be performed on the information is then
determined by the data structure.

A skilful programmer will search the user's world to find a durable
systematic understanding of users tasks, on which to develop a data
structure that is likely to support many different instances of task.
So the programmer will attempt to postpone the need for reprogramming.
Even in the best cases, and especially where programs are offered to
designers, sooner rather than later users will want to get at information that may well be stored in the computer but for which there is no
programmed access path.

Computers that understand

What can we expect of new software technology? We have now to return
to the question of who or what does the interpreting between users and
computers. We need to remove our focus from applications programs,
that is programs which perform tasks that visibly correspond to the
immediate and particular things people want doing. If we focus on
what other things computers might do, we can then consider software
developments that are aimed at getting computers to understand what
people are saying, what they are asking for?

The idea that computers should be able to interpret demands coming
directly from users, and respond appropriately, is not so improbable.
We already have experience of communications systems in which the
content of communications is conveyed in a manner that is subject to
defined and widely accepted rules, where these rules are essential to
the interpretation of content and where the rules are not thought to
restrict the content. The obvious example is grammatical rules
applied to written text. The idea that computers should be able to
understand people is not improbable, but its realisation is a long
way off. Can we use this promise?

Logic programming

We have discussed the one-to-one relationship between logical models
and software implementations. If we had a logic system that was
implemented in software and which would allow us to formulate
different logical models, so that implementation of the models would
be an automatic consequence of using the logic system, we would then
have a development that would make it easier to change logical models
and, in turn, to have computing systems that would be more responsive
to changing user demands. The logic system would consist of rules
governing the way in which a logical model may be expressed, without
limiting the content of the model or the real world application of
the model. One implementation of logic in software already exists,
in the form of the Prolog logic programming language (Kowalski 1979,
Clocksin and Mellish 1981).

Returning to our earlier example of data structures, Prolog allows us
to develop a logical model of buildings which employs the equivalent
of records and pointers, in the sense of a decomposition of whole
objects into parts that have attributes which point to other parts
(Steel and Szalapaj 1983). But by using Prolog we do not need to
make a prior decision on the totality of a decomposition; parts can
be created and related to any other parts at will. This is possible
because there is no software implementation of an explicit pointers
structure. Connections between paths are made by the expressions used
to describe the paths, and a connection exists only for as long as
its purpose is being realised. During a dialogue between the user
and the model, structures are invoked and dissolved as the user
varies the expressions that describe some thing.

Thus if we consider figure 3; we may get the expression:

    wall <= [primary_material=brick,internal_cladding=plaster]

Using generalised knowledge of the construction of such expressions, a computer can understand what an expression is meant to convey. It will know that I am talking about a thing that I call a wall which is described by the attributes of primary material and internal cladding which in this instance are brick and plaster. I can add, modify and delete attributes and their properties as my perception of the wall changes, and I can use my description of the wall as a part of other things that constitute a whole building. Later, I can recall what internal cladding has been specified for the wall by describing the access path in the expression:

    wall: internal_cladding

to get the answer, plaster. I can do all this without a programmer having anticipated that I am going to talk about relationships between walls, bricks and plaster.

What we have here is a separation between thinking about some thing and describing what we are thinking to a computer, on the one hand, and the implementation of our thoughts as software that represents our thoughts and our requests for action in a computer, on the other. The Prolog logic system is responsible for interpreting expressions from a user and, being itself a program, its task is to implement the user's logical model in software. Prolog thus is a general purpose language for conveying intended meaning as well as instructions to computers. Of course, to use the language users must know the rules by which expressions in the language may be constructed.

Prolog is the first implementation of a logic programming language and we should expect further developments of this kind. Such developments offer important advantages for designers, promising new software technology that:

a)   logical models: does not demand prior commitment to some explicit model that anticipates the actual content of object descriptions;

b)   partial models: permits incomplete models that represent the state of a user's thinking, allowing subsequent and unforeseen additions to a model;

c)   changing models: permits models to be easily modified as the user's perception of something changes, without the need for programmers making corresponding changes to program code;

d)   correct models: reduces the need to be right in a predictive sense, models may change as experience shows you were wrong, you may change your mind.

Link between now and then

How do we know when we are on the right path, so that we can expect to realise advantages of new technology? Developments in software technology take a long time, in contrast to computer manufacturing technology, and promises are inherently speculative. Yet architects can choose computing environments in which these developments are taking place, and architects can then expect to influence these developments and benefit from early results. This need not be an either/or choice; the same computing environments can also support immediate and practical computing applications.

When you choose a computing application, packaged as a hardware and software system, you are in fact making choices on different aspects of computing that will affect the ease with which you can link yourself to new developments (figure 4).

As already discussed, applications programs have to represent what you want to do as instructions that tell a computer how to execute its internal machine operations. Computer hardware is the resource that you wish to exploit.

The software environment governs how you (or your programmer) can exploit computer resources, forming the link between a user program and a computer. As designers, the things you will want to do will change, and hardware technology changes. Over time, you will want to run different programs on different hardware. Choice of software environment, made either inadvertently (as an invisible consequence of choosing an applications program) or deliberately, can have major cost implications. Seen by a user, these implications will be experienced as the cost of developing and supporting computer programs, of learning how to exploit program functions, and of making adjustments to a user's existing work-practices to match the anticipations encapsulated in a program. These implications become more severe when it is time to change a program or to change to new hardware.

A software environment consists of a low level computer operating system plus associated software tools and a range of high level programming languages. Broadly, choice of operating system is between a computer manufacturer's system or a system developed by computer users. In recent years, there has been a growing preference for the latter. Operating systems that have been developed by and for computer users should offer the following advantages:

a) system visibility: written in a high level language, the traditional barrier between operating system and user program is diminished and systems can be modified and tuned to suit particular applications fields;

b)   portability: systems are not specific to a single manufacturer's
     range of equipment, and they can be and are ported to different
     computers, thus easing the job of porting programs;

c)   support: given a world-wide user community and given system
     visibility, these systems have more support resources than can be
     provided by any single computer manufacturer;

d)   efficiency: these systems can get more out of equipment than the
     manufacturer's own operating system;

e)   software tools: as with support, a world wide effort can be and
     is focused on software development tools associated with the
     operating system, to ease the task of writing user programs;

f)   programming languages: given the above advantages, people
     engaged in development of new software technology and new program-
     ming languages are likely to be working with these systems, and
     results will be available first on these systems.

A dominant example is the UNIX* operating system. This system is so
persuasive that manufacturers of powerful new 16 and 32-bit microcomputers are now supplying their computers only with UNIX, without
attempting to develop their own operating systems. The UK programme
for advanced information technology has chosen UNIX as a preferred
operating system. The Prolog logic programming language, as a fore-
runner of new technology, has already been implemented on UNIX
(Pereira 1982). At the same time, UNIX is rapidly gaining popularity
as an environment for immediate and practical computer applications.

Thus, taking a cautious view of the simplifications necessarily contained in this paper, it is possible to relate immediate decisions on
how to get into computing to the promise of future new technology.
For designers, this promise is important. If current computing
technology were to be regarded as being mature and if the world were
to become dependent on it, then architects and architecture would
face a dismal prospect. If, on the other hand, we can recognise that
present computing is primitive and that the technology is due to
develop and change, and if architects among ordinary people can take
part in influencing that change, then we have reason for optimism and
excitement.

Acknowledgments

The views presented in this paper have emerged from work at EdCAAD
funded by the Science and Engineering Research Council, plus
experience of EdCAAD computer programs in use in architects' offices.

In recent years, this work has benefited from staff joining EdCAAD

*UNIX is a Trademark of AT&T

from the Department of Artificial Intelligence at Edinburgh University.

References

Alvey Report; "A Programme for Advanced Information Technology", HMSO, 1982.

Bijl, A., Renshaw, A., Barnard, D.F.; "House Design: Application of Computer Graphics to Architectural Practice", EdCAAD report, 1971.

Bijl, A., Stone, D., Rosenthal, D.S.H.; "Integrated CAAD Systems", EdCAAD, 1979.

Bijl, A.; "Non-Prescriptive Computing Technology for Designers", proc. Design Policy Conference, London, July 1982.

CIAD et al; "The Effective Use of Computers within the Building Industries of the European Community", EC report 1979.

Clocksin, W., Mellish, C.; "Programming in Prolog", Springer-Verlag, 1981.

Dickson, P.; "The Official Rules", Delta Books Publishing Company, New York, 1978.

JIPDEC; "Preliminary Report on Study and Research on Fifth-Generation Computers 1979-1980", JIPDEC, 1981.

Kowalski, R.A.; "Logic for Problem Solving", Elsevier North Holland, 1979.

Pereira, F.; "C-Prolog User's Manual", EdCAAD, 1982.

Steel S., Szalapaj, P.; "Pictures without Numbers: Graphical Realisation of Logical Models", PARC83.

DESIGN: DISCIPLINE OR PRACTICE?

KNOWLEDGE BASED DISCIPLINE

ACTIVITY: explicit knowledge forms the primary means for progressing from problems to solutions

ANSWERABILITY: to peers who share a common knowledge base

DISCIPLINE: formal and detached, a shared basis for assessing new developments

PROCEDURES: methodical and stable, overt exclusion of intuitive judgement

EXPERIENCE BASED PRACTICE

ACTIVITY: relies on explicit knowledge plus intuitive judgement of practitioners

ANSWERABILITY: to public who do not share a common knowledge base

DISCIPLINE: informal and inconsistent, practitioners must be responsive to a volatile world

PROCEDURES: idiosyncratic, ill-defined integration of knowledge and experience

Figure 1: Design, discipline or practice?

current technology:

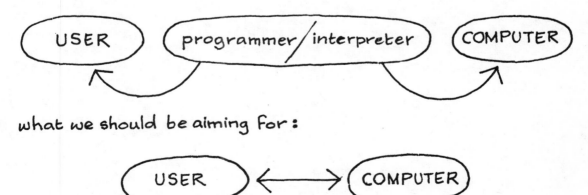

what we should be aiming for:

Figure 2: Users' access to computer resources

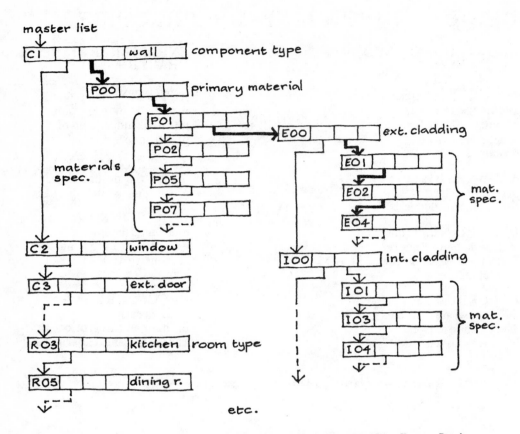

Figure 3: Example of database layout taken from EdCAAD's House Design system (Bijl et al 1971), showing access path to material of external cladding to wall of specified primary material.

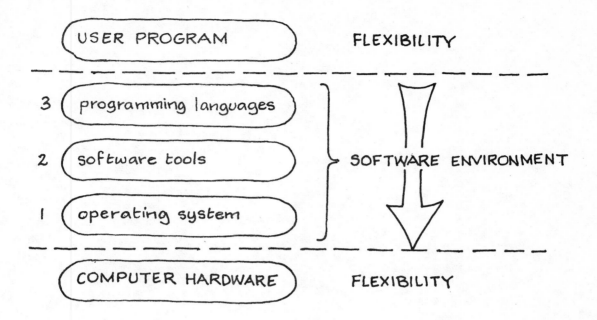

Figure 4: Software environment conditioning the way that computer hardware is made to work for users.

CASE STUDIES IN COMPUTER-AIDED
VISUAL IMPACT ANALYSIS

A H Bridges
Deputy Director
ABACUS, University of Strathclyde
UK

Two computer programs for visualising design proposals are described, and their use illustrated in three complimentary case studies.

Alan Bridges is an architect. He has worked in the CAAD field for some ten years, both developing software and consulting on CAD applications. Dr Bridges is a Deputy Director of the ABACUS CAD group at the University of Strathclyde.

Introduction

The effect of any new development on its surroundings, whether a new shop in an historic urban setting, or a powerstation in unspoilt countryside, is always a contentious issue. This is not solely due to the merits (or otherwise) of the proposed development, but rather the underdeveloped state of objective visual appraisal. Notably the accuracy and realism of traditional visual assessment methods have been questioned and new techniques which can clearly present visual evidences in sufficient detail and with known levels of accuracy are slowly replacing them.

This paper describes the use of two computer-based methods of predicting the visual impact of buildings (or other constructions) on their urban or rural surroundings. The programs BIBLE (Buildings with Invisible Back Lines Eliminated) and VISTA (Visual Impact Simulation, Technical Aid) offer the designer a two stage approach to visualisation. The first stage is the production of wire-line perspective views; these may be perfectly adequate where issues of visibility predominate or where the object has a skeletal structure (eg electricity pylons). The program output may be used directly in a photomontage or used as an accurate base from which a perspective artist may work up a presentation drawing. The second level is the production of fully coloured, textured and lit perspectives which may be used where issues of visual quality predominate. These pictures may again be photomontaged and are then complete in themselves.

The program BIBLE

The user interface of BIBLE (Figure 1) is designed to be as easy for the inexperienced user as possible. This is mainly achieved by four features:

(a)   Fail-soft design: any invalid or wrong input produces an English-language error message, apologising for the program's inability to understand the input provided and explaining what sort of input was expected, or what options were available to the user at that point.

(b)   Graphical specification of view point. This allows the user to point on a displayed plan view to a place in the vicinity of the building(s) and in effect ask -'What does it look like from here?'

(c)   Use of default parameters: all the view control parameters have default values computed by the program for each data set as it is read in. Thus it is possible to read the data file and immediately get a meaningful picture.

(d)   A command menu on the screen gives the user a visible reminder of what he can do without verbose prompts, and more detailed information can be obtained by selecting the HELP command.

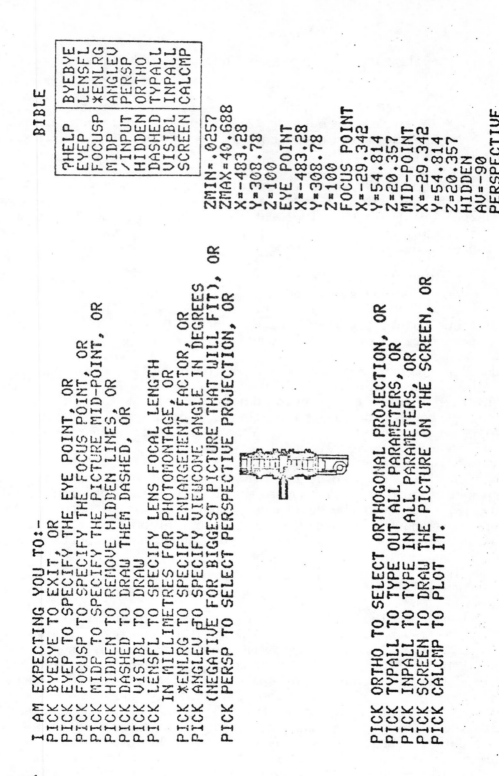

Figure 1
Screen hardcopy showing BIBLE menu, default parameters, response to HELP command, and small scale plan of building ready for user to select viewing point.

The user-specifiable view parameters and default values are as follows:

(a)   The EYE POINT from which the scene is viewed may be any point
        (X,Y,Z), inside or outside the region containing objects. X and
        Y may be specified graphically. The default is 'a long way away'
        in -X,-Y,+Z.

(b)   The FOCUS POINT which is the other end of the line of sight
        may be any point (X,Y,Z). X and Y may be specified graphically.
        The default is the middle of the scene. The focus point may be
        moved in order to obtain two-point perspectives or views of off-
        centre parts of the scheme.

(c)   The MID POINT (of the resulting picture) may be any point (X,Y,Z).
        X and Y may be specified graphically. The default is the middle
        of the scene. The mid-point is normally set the same as the
        focus point, but it may need to be different for two-point
        perspectives or non-orthogonal parallel projections.

Hidden lines may be removed (which is the default), drawn dashed, or
left in. The projection may be perspective (by default), partially
perspective (parallel verticals, parallel horizontals), or orthogonal.
Output may be to a display file, to the terminal screen or to a plotter
with the drawing produced to A1, A2, A3 or A4 size; output devices
may be changed between pictures.

A major facility offered by the program is that of producing views
which can be automatically superimposed onto site photographs. The
user simply specifies the camera position, the focal length of the
camera lens and the enlargement of the photographic print; the
resulting view is correctly scaled, positioned and proportioned for
the photomontage.

The program VISTA

VISTA is a 3-D colour perspective package with hidden surface elimination; it may be used to model any artifact composed of planar
surfaces (Fox, 1981). Although wireline perspectives, as produced by
BIBLE, can be valuable aids to visualisation, they remain indicative
and lack solidity. The use of colour to fill the surfaces improves
the 3-D impression of the drawing, particularly so if the colours
are modified according to the light falling on them and shadows
generated. The outline structure of VISTA is shown in figure 2:
a more detailed description may be found in Stearn (1982). The VISTA
database contains a hierarchically structured definition of the
geometry of the model. This definition is similar to the BIBLE
geometry definition, being composed of Bodies which contain planar
Faces, but VISTA allows another additional level of detail to be
associated with each Face. These extra elements are known as Tiles,
and may be used to model areas of different colour or features, such

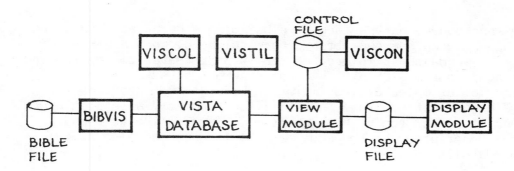

Figure 2
Overview of VISTA system

Figure 3a
Site view showing existing boilerhouse and chimney

Figure 3b
Montage showing extent to which new powerstation is hidden

as windows and doors, on the face of a building. Because of the close relationship between the geometric data required by both BIBLE and VISTA, the VISTA database is created from a BIBLE data file by running the interface program BIBVIS. This has a number of advantages - a large number of examples already exist in BIBLE format; programs for creating BIBLE geometry already exist; if the geometry exists in BIBLE format then it can be run by both programs. In addition to the geometrical description of the model the VISTA database also contains the colour details for each Body, Face and Tile in the model.

The core of the VISTA package is the VIEW module. This performs the perspective transformations, the hidden surface elimination and the colour rendering. It takes as input the description of the model as defined by the VISTA database and the required viewing and lighting parameters. The viewing parameters consist of the type of view required ie bird's eye, camera, etc, and the eye and focus positions. The lighting parameters specify the position and spectrum of any light sources (in RGB) and whether any shadow studies are to be retrieved. The lighting model in VISTA allows the user to model the ambient, diffuse and specular components of any light source, and also to vary the ratio of ambient to direct light available from that source. The output picture is written to a display file and not directly to a colour output device, this has several advantages the most important of which is that the VIEW module can be totally device independent.

Case Studies

The use of the programs briefly described above allow a thorough evaluation of design proposals to be made. Early use of the software, together with a more general description of visual impact analysis is described in Bridges (1981). Further use in live projects by designers, planners, and lay audiences in both ordinary design work and at special planning enquiries has, naturally, indicated new directions for program improvement and stimulated continuous revision and reappraisal of program capabilities.

The issue of accuracy is obviously fundamental. This has been rigorously investigated (Purdie, 1982) and a number of features, not always included in CAD perspective packages, have been incorporated in the software to take account of factors such as

~ that in long range visualisation, over 2 miles, earth's curvature and light refraction can affect the position of objects as seen by an observer.

~ that optical and other camera distortions can cause a mismatch in computer based photomontaging.

~ the accuracy of the photomontage process using BIBLE has been established and high degrees of control are respected in project work.

189

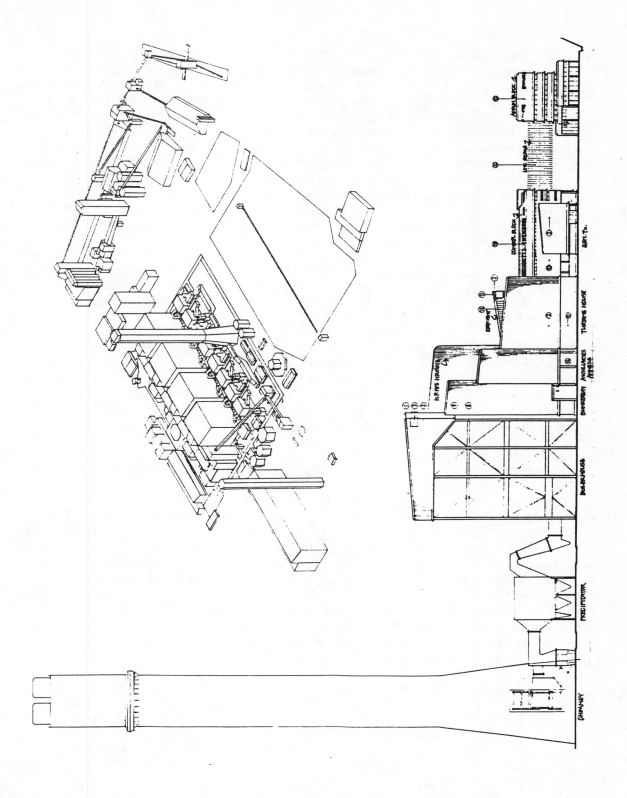

Figure 4
BIBLE perspective view of Castle Peak power station

Often though the available data is not of the standard or accuracy required. In these cases computer techniques have been developed to determine unknown or dubious data. For example in the case of the design of a second power station on the Hong Kong mainland at Castle Peak by the architects Robert Matthew Johnson Marshall, a number of viewpoints of the site photographs were unknown, having been taken from a ferry and a helicopter. The building geometry was assembled and prepared for viewing by the program BIBLE. The onshore photo-montages were drawn. To locate the XYZ viewpoint co-ordinates of the offshire and aerial photographs a program was devised to iteratively search back to the correct observer position. This procedure was based on a triangulation method with two known objects in the photographs and the computer views being fixed and the viewpoint acting as the variable. Finally, the accurate wire line perspectives (Figure 3) and the colour site photographs formed the basis of a set of finished colour montages by a perspective artist. The level of detail included was such that quite elaborate drawings of the power station itself could be produced (Figure 4).

The presentation of visual evidence at a planning inquiry can win or lose aesthetic decisions. In another case, the client, a life assur-ance company, was proposing an office development in a sensitive semi-rural landscape at Hitchin Priory, Hertfordshire and required high quality visual material to put before a local planning committee. The programs BIBLE and VISTA were employed to address two problems:

1. building scale in relation to adjacent housing (BIBLE)
2. building colour in relation to existing brickwork colours (VISTA)

Photographs from a number of vantage points around the site were recorded, and a selection made for computer montaging: black and white, and colour print film were used. The geometry data files for computer processing were compiled from 1:200 scale drawings of the proposed building and an existing wall, surrounding and intersecting the site. Control point information, known site features and surveying poles, were included for each view and surveyed in reference to the O.S. grid to the nearest 100mm. Seventeen BIBLE wire line montages were drawn on acetate and overlaid on the black and white site photographs. The program VISTA was then used to generate colour views of the proposed development (Figures 5 and 6).

In addition to the computer based montages, a number of artist's impressions were drawn for presentation purposes. The most time consuming part of this work for the artist is in the construction of the two point perspective such that the drawn building matches the position of other site objects in the photographs. This setting up procedure for the perspectives was obviated by the use of the computer wire line perspectives. More attention was, therefore, able to be given to the rendering of the final perspective, knowing that the building location and scale were accurately drawn already. Two main areas of concern resulted from this study.

Figure 5
BIBLE photomontage

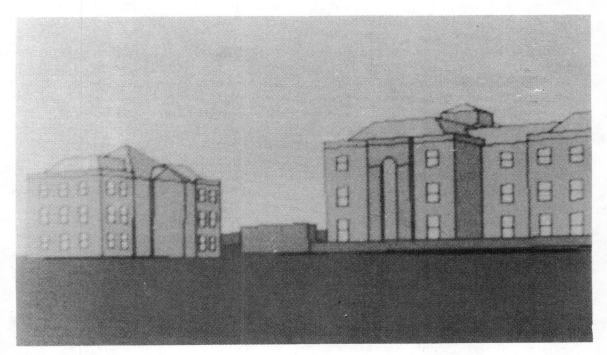

Figure 6
VISTA perspective (from coloured original)

i) Data inaccuracies. Incorrect reportage of survey data identifying
viewpoint and control point information causes delays and necessi-
tates rechecking and reprocessing the computer views.

ii) Overlaying. The difficulty in effecting a realistic colour montage
when views of the development are interrupted by foreground
features, still remains unresolved unless time consuming hand
crafted methods are used. This runs against the idea of speedy
computer based visualisation.

The theoretical issues of accuracy have already been mentioned, and,
ultimately, the validity and usefulness of a modelling aid will be
measured against its ability to predict reality. Fortunately this is
a fairly easy criterion to validate. By the simple expedient of
drawing an existing building computer predictions may be compared
directly with reality (or montages compared with photographs of
reality). This retrospective visual appraisal was undertaken on
the Architecture Building at the University of Strathclyde. The
results of the simulation, together with the actual view are shown
in figures 7 and 8. At this level of detail difficulties arise in the
convincing modelling of landscape and the simulation of window glass
and other reflective materials.

Conclusion

A number of general problems still beset these techniques - not least
the difficulty of accurate colour copying and reproduction.

Maintaining the correct colour balance and quality of hardcopy reproduction from graphics terminals has consistently proved to be a
stumbling block in the presentation of accurate visual evidence,
especially when building surface colours and textures are under examination. In the same manner, research dissemination in this field is
fraught with reproduction difficulties; even within this paper
uncertainty exists as to the fidelity of the graphics reproduced.
Significant improvements in the copying and reproduction of colour
computer graphics for visualisation in architectural design are
required if the benefits of building detailed simulation models are
to be realised.

Many techniques for visual assessment are only initiated in the later
detailed stages of design work. In contrast, there is a greater need
for methods and models to be developed and applied at the earlier
outline stages of design, where the major visual design decisions are
normally taken. Computer-based models seem best structured for continuous application throughout design from inception to completion, and
beyond in terms of retaining a model for exploring the visual
impacts of landscaping options.

Figure 7
Photograph of Department of Architecture, University of Strathclyde

Figure 8
VISTA perspective of Dept. of Architecture, University of Strathclyde

Acknowledgements

Many people at ABACUS have contributed to this area of computer
application, but the examples described would be far less convincing
without the intellectual efforts of Cameron Purdie and the coding
skills of Donald Stearn.

References

Bridges, A H (1981). Visual Modelling Using Composite Colour
Computer Graphics and Still or Video photography. Proceedings
of Computer Graphics 81, Online Publications Ltd, pp103-113.

Fox, P (1981). VISTA : A Visual Impact Simulation Technical Aid.
PhD Thesis, University of Strathclyde.

Purdie, C (1982). VIEW and BIBLE: an Accuracy Study. ABACUS
Occasional Paper no 87; University of Strathclyde.

Stearn, D D (1982). VISTA : Visual Impact Simulation Technical
Aid. Proceedings of Eurographics 82, North Holland Publishing Co,
pp333-337.

DEVELOPMENTS IN COMPUTER AIDED LIGHTING DESIGN

A W Stockmar
Consultant
LCI Light Consult International Software Engineering
FRG

The new 32-bit desktop or mini computers can be regarded
as a very useful tool to solve the problems occuring
today in lighting engineering. With their large central
memories and their efficient graphics input and output
devices they can be used not only for the calculation
of the different photometric data but also for the interactive lighting design, for graphic presentations of
illuminance and luminance distributions, and for the
creation of colour shaded images (perspective views) of
interiors taking into account the spectral properties
of lamps and reflecting surfaces.

Axel Stockmar is electrical/lighting
engineer (Dipl.-Ing. TU Berlin). From
1976-1981 he was scientific assistant
at the Technical University Berlin
(Institut für Lichttechnik). Since
October 1981 he is running his own
business as software engineer in the
lighting field.

Introduction

The use of computers in lighting design has been common practice for many years. Using large main frame computers it was possible to develop and run very sophisticated programs as for automatic floodlight aiming optimisation and for the calculation of contrast rendering factors (CRF) and equivalent sphere illuminances (ESI). During the last few years new powerful desktop and mini computers (16/32-bit) have become available which - utilized in lighting laboratories and design offices - give the lighting engineer the chance of immediate access and on-the-spot decisions during the iterative design process. With their large working memory sizes of 2 M bytes or more there is no practical limit for the number of calculation points, the number of luminaires, and the number of different luminous intensity distributions used at the same time (usually 500 calculation points, 600 luminaires, and between 3 and 5 intensity distributions respectively). With the new fast 32-bit processors it is possible to calculate up to 2500 illuminances per second, so that even large lighting schemes can be evaluated within some few minutes.

As these computers are usually equipped with high quality graphics input and output devices they can be used not only for the calculation of the different photometric data but also for the interactive computer aided lighting design and for the graphic presentation of illuminance and luminance distributions. This is of particular interest for the lighting specialist: Working together with architects, consulting engineers, and contractors he is now able to show his partners how his lighting system works and how the light will be distributed within a space in a 'language' all parties concerned can understand.

Interactive computer aided lighting design

The calculation of photometric values - e.g. horizontal, vertical, cylindrical, and semi-cylindrical illuminances, surface luminances, or contrast rendering factors - requires the knowledge of the luminaire layout, the geometry of the space, and the surface reflectances. If an interior has a rectangular shape, and if the luminaires are arranged in a regular pattern, it is usually adequate to use a keyboard as input device for the room dimensions, the room surface reflectances, and the number of the equally spaced luminaires in x- and y-direction. If a room has a non-rectangular shape, if parts of the interior (working areas) are to be considered separately, or if the luminaires are arranged in irregular patterns, the use of

digitizers, graphic tablets, light pens and/or CRTs is
preferable for the input and correction of the different
data. Figure 1 shows the plan of a rectangular room with
linear luminaires and asymmetric point sources arranged
to meet the lighting requirements of the three working
areas. In this case the simultanuous use of a CRT as
alpha-numeric display unit and raster graphic device
makes it very easy to position the working areas (with
narrower grids of calculation points) and to arrange/
rearrange the suitable luminaires in the right order.
The number and shape of the elements of a suspended ceiling have been calculated for the non-rectangular room
given in figure 2. Here the use of a digitizer is advis-
able for getting in the co-ordinates (x,y) describing the
outer contour of the interior, and the start point and
direction of the ceiling system.

For the interactive design of a tube/track lighting system
(figure 3) or a floodlighting scheme (figure 4) the use of
a light pen or a graphics tablet is very efficient. If
parts and/or complete modules of the tube/track lighting
system can be chosen from a menu and arranged by moving
e.g. a light pen, the design of such a (more complicated)
lighting system can be carried out easily and with great
flexibility. The main problem in floodlighting design
consists of the appropriate aiming of the floodlights to
achieve a visually acceptable brightness pattern. This
design problem can be solved conveniently using a light
pen to position a tracking marker (cross) to a chosen
aiming point while the co-ordinates are displayed continuously. From the digitized values the horizontal and
vertical settings of the floodlight are evaluated, the
illuminances and uniformities are calculated due to the
symmetry properties of the installation, and an iso-lux
diagram is plotted by linear interpolation along the grid
lines. If the results are not satisfying the floodlight
can be re-aimed using the light pen as often as desirable;
otherwise the interactive design process can be continued
with the next floodlight of the same or another type.

The calculation of the illuminance distribution of a tube/
track lighting system in a non-rectangular room has to
take into account the shading effects of parts of the
walls for particular reference points (fast processor).
The shading of the illuminance distribution on a non-
rectangular area like the running track of a stadium
(figure 5) requires special interpolation routines and
area filling graphic procedures.

Perspective views

The luminaire layout in an interior is given by the number
and type of the luminaires, the co-ordinates (x,y,z) of
their central points, and the orientation, tilt and turn
of the luminaires with respect to the utilization plane.
Using a perspective presentation (here one-point perspective, cone of vision 30°) it is possible to show not only
the luminaire layout but the reference points on the different room surfaces as well. Sub-surfaces of interest
like windows, doors, or blackboards can be presented in
the same graph giving a more realistic image of the
installation (figure 6).

If the individual direct and indirect components of the
illuminances at the reference points have been calculated,
shadings of the luminance (brightness) distributions can
be obtained by suitable interpolation procedures (assum-
ing perfect diffus reflecting surfaces). These shadings
with adjustable 16 (or more) luminosity ranges can be used
for the comparison of different lighting systems (figure 7
and figure 8), or for the simulation of daylight/electric
light interactions under varying conditions.

Influence of the spectral power distribution of the lamps on the colour appearance of an interior

The luminance of a particular surface can be calculated
under spezified conditions following the equation L=q·E,
where q is the luminance coefficient and E the illuminance
on the surface. If the luminance coefficient is a function
of the wavelength λ , the luminance L should be calculated
using the formula:

$$L = K_m \cdot \int q(\lambda) \cdot E_e(\lambda) \cdot V(\lambda) \cdot d\lambda$$

K_m..... maximum spectral luminous efficacy

$q(\lambda)$... spectral radiance coefficient

$E_e(\lambda)$.. spectral irradiance

$V(\lambda)$... relative luminous efficiency function
for the CIE standard observer

This equation allows to take into account the spectral
composition of the irradiance at a particular point on
the room surfaces due to the spectral power distributions
of the lamps installed,   the spectral interreflection
of the light within the room (to be calculated for up to
81 wavelengthes), and   the spectral reflectances of the

room surfaces.

To create colour shaded images of the luminance distributions and to show the changes in the colour appearance (shift of the chromaticity co-ordinates) of an interior a colour model has been developed which converts the calculated chromaticity co-ordinates into values of hue, saturation, and luminosity available on the CRT (96 hues, 16 saturations, 16 luminosities, i.e. 4913 colour shades).

The spectral reflectances of 36 samples (each of them for five saturations) have been measured so that at the moment the colours of the room surfaces can be choosen from a variety of 180 different spectral reflectances. If the chromaticity co-ordinates at the reference points have been calculated and converted into values of hue and saturation, the same interpolation procedures which were used for the shadings of the luminance distributions in the perspective views (figure 7 and 8) can be utilized to obtain colour shaded images. Using different types of lamps the colour appearance of an interior will change remarkably. It is hoped that using colour shaded images at the design stage will help to design better colour balanced lighting schemes.

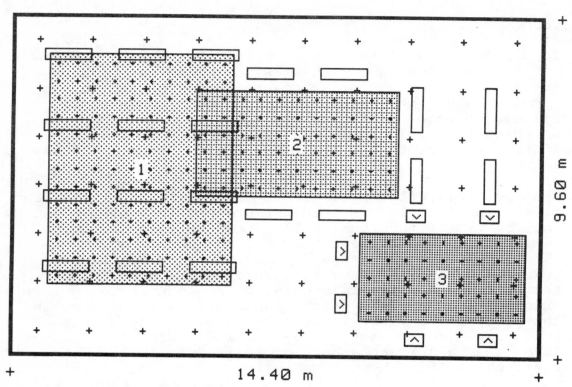

Figure 1   Luminaire arrangement, working areas

9.60 m

14.40 m

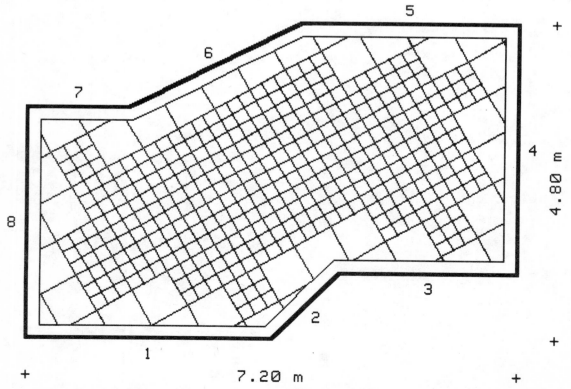

Figure 2   Suspended ceiling elements, non-rectangular room

4.80 m

7.20 m

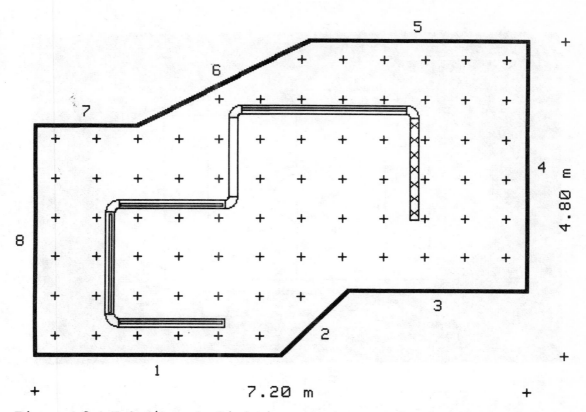

Figure 3 Tube/track lighting system, calculation points

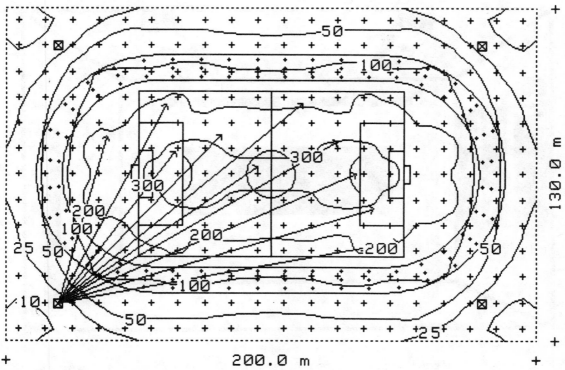

Figure 4 Stadium, aiming points, iso-lux contours

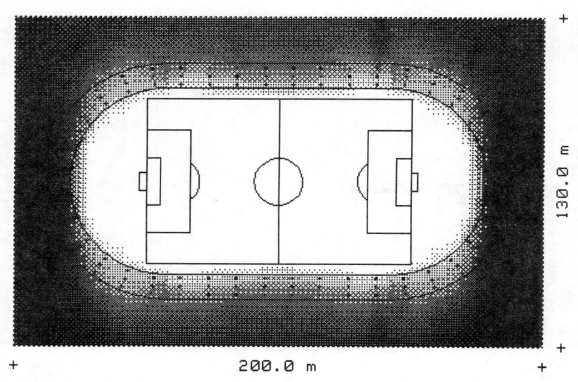

Figure 5   Stadium, shading of illuminance distribution

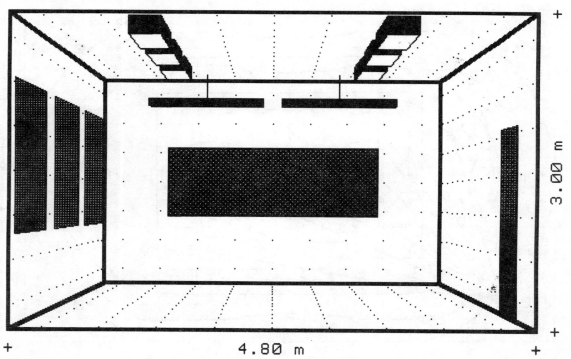

Figure 6   Perspective view, luminaire layout, sub-surfaces and calculation points

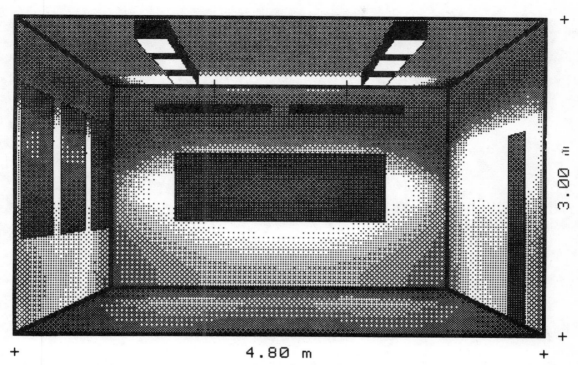

Figure 7   Perspective view, luminance distributions on
ceiling, walls, floor, and sub-surfaces

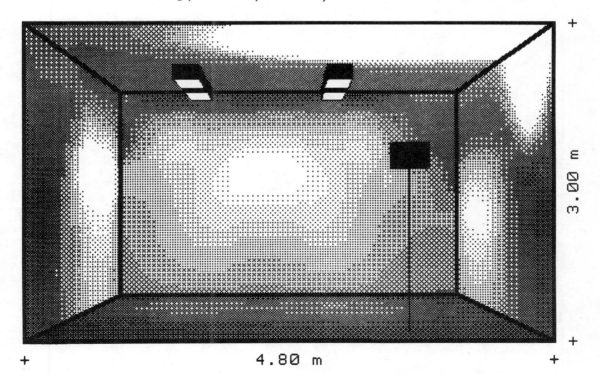

Figure 8   Perspective view, combined direct/indirect
lighting system, shading of luminance distribution

WHAT'S WHAT AND WHAT'S WHERE: KNOWLEDGE ENGINEERING IN THE REPRESENTATION OF BUILDINGS BY COMPUTER

John S Gero
V Tuncer Akiner
Antony D Radford
Computer Applications Research Unit
Department of Architectural Science
University of Sydney
Australia

Knowledge engineering allows for the encoding of both numeric and symbolic knowledge as inferences. It provides a fundamentally different means of representing buildings than do traditional data structures and databases. A prototypical knowledge engineering reasoning system which reasons about topological relationships, geometric entities and attributes of buildings is described. It is applied in the analysis of an existing small hotel. Using knowledge engineering we can expect future CAAD systems to be different to the ones with which we have become familiar.

John Gero, Ph.D., is Director, Tuncer Akiner is a doctoral student, Tony Radford, Ph.D., is Associate Director, Computer Applications Research Unit, Department of Architectural Science, University of Sydney.

1.   Introduction

Fourth generation systems, based on the notion of
developing increasingly detailed descriptions of buildings
in databases, do not have the capacity to provide
knowledge about buildings. An ideal representation would
allow us to find any characteristic which is immanent in
the building itself. New tools from the artificial
intelligence area of **knowledge engineering** are proving to
be useful in developing symbolic representations of
buildings which explicitly encode knowledge about the
building. Such fifth generation systems make use of
declarative representations as against process or
procedural representations. Such representations attempt
to describe the building in terms of what it is. The
difference may be thought of as the difference between
performance and prescriptive specifications.

2.   Explicit Knowledge Representation

Knowledge, as we use the word here, is to do with the
structuring of facts and the relationships between facts.
In a traditional system for the representation of
buildings by computer, facts are stored explicitly in a
database. Examples of facts in this context are the co-
ordinates of a point, the end points of an edge or the
colour of a surface. Traditional databases contain no
corresponding explicit representation of knowledge.
Instead, the knowledge about relationships which is
necessary to model a building is defined implicitly by the
organizational structure of the database. Thus an object
file might refer to a line file, which in turn refers to a
points file, which contains the co-ordinates of the
vertices of the building component spaces or objects. The
expression of the relationship between vertex and object
is contained within the computer code in which the system
is written. Since all knowledge is represented
implicitly, all relationships of interest have to be
defined and coded as procedures at the time of writing the
computer program system. Additions or alterations to
these relationships entails revision of the program
source.

A representation of buildings which will allow us to
reason about spaces and objects requires a manipulatable
knowledge base to which knowledge about relationships can
be added and removed in much the same way as facts can be
added and removed with a traditional database
representation. In our work towards the description of
topological relationships we have used inference as a
structure for representing knowledge. An inference is a

conclusion that can be drawn from certain premises or propositions. To be able to reason using inferencing we need to formalize the representation and operation of relationships between propositions and inferences. Kowalski (1979) proposed first order predicate logic as a subset of traditional logic which directly encodes inferences as statements of the form:

    if X then Y.

The grouping of such inference statements into what is known as a production rule provides a means of encoding knowledge in a way which clearly separates knowledge from facts. For example:

    Y if X
      and Z

is a production rule for inferring the fact Y from the facts X and Z given the knowlege encoded in the production rule. For example, if we have polyhedral objects we can readily infer which vertices make a face if we have the vertex information in a facts base. Knowing the faces we can infer which vertex pairs form edges. Knowing the edges and faces we can infer the entire topology of an object from a factual knowledge of only the vertices. Thus a knowledge base and a facts base can then exist as separate entities.

An example from TOPOLOGY-1 will illustrate the use of first order predicate logic in the description of relationships. The DIRECTLY UNDER predicate establishes whether an object or space A is directly below an object or space B by using the following production rule:

    A is directly under B
      if A is under B
      and A is next to B.

To use the DIRECTLY UNDER rule the system must establish the relationships UNDER and NEXT TO. The simplest way is to look to the facts base; if the facts already exist that:

    A is under B
    A is next to B

then the DIRECTLY UNDER rule has all the information necessary to establish a new fact (which could be added to the facts base) that object A is directly under object B. If these facts do not exist in the facts base, then the system must look to the knowledge base to establish the meaning of the relationship UNDER and NEXT TO. Thus, the knowledge base allows the system to establish facts as and when they are needed.

Although any computer language can, in theory, be used for the encoding of first order predicate logic, most computer languages have been developed for a very different conception of program execution procedures and their use is clumsy. TOPOLOGY-1 is written in Prolog (Clocksin and Mellish, 1981), which is the principal existing computer language in which logical inferences can be expressed directly. In Prolog the DIRECTLY UNDER rule could look like this:

```
directly_under (A,B):-
  under (A,B),
  next_to (A,B).

where  :- can be read as "if"
       ,  can be read as "and"
       .  can be read as "end".
```

A knowledge base may remain valid for a whole class of situations, although we might distinguish between logical knowledge (the domain of knowledge which is universally valid) and experiential knowledge (the domain of knowledge derived from experience or practice in a restricted domain). For a particular house, for example, we might enquire whether the kitchen is directly under the bathroom. In Prolog this might be done as:

```
? directly_under (kitchen, bathroom).
```

to which the response will be either 'true' or 'fail'. Fail means 'not proved', often signified by a simple ':' indicating readiness for more input, rather than 'false' since failure may result from inadequacy in the building description rather than some other room being underneath the bathroom. The relationship DIRECTLY UNDER remains unchanged for all houses and for all buildings, whereas the fact of particular locations for the kitchen and bathroom will be peculiar to this particular house.

3.   TOPOLOGY-1:   A Prototypical Reasoning System

3.1   Aim of the System

TOPOLOGY-1 is aimed at developing the core element of an interactive, knowledge based CAAD system to support the design activity of an architect. It is an inferencing system for physical object description and manipulation, space description and spatial manipulation. It is concerned with the external dependencies approach in geometric modelling, i.e., an approach at the "meta object level". The meta object level in geometric modelling concerns object to object and groups of objects to groups of objects types of relationships. We employ topology within objects at a single object level and topological relationships between objects in the process of manipulating these objects and spaces and inferring relationships. Thus, our concept of "topological attributes" expresses some form of spatial relationship between objects and spaces and their various combinations, such as "adjacent to", "above" and "under".

TOPOLOGY-1 at this stage is capable of making inferences about topological relationships, geometric entities, attributes of objects and spaces and provides support for the architect in design appraisal. It is a system which incorporates declarative attributes, explicit knowledge representation and inferencing capabilities in the domain of logical systems. It embodies some of the characteristics of knowledge based systems which we believe will be part of the CAAD systems of the future.

3.2 Initial Facts Base

The initial facts base contains facts that are input to the system as a **priori** facts. These types of facts are generally associated with attributes of objects and spaces such as colour, direction, price and size as shown below.

    colour (wall_n brown).
    direction (a_wing, north).
    price (door_1, 100).
    space (name, origin, length, width, height).

3.3 Inference System as Knowledge Base

The knowledge base of TOPOLOGY-1 contains various types of knowledge.

(i)   Knowledge for characterizing individual objects

Knowledge about the structure of a single object can be readily broken into three categories:

    (a)   knowledge about object topology - in traditional
          systems these are usually stored values in a
          predefined data structure within the database.

(b)   knowledge about object geometry.

(c)   knowledge about object attributes.

(ii)   Knowledge for characterizing relationships between objects

(a)   topological relationships.

(b)   geometrical relationships.

(iii)   Knowledge or characterizing groups of objects

Here we are concerned with knowing if a group of objects has a particular meaning. For example does it create a frame, a space, or what type of space.

(iv)   Structure of a single space

A single space can be thought of as being similar to a single object except that it is hollow and bounded by walls, floor and roof objects so the same structural characterizations apply as for single objects with the addition of a wide range of attributes.

(v)   Knowledge for characterizing groups of spaces

This type of knowledge is about linking individual spaces to create groups of spaces. Buildings may be thought as groups of spaces, hence, knowledge about such groups is fundamental to knowledge about a building. As with groups of objects we are interested in knowing the meaning of a group of spaces. This is knowledge which is domain dependent, i.e., it does not depend on the particular building in question but applies to all buildings which can be characterized this way.

3.4   What's What and What's Where in the Steampacket Hotel

The Steampacket Hotel is a two storey brick and timber building built in 1971 in Nelligen near Canberra, Australia. The architects' plans are shown in Figure 1 whilst the abstracted spaces with their associated names and floor level are shown in Figure 2.

The initial facts base contains the name, size and location of each space in the building and the location of doorways between spaces. The knowledge base, TOPOLOGY-1, has been described generically in Section 3.3. From the knowledge and facts bases we can "discover" what's what and what's where.

211

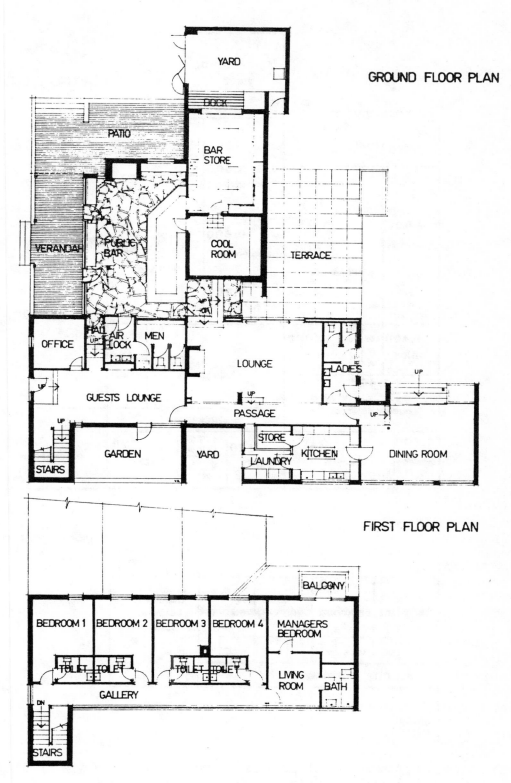

GROUND FLOOR PLAN

YARD

DOCK

PATIO

BAR STORE

VERANDAH

PUBLIC BAR

COOL ROOM

TERRACE

OFFICE

HALL

AIR LOCK

MEN

LOUNGE

LADIES

UP

GUESTS LOUNGE

UP

PASSAGE

UP

UP

STAIRS

GARDEN

YARD

STORE

LAUNDRY

KITCHEN

DINING ROOM

FIRST FLOOR PLAN

BALCONY

BEDROOM 1

BEDROOM 2

BEDROOM 3

BEDROOM 4

MANAGERS BEDROOM

TOILET TOILET

TOILET TOILET

LIVING ROOM

BATH

GALLERY

DN

STAIRS

Figure 1: Architects' plans of the Steampacket Hotel, Nelligen near Canberra, Australia

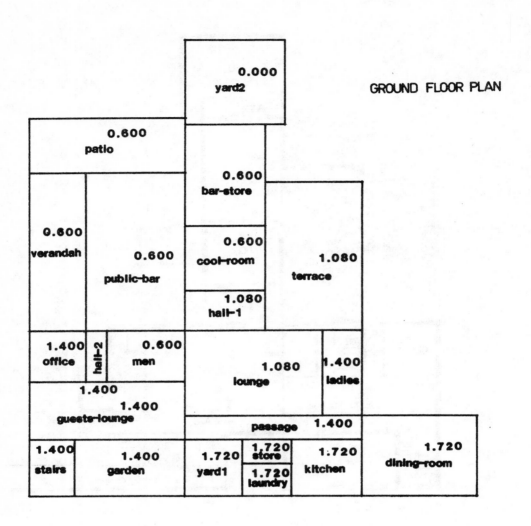

GROUND FLOOR PLAN

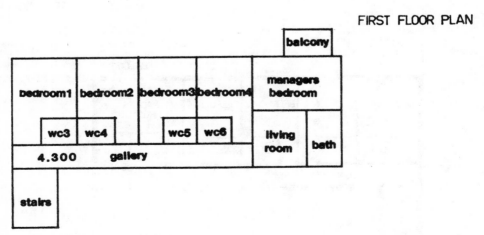

FIRST FLOOR PLAN

Figure 2: Abstracted spaces with their names and floor
levels for the Steampacket Hotel.
Architects: Fisher, Jackson and Hudson

For example we want to know whether we can easily move chairs from the lounge to the terrace for summer use. Thus, we ask whether these two spaces are at the same level:

```
user:      ?same_level(lounge,terrace).
system:    true
```

After a long night in the bar patrons find it difficult to negotiate steps. What rooms can they walk to without using steps:

```
user:      ?same_level(public_bar,Rooms).
system:    Rooms=[men, verandah, cool_room, bar_store,
           patio]
```

A female customer on the verandah unable to locate a waiter, decides to search for the kitchen. Where is the kitchen and how can she reach it.

```
user:      ? reach (verandah, kitchen, Spaces).
system:    Spaces=[verandah, public_bar, hall_2,
                   guests_lounge, passage, dining_room,
                   kitchen]
           Spaces=[verandah, public_bar, men, hall_2,
                   guests_lounge, passage, dining_room,
                   kitchen]
           Spaces=[verandah, public_bar, hall_1,
                   terrace, lounge, passage,
                   dining_room, kitchen]
           Spaces=[verandah, public_bar, hall_1, lounge,
                   passage, dining_room, kitchen]
```

From this we can observe that one of the four paths involves passing through the men's toilet - an undesirable route. It could be eliminated in two ways. Either by adding knowledge to the system or by rephrasing the query as:

```
            ?reach(verandah, kitchen, Spaces), not
                  (member (men, Spaces)).
```

The dining room often overflows at lunch time what other spaces are adjacent to the kitchen:

```
user:      ?adjacent_to (kitchen, Space), not
                          (Space=dining_room).
system:    Space = store
           Space = laundry
           Space = passage
```

A passerby arrives late and wishes to know if the only available room (bedroom 1) contains a toilet:

```
user:     ?inside (toilet, bedroom_1).
system:   true
```

(toilet is a list of all the wc's).

Suppose there is water dripping through the ceiling of the office. We want to know what is the space on top of it:

```
user:     ?on_top_of (Space, office).
system:   Space = bedroom_1.
```

What spaces have direct access to the stairs:

```
user:     ?access (stairs, Space).
system:   Space = gallery
          Space = guests_lounge
```

4. Discussion

Knowledge engineering techniques, particularly first order predicate logic, provide the opportunity to encode knowledge as inference and, hence, to build declarative descriptions of objects. Such descriptions provide a fundamentally different form of object representation. One in which we store knowledge about an object rather than simply a specific set of facts which is a particular representaiton only. Thus, we can add to the knowledge base and infer novel facts. This addition can be achieved without altering any of the existing knowledge. Unlike traditional representations, knowledge-based representations allow us to carry out symbolic computing (i.e. computing without numbers) and this opens up new fields (Gero, 1983). It appears that we will be able gradually to build up considerable knowledge about buildings so that all the immanent characterizations of buildings will be represented in the computer. We can expect future CAAD systems to be fundamentally different to the ones with which we have become familiar.

5. Acknowledgements

This work is supported by the Australian Research Grants Scheme and by a Special Projects Grant from the University of Sydney.

6. References

Clocksin, W.F. and Mellish, C.S. (1981). Programming in Prolog. Springer-Verlag, Berlin.

Gero, J.S. (1983). Knowledge Engineering - Future Uses of Computers in Engineering. Computers and Engineering, I.E. Aust, Canberra.

Kowalski, R.A. (1979). Logic for Problem Solving. North-Holland, London.

PICTURES WITHOUT NUMBERS: GRAPHICAL REALISATION OF LOGICAL MODELS

S W D Steel
Research Assistant
P J Szalapaj
Research Student
Department of Architecture
University of Edinburgh
UK

We see lines as being the primary drawing objects from which the graphical representations of building objects are constructed. Some of the operations that may be needed for manipulating lines are discussed.

It is necessary to structure object representations in logical models which reflect the ways people such as architects and engineers think about those objects. The types of structures we envisage are discussed.

Sam Steel, Research worker at EdCAAD in Edinburgh University. His background is in artificial intelligence and philosophy. (Mathematics has applications to the numerical descriptions of buildings; philosophy, to their logical and symbolic descriptions.) He has worked on computer analysis of natural language and in the professional theatre.

Peter Szalapaj, Research student at EdCAAD, Edinburgh University. Has a background in the disciplines of mathematics and computer science (including AI). Has taught maths/computing, and has experience of architectural computing research at UWIST.

1. Drawings

We have observed that the principal means used by architects to convey the complexities of a building project is by drawing. In order to investigate what kind of information manifests itself in the form of architects' drawings, and to study how the drawings evolve during the course of a project, we have co-operated with architects in analysing their drawings for a completed housing development.

We found a variety of drawings prepared for different purposes, from the early sketch drawings which were primarily an aid to the architect's own thinking, through to presentation drawings intended for different people at different stages in the design, and finally production drawings.

Initially we focused our attention on house design rather than site layout drawings. We were also interested to obtain any form of data that would naturally be associated with drawings but not be part of them, such as specifications, schedules and bill of quantities.

Ideally, we are aiming at an integrated design system, whereby all the data necessary to describe a design should be machine resident in a data base which is complete, consistent, and non-redundant. The conventional method of recording design information, briefs, drawings and schedules possesses several drawbacks. First, because the information is not integrated, it is necessary to perform correlations between different forms. Secondly, a great deal of redundant information may be generated and remain in existence. Next, different professions require different subsets of information in different formats, which requires appropriate translations of selected information. Finally, the revision of design data to remove obsolete data is often performed inefficiently if at all (1).

Let us now examine copies of two of the drawings in detail, to discover the purpose behind the information that is to be conveyed by them, the person to whom the drawings are to be addressed, and the material to be communicated.

Example 1: A sectional elevation

Figure 1 was one of a set of drawings by the architects which was given to the structural engineer after preliminary sketches had been made, in order that he could provide advice on the suitability of the proposed structures. In this set of drawings, the architects were denoting the walls which they thought at that time would be the primary structural load-bearing walls. They were also denoting the floor material. The shaded areas represent doors, structural walls and floors. The dotted lines are the other flights of the stairs so that the stair section is taken on one flight, the other flight is shown dotted. The dotted lines at the top represent the top floor.

In constructing such a drawing, the architect has to be aware of what kind of knowledge the structural engineer possesses in order to be able to distinguish such features as flights of stairs, doors, walls and openings. It would be desirable for drawing systems to represent such objects so that their topologies and geometries form only two facets of richer representations. Such representations may have knowledge of the objects' physical properties, their relations to each other, and so on.

The desirability of having such embodied knowledge within a drawing system would not only have a beneficial effect upon the user interface in that it would be possible to refer to specific objects in order to expand upon their design (rather than to manipulate groups of lines devoid of meaning other than their screen co-ordinate representations), but more importantly, such an object-based representation would constitute the core of the computer's internal representational system, replacing the more conventional representations which are based upon whatever software happens to produce graphical output most efficiently with respect to the hardware that it is running on.

Example 2: Floor plans

Figure 2 shows a part of an engineer's drawing of floor plans. The purpose of the drawing is to show all the structural concrete work, which consists of floors and stair flights and landings, and these generally are dimensioned in plan and section so that their location in the building can be seen and checked against the dimensions of the building, and they will probably be used by the manufacturer of the precast units. The dotted lines indicate the extent of the support provided by walls below the floor.

It is interesting to speculate as to how the engineer may have constructed such a drawing using the implements at his disposal.

First draw two feint parallel horizontal lines whose exact length is not important, at the required separation. These would have been done solely with the aid of the T-square and a pencil, and are not visible on the final drawing as they would have been rubbed out. They are the lines that would give rise to lines 4 and 1, and lines 5 and 8.

On the lower line, two points would have been marked whose separation was the same as the distance between the lines since the final figure is intended to represent the intersection of walls of the same type.

Using the set-square, two feint vertical lines are drawn through these points to cross the first two lines. All such feint lines are termed construction lines, and to bring out the required shape they have to be strengthened where necessary. This is usually done by inking-in where necessary, and in this case dashed ink lines are used to produce lines 1-8.

2 Computer draughting facilities

We are now in a position to propose the computer draughting facilities that we are intending to present to architects.

2.1 Lines - 'pencil' and 'ink

"For the present then let us content ourselves with the most primitive of elements, the line. At the dawn of civilisation, when writing and drawing were the same thing, it was the basic element."

Paul Klee

We see lines as being the primary drawing objects from which the graphical representations of building objects are constructed. From the discussion of example 2 above, it seems intuitively obvious that there should be a distinction in computer draughting, just as there already is in conventional draughting, between 'pencil' and 'ink' lines.

Pencil lines are construction lines that are used to position the ink lines that appear in finished drawings. They are presented as effectively infinite lines extending across the full width of the screen for whatever object is being drawn. The intersection of any two pencil lines produces a construction point which may be used subsequently to delimit an ink line. All ink lines must lie between two such construction points.

We have done away with the traditional computer draughting approach in which drawing takes place on a fixed grid, typically square grids with uniform intervals of 300mm and 100mm for house design. Pencil lines can be viewed as a more general case of grid lines, in which the grid pattern is infinitely variable, and every instance of a pencil line is positioned according to some particular anticipation of the final ink lines. Pencil lines can either be horizontal, vertical, or inclined. Once a set of pencil lines has been constructed, it is then possible to traverse them using ink lines to determine the desired shape or drawing.

Drawing in 2-D in order to represent a 2-D subset of 3-D space such as a plan or section, is sufficient for most purposes in architectural practice. A line drawn in the X-Y plane which is to represent an edge in 2-D space, has two real world dimensions associated with it: its length and its angle relative to a bearing. These should not be confused with the length and angle of a line as produced by a drawing system.

It is only ink lines that can bear both real world dimensions, since pencil lines are effectively of infinite length. Pencil lines do have angles however, and, since it is they that are drawn first, they determine what angles the ink lines shall have. Consequently, we associate angles with pencil lines, and lengths with ink lines.

Upon completion of the ink lines representing a new shape, we make no
assumption about the real world dimensions of any of the lines contained in it. However, at this stage all ink lines have names. It
should be possible to attach numeric values representing real world
dimensions to these names at any subsequent stage in the drawing
whenever they are referred to. The angle dimension of an ink line
can be derived from those of the pencil lines associated with it.

Furthermore, the dimensions of lines can be expressed in terms of the
dimensions of other lines. Shapes can be parameterised so that only a
minimum number of dimensions are required to determine all the line
dimensions for a given shape.

Only shapes that are fully dimensioned can be drawn to scale. Otherwise, shapes retain their original graphical representations for the
purpose of illustration.

Example 3: Illustration of pencil/ink line drawing

Suppose we have constructed the shapes shown in figure 3a and figure
3b. Each pencil line in both shapes has associated with it a symbolic
real-world angle as shown. Each ink line has a symbolic real-world
length. The real-world angles need not necessarily be equal to the
screen angles. Figure 3a has one real-world length, y, which should
also be given to the line opposite because of parallelism. Figure 3b
has real-world lengths a,b,c.

Suppose figure 3a is stretched as shown in figure 4a, and that two
further pencil lines are added to this new shape as shown in figure
4b, in order to provide figure 3b with points for it to map on to for
the purposes of a composition. The stretching may be carried out by
indicating points on the screen on to which the original points may
be mapped. In figure 4a, parameterisation has taken place with
respect to real world lengths.

In order to arrive at the shape shown in figure 5, we require a
transformation of the dimensions of figure 3b relative to figure 4b.
Although figure 5 is shown without pencil lines in order to indicate
the shape, the pencil lines upon which this shape has been constructed
remain an integral part of its representation.

2.2 Inferred dimensioning

Once there are named lines that bear symbolic dimensions and angles,
it ought to be possible to state relations between them. These
relations should be kept even when the drawings change. For instance,
consider a drawing like figure 6a. A house is 40' wide, 20' of that
is sitting room, 20' is kitchen. If the width of the sitting room is
increased to 22', what happens? Do you get figure 6b or figure 6c?

Consider figure 6a again. How does one dimension it? Suppose the width BC is 20'. This is the dimension of the sitting-room by itself. Then one can either:

1   Declare the length of the ink-line segment AC, which is the total width of the house, to be fixed at 40'. The width of the kitchen follows by subtraction.

2   Declare the length of the ink-line segment AB, which is the width of the kitchen, to be fixed at 20'. The width of the total house follows by addition.

What happens if you widen the sitting-room depends on which of these has been chosen. If the first, then the width of the house is constant, and so the kitchen will shrink. If the second, the width of the kitchen is constant, so the width of the house will increase.

The great advantage of inferred dimensioning lies in its use in the attachment of objects discussed next.

2.3   Attachment facts

Imagine that both a bath and the walls of a bathroom have been drawn (figure 7a). Suppose the bath is now to be put into the bathroom. The bath can be located relative to some fixed point in the bathroom - say 2' from the lower left-hand corner (figure 7b). Now suppose the bathroom changes width, from 5' to 6'. What happens to the bath? It is still 2' from the origin, so it gets stranded in the middle of the enlarged bathroom (figure 7c).

What should have happened is that the right-hand side of the bath and the right-hand wall of the bathroom should have been attached to each other. Thus when one moved, the other would have been dragged with it. How is this done? Figure 7d is like figure 7a. If the construction points are attached as shown, the pencil lines on which lie the right-hand sides of the bath and bathroom will be declared to be the same, and if one of them is moved in the composite drawing (for instance by being declared to lie 5' not 6' from the other side of the bathroom) they will move together to produce, not figure 7c, but figure 7e.

This answer should be derivable from attachment facts stated during the construction of a drawing, and which indicate how different parts of a drawing are related. They are statements about which construction points on one drawing go with which construction points on another. When attachments are made:

1   the lengths between pairs of pairs of points in the drawings that you have attached to each other are made symbolically equal to each other;

2 the pencil lines on which pairs of pairs of points lie are declared
   to be colinear in the combined drawing. These facts will interact
   with numerical dimensions of the picture to fix the final drawing.

2.4 The grouping of lines and attachment facts to form objects

When talking about buildings, they can usually be thought of in terms
of their decomposition into parts, as was illustrated by the architects' drawings. It should be possible to describe such parts, draw
them, and to describe how they themselves can be further decomposed
into other parts.

As we are primarily concerned with graphical input, it is the drawing
that takes place first in the manner we have indicated, with lines as
the primary drawing objects. Lines drawn on a screen refer to things
in the real world. These happen to be the boundaries of surfaces of
objects. A surface lies between that part of space occupied by an
object, and the rest of the space outside it. Just as surfaces of
objects exist in the real world, so do lines which separate one part
of an object from another, both of which can be seen to exist. In
other words, lines are not figments of our imagination which we think
of as strings that have become infinitely thin. In the same way,
points should not be thought of as being very small particles. Thus
lines and points in the real world define the surfaces of objects.

As a consequence, it should be possible to group lines together, first
to identify the boundaries of surfaces which constitute the parts of
objects, and subsequently in order to identify the objects themselves
by grouping the parts together, and stating the relations between them
by means of attachment facts.

If we are aiming for an integrated representation of objects, then the
primary graphical representation of object topologies/geometries
should be structured according to the way they fit into a logical
model.

3 Modelling objects

3.1 Abstract and graphical objects

We have already observed that sometimes it is necessary to refer to
objects by abstract names such as "the third floor bathroom of the
five storey block", and on other occasions the graphical representation of such an object is required. In both cases, there is a
hierarchical breakdown of a high-level object into the lower-level
parts from which it is constructed. It is easier to talk about the
abstract object hierarchy, which in the previous example, might look
something like:

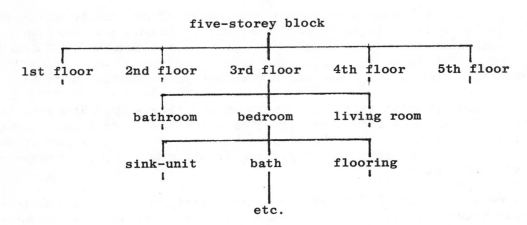

For each line-set topology which has been obtained as a result of drawing, there has also to be a breakdown of the line-set into its abstract object hierarchy, each part of which is defined in terms of a topology. In other words, there is a mapping from abstract parts on to topological elements.

It is the logical model which is responsible for handling transactions between abstract object hierarchies and the topologies of their parts. A graphical/textual interface is needed to construct and update them. It is possible to construct both graphical and abstract object hierarchies simultaneously by naming objects as they are drawn.

3.2 Kinds

A way of defining types of object, and making copies of those types, is essential for any drawing system. We have such a mechanism, but it is rather different from the usual. We believe that types and objects are the same sort of entity, which we call the <u>kind</u>. This could be thought of as being short for "kind of thing".

In existing drawing systems a type called, say, "door" might be defined. Later a copy of it is made, which is then planted down in some other drawing - say "front-wall". The copy will have a name - perhaps something like "door/93". If the door type has parameters, say "height" and "material", these must be filled in when the copy is made. This copy is not a type. A copy cannot be copied to produce another sort of door.

Since we make no distinction between types and copies, the kind "door" could be instantiated only partially, so that the "height" is 7'6" but the material is unknown. This can be both planted in another drawing, and also further instantiated to give another kind of door used in another drawing. The usefulness of such a mechanism is illustrated in the following example:

On a housing estate all doors might be roughly the same, in material, construction, and supplier say. Now suppose there are two sorts of building. Then all those in one sort may be of height 7'2", and all those in the other be 6'10". But they are otherwise both copies of the kind "door". But in each sort of building, the doors on each floor may be one particular colour. So all the doors on floor 2 of block type 1 will be copies of the kind of door of block type 1, which are in turn copies of the kind of door common throughout the estate.

Kinds can have named parts. For instance, a door may have parts called "door_knob" and "stile". The thing that is the "door_knob" part of the door will probably be a door_knob. Don't be misled by the similarity of the name of a part and the name of the thing that is that part. A roof could have a part called "left_wallplate" while the thing that was that part was a beam.

But there are other aspects that a door may have that are not really parts in the ordinary sense. A door may have a "colour" and a "height" and a "made_to_BSI_standard" property. The colour could be red, the height could be 200cms and the "made_to_BSI_standard" property could be "yes". All these facts about a door should be treated in the same way. So we generalise the notions of a part of a kind, and an aspect or a property of a kind, into the notion of a SLOT of a kind (2). The thing that goes in the SLOT is called a FILLER. You can have a slot called anything you like. Any filler can go in any slot. Slots have no meaning beyond their conventions of use. Here is the door example in these terms:

SLOT	FILLER
door_knob	DOOR_KNOB
stile	*
colour	RED
height	200
made_to_BSI_standard	yes

(The filler "*" for the slot "stile" means that no explicit filler has yet been inserted.)

3.3 Parts and relative names

Occurrences of kinds do not have their own proper names. Instead they are given names relative to the highest part in the hierarchy of parts that they occur in. If a copy of "door" fills the "main door" property of an assembly called "wall", it will be called "wall:main-door". If that door contains a door-knob, and that door-knob is a copy of Messrs Bloggs "Queen Anne's Pleasaunce", it is not called "Queen Anne's Pleasaunce/7" but "wall:main_door:door_knob". At the same time, the type of door knob is derivable from the description of the part "wall:main_door: door_knob".

Relative naming is an access mechanism which reflects the hierarchical nature of the decomposition of an object into its parts. Relative names are a way of telling you where to look for the facts that you are interested in, without having to duplicate them for each object of which they are true.

4 Choice of implementation

The most successful and precise language ever developed to express inference procedures is modern formal logic (3). This is not a programming language, but a mathematical formalism. It does have the admirable properties, however, of being both precise enough to be understood and manipulated by computers, and natural enough to be regarded as a simplified form of natural language. Obviously we want to use computers to exploit their excellent storage facilities, and the most promising implementation of logic so far is Prolog.

At present we are implementing some of the facilities described for the graphical input and for object modelling. We are using Seelog, a graphics front end to Prolog based on GiGo, an event-based graphics system, in conjunction with EdCAAD's own implementation of Prolog in C.

5 Summary

We consider drawings to be paramount in the representation of buildings. We have looked at architects' drawings in order to determine what is depicted by them, and what techniques are used to achieve this. One immediate consequence was to adopt the pencil/ink line representation as a useful method of input, and which also allows us to consider lines as symbolic objects with respect to their dimensions, since there is no notion of drawing on a fixed grid and hence symbolic values have to be given.

In order to be able to propagate changes in the dimensions of parts of a drawing to other parts of the same drawing, it is essential to be able to state how the parts are connected to each other, and we do this by means of attachment facts. Graphical objects are sets of lines together with attachment facts. A building may also be thought of in terms of an abstract object hierarchy, and our aim is to integrate abstract and graphical representations. We call the general object a kind, which is described in terms of its slots and fillers. The parts of a kind are also kinds and are accessed by means of relative names.

Finally, we have chosen Prolog as the implementation language because of its closeness to modern formal logic which has a rigorously defined semantics.

Acknowledgments

This work was funded by the Science and Engineering Research Council. We wish to thank the Scottish Special Housing Association for their time, and cooperation in providing drawings. We are grateful to our colleagues at EdCAAD for their support and encouragement.

References

1   Bijl, A., Stone. D., Rosenthal, D.; "Integrated CAAD Systems", EdCAAD, 1979.

2   Minsky, M. "A Framework for Representing Knowledge", in The Psychology of Computer Vision, Winston P.H. (Ed) McGraw Hill, 1975.

3   Kowalski, R.A.; "Logic for Problem Solving", Elsevier North Holland, 1979.

Fig.1　A sectional elevation

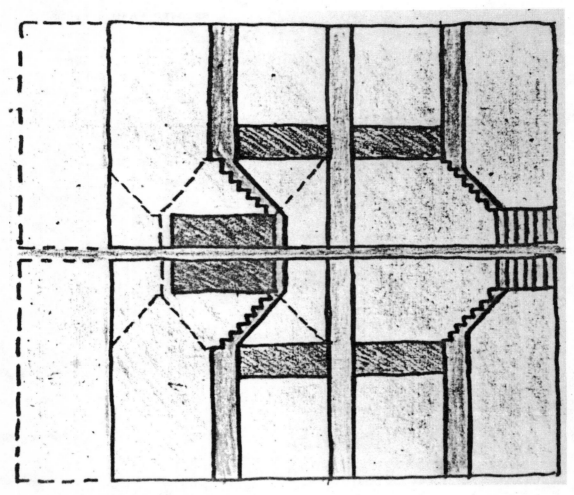

Sectional elevation 3

fig.2 Floor Plan

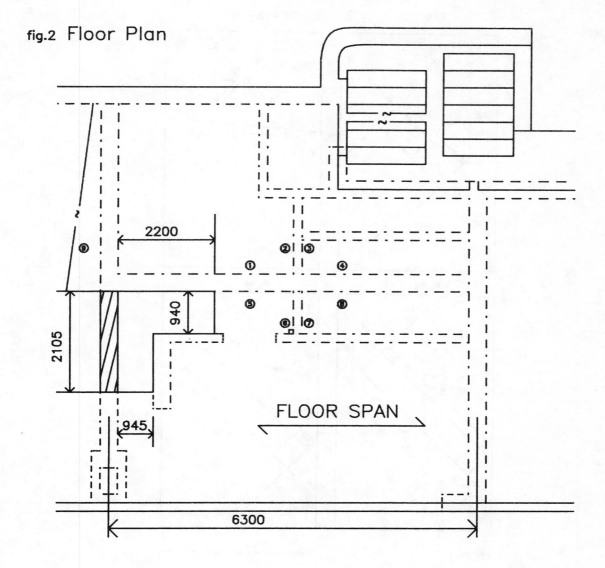

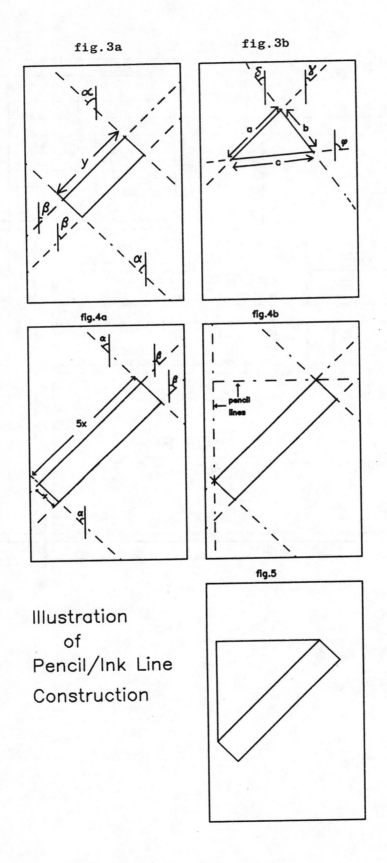

Illustration
of
Pencil/Ink Line
Construction

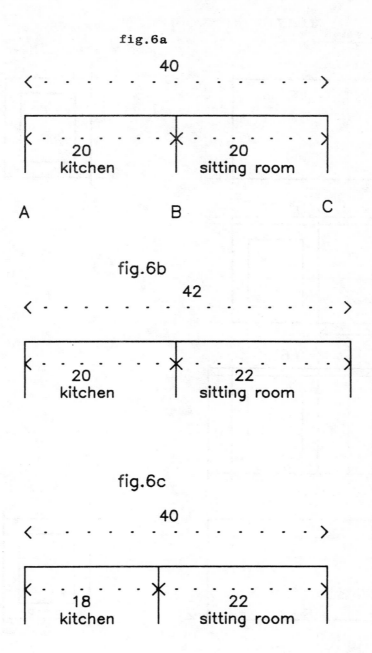

fig.6a

fig.6b

fig.6c

fig.7

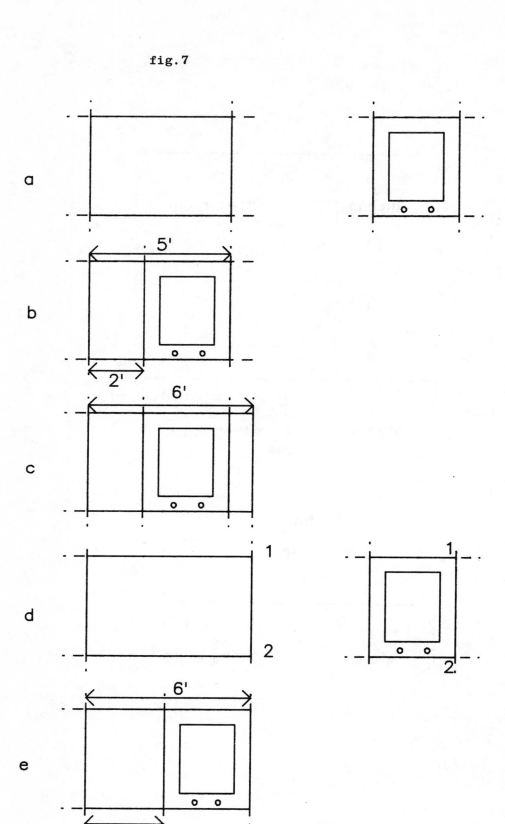

DEALING WITH UNCERTAINTY & IMPRECISION

John Lansdown
Chairman
System Simulation
UK

If we are to make fullest use of Expert Systems in the construction industry, they must be capable of dealing with both uncertainty and imprecision and yet still produce useful results. This paper briefly discusses some of the ways of doing this.

John Lansdown is an architect who has used computers in his work since the early '60s. As far as architectural computing is concerned, he has been specialising lately in the examination and development of Expert Systems and is author of the RIBA Conference Fund Report on the subject.

INTRODUCTION

Although a great deal of construction industry knowledge is of a type that can be expressed in the concrete IF-THEN form outlined in part 2 of the author's Expert Systems Report (RIBACF82) and can be treated in strictly deterministic terms, it frequently happens that we have to deal with imprecise and uncertain matters. For example, it is not always possible for us to answer a question like 'Is the soil cohesive?' with a simple 'Yes' or 'No'. We might need to reply with answers such as 'partly', 'almost', 'to a small degree' on the one hand or, say, 'with probability of 0.7' on the other. In the first case we are sure that an element of cohesiveness is present but feel that it would be misleading to say so without qualification. In the second case we are not certain that any cohesiveness is present but feel it is more likely than not. (Of course, in practice, we might further complicate the issue by saying something like 'I am almost certain that some degree of cohesiveness is present'.)

If we are to develop and exploit the use of knowledge-based computer systems, they must be capable of dealing both with the imprecision, or 'fuzziness', of the first case and the uncertainty, or probability, of the second and yet still produce useful results.

IMPRECISION

Perhaps we have a system which puts the question, 'Is anyone on the staff experienced in hospital planning? (Answer YES or NO)'. Here, the program works on the assumption that staff come in two distinct and separate classes - experienced and inexperienced. In the language of classical set theory, and as far as this form of experience is concerned, staff are assumed to be members of disjoint and exclusive sets (Figure 1). The question is founded on the notion that someone cannot be both experienced and inexperienced at the same time, and we might be given some guidance on making the choice as to which category a particular person belongs, for example, someone with less than three years experience might be classed as 'inexperienced'. However, as it makes complete sense to speak of someone being 'slightly experienced', 'rather inexperienced' or 'totally experienced', most of us would believe that being experienced is not something that can be divided into two separate packets, but a continuum which is better expressed in the form of Figure 2 than Figure 1 or, perhaps, by a number of loosely defined packets as in Figure 3.

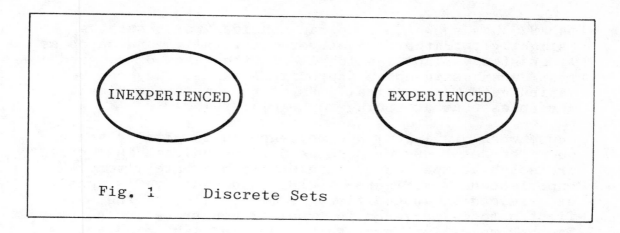

Fig. 1   Discrete Sets

Fig. 2   Continuum

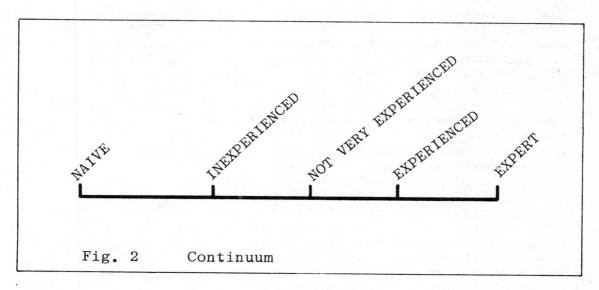

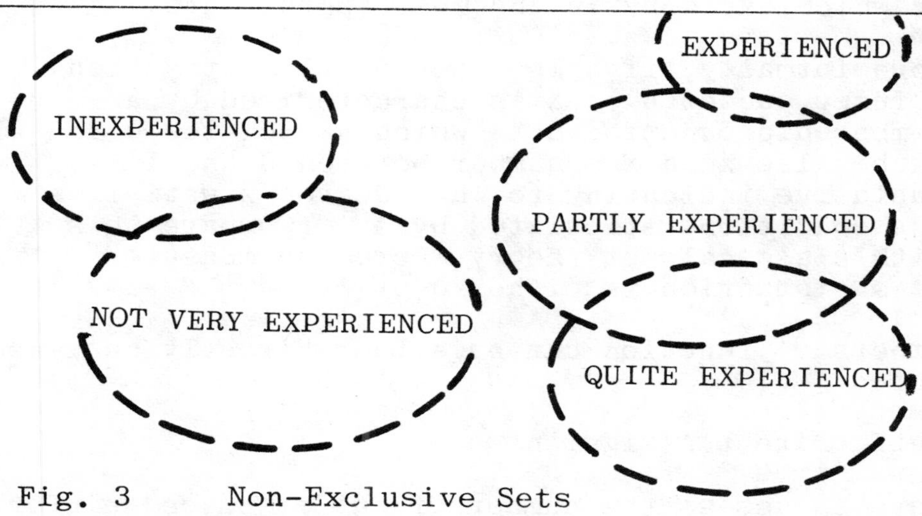

Fig. 3   Non-Exclusive Sets

ZADEH75 has shown that we can consider words such as
'slightly', 'rather', 'not very', 'totally' and so on as
linguistic variables which lie in the range 0 to 1 and
that, when assigned an appropriate value, they can be
manipulated mathematically as if they were numerical
variables (but according to special rules).

Thus, when dealing with experience in hospital planning,
we might set a number such as 0.8 to indicate the concept,
'reasonably experienced' and 0.9 to indicate, 'very
experienced'. A figure of 0.3 could indicate 'slightly
experienced'. In addition, we might allocate the same
figures to 'experience in tropical countries'. Then, by
Zadeh's rules for fuzzy sets, when we wish to calculate a
figure indicating the degree to which the condition
'reasonably experienced in hospital planning AND very
experienced in tropical countries' is satisfied, we take
the minimum of the two appropriate values, that is
$\min(0.8,0.9)=0.8$. If we want a figure to represent,
'reasonably experienced in hospital planning OR very
experienced in tropical countries', we take the maximum of
the two values, that is $\max(0.8,0.9)=0.9$.

Bear in mind that we are neither being ambiguous nor
general when we say such things as 'someone is slightly
experienced' or 'the bedroom is very small'. As DUBOIS79
points out, a description is ambiguous if it denotes
several different concepts at the same time and general
when is applies to a multiplicity of concepts having only
a common essential feature. Neither is the case in our
examples where the statements are simply fuzzy or vague
in the sense that, if we have a set of categories into
which an object or concept might possibly fit, it is not
clear which category is the most appropriate.

> More formally, if X is a set of elements, then
> a fuzzy subset A of X is characterised by a
> membership function M(X) which associates with
> each value x in X a number between 0 and 1
> inclusive indicating to what degree x satisfies
> the conditions stipulated by A. (Compare this
> with classical set theory where the measure
> of satisfaction is either 0 or 1.)

A membership function can be either directly assigned or
computed.

EXAMPLE: Direct Assignment

We have to assess the number of out of place reinforcing
rods in a beam where the membership function for a small

number is defined as:

   1/0   0.8/1   0.6/2   0.2/3

(Read this as, if 0 bars are misplaced, then the function
is 1, if 1 bar is misplaced, the function is 0.8 and so
on.)

EXAMPLE: Computed Assignment

We have to assess the size of bedrooms where the membership function for a small bedroom is defined as:

$$\begin{cases} 1 & \text{if area} \leq 6 \text{ sq m} \\ 1/(1+((area-6)/2.5)**2) & \text{if area} > 6 \text{ sq m} \end{cases}$$

(Thus, if area is 8 sq m, the function is 0.61 and if
area is 12 sq m, the function is 0.15)

It is also possible to compute other membership functions
from these. For example, 'very small' might be defined
as (small)**2 and 'more or less small' as (small)**0.5
(MIZUMOTO79).

Fuzziness can also be introduced into the IF-THEN
productions of RIBACF82. For example, if we have the
fuzzy variables A, B, C and the items X and Y, the
statement

    If X is A then Y is B else C

can be interpreted in fuzzy set theory as

    (A and B) or (not A and C)

where (not A) is given by (1-A).

An instance of this is:

IF design 1 IS reasonably cheap
THEN the client's satisfaction IS high
ELSE the client's satisfaction IS medium

Here, X = design1
      Y = the client's satisfaction
      A = reasonably cheap = say 0.7
      B = high   = say 0.85
      C = medium   = say 0.6

Then

    (A and B) or (not A and C)

reduces to max(min(0.7,0.85),min(0.3,0.6)) = max(0.7,0.3) = 0.7 which is the membership function for this condition.

YAGER80 outlines the way in which this approach can be used to choose between sets of options which are fuzzily defined. Using his technique, we are able to deal logically and objectively with an expression such as: 'IF a given design is reasonably cheap AND more or less fulfils the brief AND can be built in about 12 months OR is very cheap AND almost fulfils the brief THEN the client's satisfaction is high ELSE it is low'.

The ways in which we can incorporate such fuzzy knowledge and understanding into Expert Systems needs further work but it is clear that even the present methods could provide us with valuable tools for more realistic and intelligent programs.

UNCERTAINTY

Uncertainty is different from imprecision. When we say, 'There is a 70% chance of the tenders for our latest scheme coming in under budget', we are not being fuzzy but are stating our level of confidence in the outcome of an uncertain event. Many Expert Systems have ways of dealing with probability in order to allow their users to say something about uncertain happenings and for the system to convey the degree of certainty of its conclusions. However, although the mathematics of probability is well-understood, uncertainty is not easily handled particularly when, as is likely to be the case, the assessment of chances is both subjective and conditional in a way which makes the likelihood of one event dependent on the likelihood of another.

In theory, Bayesian probability analysis is ideal for these circumstances as it links probable cause with effect and allows the orderly reassessment of probabilities based on the acquisition of new knowledge. In essence, it can be summarised by the statement: 'If the evidence is true to some degree then the hypothesis is true to some degree'. However, in practice, the strict application of Bayesian theory to real problems is not easy and most of the Expert Systems which handle probability use modified methods.

The Prospector Expert System is a case in point. This system was originally designed to assist in exploration for minerals (GASCHNIG81) but has since been used in other applications. In Prospector-type Expert Systems, probability is taken care of by what are called 'plausible relations' wherein cause and effect are associated. For example, a plausible relation (unfortunately, imaginary) could be:

If ground works tenders are below budget then it is usual for the whole tender to be below budget.

This relation can be expressed diagrammatically as in Figure 4.

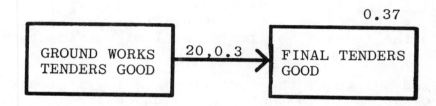

Fig. 4   Plausible Relation

Associated with each effect is a number representing the probability that the effect will occur if nothing else is known. In Figure 4, the prior probability is given as 0.37 indicating that, with nothing else known, we can only be 37% certain that the tenders will come in under budget. Associated with each relational arc are two numbers: the first number is called the measure of sufficiency (LS); the second number is called the measure of necessity (LN). In Figure 4, the LS is 20 and the LN is 0.3. These figures are used to reassess the probability of the effect once the probability of the cause is known. In order to do this the 'odds-likelihood' form of probability is used. Here,

Odds = Probability/(1 - Probability) and

Probability = Odds/(1 + Odds).

Thus, if it is known that groundwork tenders are <u>below</u> budget, we can use this fact to multiply the odds in favour of the whole tender being below budget (WTBB) by the LS factor of 20. Then the prior odds of WTBB are 0.37/(1-0.37) = 0.587, giving the final odds of 0.587*20 = 11.74 corresponding to a final probability of 11.74/(1 + 11.74) = 0.92.

If, on the other hand, it is definitely known that the ground work tenders are <u>above</u> budget, we can use this fact to multiply the odds in favour of WTBB by the LN factor of 0.3. Then the final odds are 0.587*0.3 = 0.176 corresponding to a final probability of WTBB of 0.15.

In addition to uncertainty in the outcomes, it sometimes happens that users are uncertain about the presence or absence of the cause. Prospector takes care of this by allowing users to express their certainty on an arbitrary scale between 5 and -5, where 5 means absolute certainty that the cause or evidence exists and -5 means absolute certainty that the cause does not exist. Figures in between these extremes can be used to express varying degrees of certainty or uncertainty. These figures are converted by the system into probabilities and are applied to the results to give a level of confidence in the final conclusion.

The major advantage of the logical necessity/logical sufficiency approach is that both evidence for and evidence against a hypothesis is given adequate weighting. It can readily be seen that a very small figure for logical necessity greatly effects the probability of a positive conclusion. Thus, the lower the LN figure, the greater is the necessity for the evidence or cause to be present. Similarly, a very large figure for logical sufficiency increases the chance of a positive conclusion so that the existence of evidence with a high LS figure is sufficient to point to the conclusion. (For the methods of arriving at these figures and a more detailed exposition of the techniques the reader is directed to REBOH81).

However, the disadvantage of the Bayesian approach is the considerable work that is needed to set up the prior probabilities and the figures for logical sufficiency and necessity. It must be difficult enough to get experts to assess these measures in scientific subjects such as geology and medicine. In construction industry work, where mathematical techniques are largely ignored, the problems look too formidable to make it feasible to use the Prospector (and similar) Expert System approach. Thus much development work still needs to be done to allow probability to be readily included into Construction Industy Expert Systems and I suggest it is a subject for further study.

REFERENCES

BOND81: Machine Intelligence A Bond (ed) Infotec State
of the Art Report Pergamon Infotech 1981

DUBOIS79: An Outline of Fuzzy Set Theory D Dubois and
H Prade in GUPTA 79

GASCHNIG81: PROSPECTOR: An Expert System for Mineral
Exploration J Gaschnig in BOND81

GUPTA79: An Introduction to Advances in Fuzzy Set Theory
and Applications M N Gupta et al (eds) North-Holland
Publishing Co 1979

MIZUMOTO79: Some Methods of Fuzzy Reasoning M Mizumoto
el al in GUPTA79

REBOH81: Knowledge Engineering Techniques and Tools in
the PROSPECTOR-Environemtn R Reboh SRI DATALOG File
81-620 SRI International Calif 1981

RIBACF82: Expert Systems: Their Impact on the Construction
Industy John Lansdown RIBA Conference Fund London 1982

WANG80: Fuzzy Sets Theory and Applications to Policy
Analysis and Information Systems P P Wang and S K Chang
(eds) Plenum Press NY 1980

YAGER80: Satisfaction and Fuzzy Decision Functions
R R Yager in WANG80

ZADEH75: The Concept of a Linguistic Variable and its
Application to Approximate Reasoning Information Sciences
8 and 9 1975 and 1976

A STANDARDS DATABASE

J S Widdowson
Group Manager
Information Department
British Standards Institution
UK

Technical requirements including standards, constitute a critical source of information to industry and particularly to the Building/ Construction field. The current situation on bibliographic databases is reviewed. The services currently available from the British Standards Institution are described with special mention of the Database Development Project and its prospects for the future.

John Widdowson is Group Manager of BSI's new Information Department at Milton Keynes. His responsibilities include enquiries, the merged Library, and Database Section. Following education training and work in marine and power engineering, in 1970 he joined BSI as a THE Consultant Engineer. Promotion to Head of its Information Section involved the development of practical information systems to suit industrial clients and an active international role. The development of BSI's database system started in 1977 with work on the ROOT Thesaurus.

Why do buildings fall down?

Human error is the first cause that springs to mind and if a mistake is made in complying with an appropriate specification then better control of the work-force is the only cure. However, if the design itself was unsound then you have a major problem and it was in this context that the value of nationally accepted standard specifications became a valuable contribution to the design and erection of good buildings.

The "Good Old Days" when **technology** moved slowly and the memories of your professional staff could keep track of relevant standards and regulations are going if they have not already gone.

My building colleagues tell me that today a bigger problem than building collapse is building performance where problems are complicated by the use of untried materials (foams, plastics, sealants, etc). Even improved performance can lead to problems in other areas (improved insulation and draft proofing giving rise to condensation). But the world is a small place and it is often the case that problems experienced in another country yesterday which have resulted in new standards or regulations will throw light on the best way of resolving the new problems before they become serious.

Further, in a world where cost effective design and construction is the only way to remain in business, perhaps a new American, German or Swedish development would reduce the cost of your buildings and the existence of an established, nationally accepted design criteria, published in an authoritative standard, could give you leverage to get an alternative design configuration accepted.

So, in today's world accurate knowledge of the current standards and regulations affecting your product or construction is critical and systems to provide information on national or world standards and regulations are a tool which is increasingly important in ensuring that you maintain your position in the market place.

What is a bibliographic database?

In layman's language a bibliographic database is an information tool that permits the retrieval of references to documents. The online bibliographic database permits inter-action between the searcher and the system by the initial question being almost instantaneously answered, enabling the enquirer to refine his question to obtain the collection of document references most relevant to his problem. The bibliographic database will normally be mounted on a host computer which offers access to members of the public who own appropriate terminals via telecommunication lines.

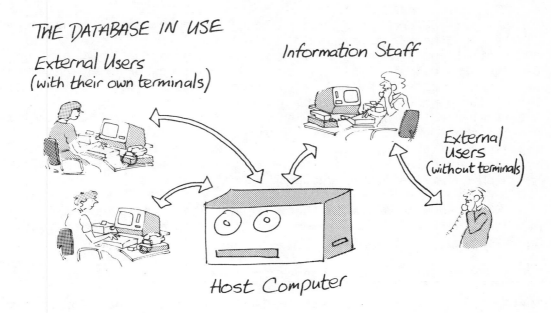

THE DATABASE IN USE

External Users (with their own terminals)

Information Staff

External Users (without terminals)

Host Computer

As the above diagram shows, while the enquirer can use the database direct, problems can also be solved by professional intermediaries.

Bibliographic databases are not new with the early samples available for inhouse use in the early 1960's, with public access developing around 1972. The principal databases made available over the years have contained references mainly to scientific and technical journal articles of the sort conventionally contained in abstracting or indexing journals. The benefit of the online system was the speed of access to enormous bibliographic files now risen to over 77 million references and increasing at the rate of 9 million items per year.

These tools have been invaluable to the scientific and research communities to enable them to trace new developments of particular interest to them. However, the scale of the systems meant that guaranteed retrieval of all relevant information was unlikely but did not concern many of the users as the references retrieved could be used as a starting point for manual research.

The field of technical requirements covering laws, regulations, codes of practice, standards and similar technical documents which prescribe the method of design, operation or use of an item of equipment or service are a different category of information. The problem here is not so much the size of the collection (though over $1\frac{1}{2}$ million documents are thought to exist around the world) but relates to change. All standards and regulations are modified in the light of experience or new technology. It is the ability of the online database to accept updated information and within days make it **available** to the client which is the major reason for the development of new bibliographic databases, covering the fields of standards and regulations.

For the professional designing buildings, structures or products to
comply with the **requirements** in force in any country or state, it is
of critical importance that all relevant information is identified
to him. The omission of even one significant law or standard could
cause the product to be refused the required approval. So with
technical requirements databases, a new standard of quality in
retrieval needs to be sought. Further, there are other facts which
the searcher may wish to refer to in defining his problem such as
the date when the regulations or standards were in force, the
availability of a certification or approval system, or the countries
in which he wishes his products to be sold, etc.

These are the special facts that make a bibliographic database for
standards and regulations a more complicated tool than its scientific
and technical equivalent.

The state of the art on standards databases

The British Standards Institution has the oldest information systems
covering both British and foreign standards and regulations through
the activities of the BSI Library (previously at Park Street) and
the Technical Help to Exporters Information Section (previously at
Hemel Hempstead) now merged together at Milton Keynes. However,
these systems were manual, not computer-based and though they
provided an excellent start, they did not have the speed of
response or comprehensive data element recording capability now seen
as essential.

Standards were included on engineering biased databases such as
Inspec, NASA and INIS but were not complete or sufficiently current
to meet the needs of the designer.

DIN and AFNOR, the German and French standards bodies, were two of
the first organizations to realise the significance of a
bibliographic database as a tool for their publications and
instigated work in the late 1960's. The International Standards
Organizations saw the logic of developing common systems rather than
a series of nationally unique structures and established a series of
activities which culminated in a feasibility study on the
establishment of an ISO information network produced with the
support of UNESCO under the UNISIST programme in 1975. Currently,
ISONET has developed as a standard information system, with
recognized thesauri (one of them the BSI ROOT Thesaurus) and a
manual undergoing its final development.

Nationally some 20 bibliographic databases, specifically covering
technical requirements, have been produced. NORIANE developed by
AFNOR and available on the French Telesystemes and European Euronet
networks and DITR, produced by DIN and used by a number of standards
bodies to provide authoritative information on German standards and
regulations are the best known of the ISONET systems. However, the

national priority to produce their systems within a national deadline
has reduced the extent of compatibility.

The information industry, particularly in the USA, has produced some
databases but they are based on old manual systems and lack the
extent of data elements or currency required of a modern standards
database system.

However, a new generation of databases,with BSI at the forefront,
are being produced which take advantage of the experience gained to
date and developed in the ISONET proposals so that the future
prospects for compatible systems are good.

Services available from BSI

My article in the August issue of BSI News will have given some of
you an insight into the background, structure and operation of the
new BSI Information Department at Milton Keynes.

The opportunity to establish professional sections to handle
enquiries, the merged BSI Library, and the new Database Section
has permitted the development of an information structure second
to none in the world.

The Technical Help to Exporters service continues to offer the
specialist engineering interpretation so essential for accurate
design of equipment to meet the needs of foreign countries and it
is supported in an improved manner by the Information Department
with its growing skills in the use of all relevant online
information systems.

On the database front, BSI was late in entering the field because of
the quality of its manual systems but early in the 1970's saw the
prospects for an ISONET system. From 1977 we contributed
significant resources, resulting in the production of the BSI
ROOT Thesaurus as a multilingual controlled vocabulary for industry
and the specialist field of technical requirements.

In 1981 a small-scale project to encourage the development of a BS
database was established which gained the support of the
Department of Industry and permitted the setting up of the current
experimental database project. This resulted in a test file being
mounted on a public access host for demonstration purposes in
September of this year.

The BS Experimental Database

The initial Development Project report proposed concentrated on the
need to provide a better information retrieval tool, initially for
information on British Standards but with a system capable of
handling other UK standards and technical requirements, overseas

information and exchange within ISONET.

Additional benefits of the database were envisaged as being the increase in efficiency within BSI by a more systematic method for producing printed publications and the prospect to produce a whole range of special publications and services for any group or individual enquirer. All this would lead to an increased use of standards in the UK and overseas as well as providing assistance to standards-makers.

To produce the experimental database, the first task involved in-depth analysis into the existing BSI operation, state of the art of bibliographic databases, particularly those within ISONET, and an analysis of the required content and practical problems involved in establishing a BS database covering both the intellectual description of the document and its conversion into a mechanized database. The project identified that, though BSI's Information Department was the best agency to carry out the analysis and provision of data, and organize the testing of the database and its search capabilities, the functions involving the conversion of the data into a neutral database or the provision of online access and search facilities were tasks best handled by external agencies. Following an investigation of available assistance, arrangements were made for Peter Peregrinus Limited (the producers of the Inspec database for IEE) to design the system for validating the data supplied by BSI and formatting it on the computer, and Pergamon Infoline to mount the database for public access, developing additional software for special search requirements as necessary.

The Department of Industry approved the project and agreed to provide 50% of the cost of the project.

Over the course of the project, the team, headed by Stella Dextre, now Head of Database Section within the Information Department, has completed the rigorous analysis of the current situation to ensure that the BS system meets the higher standards of current practice and even exceeds them.

The results of this analysis were a specification developed in conjunction with PPL, and the production of rules for the allocation of descriptors and other system instructions. The input procedures using the Wordstar package on our Superbrain were also developed.

Then a representative sample of British Standards were collected, together with a subject set relating to electrical power engineering, and samples of other standards and regulations, and this collection of documents systematically described and indexed in accordance with the experimental system. The results of this work, developed as an exchange tape by PPL have been supplied to PI and loaded for test purposes.

The database contains special features necessary for technical requirements. Over 150 fields have been established to provide the user with complete, user-friendly information. About 40% of these are directly searchable, including ROOT descriptors and words in the title and abstract, the availability of certification or approval systems, the identification of a whole range of documentary relationships with international, foreign and national documents, particularly those cited in legislation. The document identifier is a critical element for standards and regulations and we have had to introduce a special facility to simplify using it as a search key. Standards contain designation codes for grades of steel or levels of electrical safety, which may be well known to the expert but cause a major problem to the uninitiated and these codes are searchable on the database system. Dates abound so that the situation at a particular date or the facility to identify what has changed since the last search was made, is present. Language, price information, data on reference materials, titles in other languages, and indication of the inclusion of a document in a variety of other publications are also contained on the database, so that from a whole range of criteria it is possible to isolate the specific collection of documents required to resolve the enquirer's particular problem.

Further details and the results of the experimental usage will be presented to the delegates attending the "standards database" session at PARC '83.

The computer provides those who need reliable information on standards and technical requirements with a powerful tool uniquely capable of handling the complex information with its constant updating and requirement for total accuracy.

It is, however, only as good as the system applied to it and the creation of a Development Project was justified in an attempt to develop the best possible system.

A final specification and business plan will be produced as the final stage of the project towards the end of 1983 which, it is hoped, will constitute the programme for the creation of the full BS file over the next 2 years. A shorter time period can be envisaged if appropriate resources are provided and further discussions must take place to identify whether the addition of Government Technical Regulations, other standards or foreign information has the highest priority to augment the BS file.

Development will not, of course, end there. The exploitation of the system through the development of new services and publications, must be followed through.

Document ordering procedures will inevitably be developed with the online system but more advanced electronic printing and full text retrieval systems are also possible in the not too far distant future.

In the successful development of the database system and planning of future development, the common denominator is feedback from our clients. You must tell us what your needs are and how we can help you meet them. We will ensure that the best possible information supply systems for all your technical requirements needs are available from the British Standards Institution Information, Services and Marketing Division at Milton Keynes.

RETRIEVAL LANGUAGES AND DATA STRUCTURES

R M Rostron
Partner
Hutton & Rostron
UK

The application of computers in the processing and retrieval of
information depends on the precise and ordered use of language
despite their ability to search text freely. The concept of
'underware' is introduced for the organisation of data. Various
types of classification, terminologies and coding systems are
described. The importance of data structures as an extension of
retrieval languages is illustrated with examples taken from
bibliographical and product data bases

Michael Rostron MA, B Arch, ARIBA is an
architect with a particular interest in
data processing. His practice is well
known in this field; current projects
include the processing and production of
the English Full and Medium Editions of
the Universal Decimal Classification;
the BSI Root, the ISONET and the ECCTIS
thesauri. The firm produces a number of
national directories and bibliographies
and has developed its own software for
data base management and publishing

ACCESS TO INFORMATION

Developments in information services, new forms of information (eg on-line, microfilm) and classifications pre-suppose that the user knows what he is looking for. These systems do not help the user to formulate questions or investigate his problem. Traditional sources of guidance such as codes of practice, standards and, to some extent, building regulations are inconsistent in coverage, lack a systematic arrangement and fail to provide the user with reference in depth to solve his problem when his need is most acute. It is also in the nature of such publications to be slow in production and review. Building failures due to oversight are not uncommon and information systems organised to support the professions will gain value as liability insurance becomes more expensive

The cost of failure is high in economic, health and safety terms; for example, the professional and public concern about concrete failures, flat roofs, condensation and the toxic products of burning plastic. Research and experience is often available in time to avoid failure but is not applied. This is usually due to lack of information at the point of decision, and haste on the part of the designer, specifier or contractor. Carelessness may occasionally be involved as may poor presentation of the information. Ideally a user of an information system should not be able to ignore relevant facts or miss a reference. Such a system should be under constant revision. What are needed are systems which integrate the sources of advice and information with the procedures of design and construction to ensure that no reasonable reference or method is overlooked

Retrieval

Classified, alphabetical or numerical arrangements are the main means by which information is organised and retrieved by users aided by notations, keywords and codes. These methods originate in the need to store discrete items in some formal arrangement for searching. Typically these are:

1 Subject grouping: access by pre-coordinate classifications, eg UDC, SfB, using an alphabetical and/or numerical notation

2 Alphabetical sequence: access in the chosen precedence using terms from either general use or a controlled vocabulary (eg keywords) and nouns for authors, titles and places

3 Numerical sequence: access using serial or accession numbers, codes (eg from a classification) or dates

These systems are particularly appropriate to libraries and, indeed, most have been devised by librarian subject specialists rather than professional users. They are passive in character and do not direct the enquirer; this usually has to be done by a librarian who, however specialised, cannot have the depth of knowledge or relate to the problem as can the professional concerned

Process related retrieval

Subject classifications and indexes are not the only way of arranging information. Collections can be organised by size, character, source and age, for example. In most cases these arrangements are thought of as a convenience in storage and bear no relation to the process of enquiry or the use of information, still less to successive stages in the application of information. An alternative to these storage dominated systems would be to apply the sequence arising from a particular process, for example, any size, character or type of information applicable to a particular activity

Information systems geared to particular work sequences and thought processes are rare. These may be in the form of learning programmes, diagnostic questions and answers, or check lists. Each of these uses information dynamically to stimulate the enquirer or the decision, or further search

Process orientated (dynamic) information is not exclusive and can, by reference, take users to passive collections of classified and indexed information. This is facilitated in computer based systems by the speed at which alternative sources of information can be displayed. Mechanisation does not change the nature of information. However, its power to collect, analyse, synthesise, retrieve and revise information facilitates a dynamic approach and makes possible the creation of 'expert' systems

The 'underware' of information systems

The uses and value of hardware, firmware and software are familiar and recognised aspects of computer systems. Unfortunately, the disciplines involved in organising the data and the subject terminology of users is less well defined. The importance of a comprehensive approach to information retrieval, economy of collection storage, manipulation and multiple use justifies the introduction of the concept of 'underware' for all those aspects of computing related to the organising data

CLASSIFICATION, CODING AND INDEXING

Classification is a method of collecting together similar ideas
and coding is a method of identifying each item of the collection.
It follows, therefore, that a code or coding system is not a
self contained entity, but an adjunct to a classification in the
form of a notation and that the form of any coding system depends
on the layout of the classification

An index, on the other hand, is an arrangement of specific ideas
or items ordered in any manner (eg alphabetically) convenient
for use

There are two types of classification in common use - the
hierarchical classification, in which classes are arranged in order
of importance, and the faceted classification, in which classes
have equal rank. Both are pre-coordinate classifications, as the
concept relationships are defined by the system and not by the user

Hierarchical classification

The Dewey and the Universal Decimal Classification (UDC) are the
most familiar of this type. The principle employed is that any
body of knowledge may be divided into a series of primary
independent classes. Each of these primary classes may be further
divided into secondary classes, each secondary class into tertiary
classes and so on. Every class series thus breaks up knowledge into
progressively precise parts and one of the virtues of this method
is that any required degree of detail can be attained by adding
further class series

An hierarchical classification has a tree-like structure, each
branch forking into a further series of branches as far as
necessary. In a decimal system such as UDC, every additional class
series increases the number of items tenfold. The nine digits of
UDC therefore make available 10^9 or 1000 million separate entries

Although the hierarchical type of classification achieves its
primary aim of grouping similar ideas or concepts together and
subdivides these classes as finely as desired, it presupposes
that the method of forming the groups and subgroups is an absolute
operation, since the classification itself dictates the grouping

255

Consider the following groups:

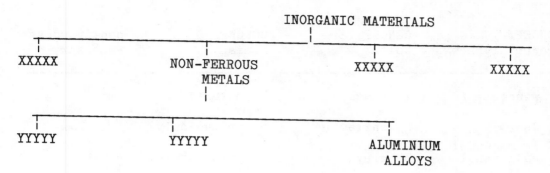

This states, quite correctly, that aluminium alloys are part of the class of non-ferrous metals which, in turn, are part of the class of inorganic materials. This grouping is an inherent and inflexible characteristic of this (hypothetical) classification and is acceptable if we want to regard aluminium alloys in this way. But if we want to regard aluminium alloys as part of the class of incorrodible materials, for example, the classification is no use to us, since it has already dictated the way in which we must regard the metal. However far the branches are forked, the earlier division into classes is fixed

The main disadvantage is that the class groupings can be defined in only one way and that the classification consequently determines from what viewpoint information shall be considered

A consequence of this is the difficulty of sorting and comparing data. Suppose we are examining dwellings. All dwellings might be divided into houses and flats, and responsible authorities into public and private. We should then need to find a method of arranging information to enable data to be extracted on 1, a particular type, for example, local authority flats, or 2, a more general group, for example, all private dwellings, or 3, a still larger group, for example, all houses, or 4, the total, ie all dwellings. This could not be done with a hierarchical classification which at some stage would divide buildings either into local authority buildings and private buildings, or into houses and flats

Faceted classification

A faceted arrangement of information overcomes this problem by creating a series of general concepts which, unlike the classes of a hierarchical classification, have equal weight. Each general group is then subdivided into separate characteristics and identified by means of a symbol or code

The following example will illustrate the principle:

CONCEPT 1 Product type	CONCEPT 2 Colour	CONCEPT 3 Finish	continued as necessary
A window	1 black	a natural	
B door	2 white	b primed only	
C wall panel	3 grey	c paint system	
D spandrel	4 red	d sealer	
E rainwater pipe	5 blue	e decorative laminate	
F staircase	6 yellow	f sheet steel	
continued as necessary	continued as necessary	continued as necessary	

The concepts 1, 2, 3, 4 .... etc are independent and exclusive and can be as numerous as necessary. Similarly the subdivisions of each concept can be continued (and added to) as far as necessary

In use, any item is described by selecting one characteristic from each concept group and using the code numbers or letters to make a notation. For example, a spandrel coloured blue by painting would be coded D5c, a door covered with white decorative laminate would be coded B2e and so on. The most familiar system of this type is the SfB

There are three important advantages of the faceted arrangement over the hierarchical classification. Firstly, all possible combinations of characteristics are catered for. Even in the short extract given above (3 concepts, each with 6 characteristics) each of the six product types can be combined with six colours and six finishes to identify $6 \times 6 \times 6 = 6^3 = 216$ different combinations. Five concepts each with 10 characteristics would identify $10^5 = 100000$ items, or as many as an entire hierarchical classification with five class series

The second advantage is that new concepts and characteristics can be added at any time in order to keep abreast of technical developments or to accommodate new products or other items.

Thirdly, a faceted arrangement enables "sortations" to be made on any concept. For example, it would be possible in the example given to group together all painted products (by gathering together all codes containing a 'c') or all blue products (code 5) and so on. This choice of groups is not possible with the hierarchical classifications which limit the grouping methods to the defined classes

FUNCTIONS OF CLASSIFICATION

Three primary functions can be discerned:

a)   organisation of knowledge

b)   identification of ideas

c)   analysis of data

Organisation of knowledge

Knowledge must be organised in order to make intelligible communication possible. A sentence is constructed in an organised manner. Further, organisation is necessary for convenience of use. A dictionary would be complete if the words were arranged at random but of little use. A standardised arrangement (of which a classification is an example) is necessary

Identification of ideas

Ideas can, of course, be identified by words, which are merely labels for ideas. But words are often imprecise labels. 'Base', for example can mean support, bad, servile, headquarters, fundamental etc

Because a classification is concerned with an arrangement of ideas rather than words, it is able to isolate the real content of an idea more precisely than a mere description in words. Having isolated the idea we can, of course, then describe it in any convenient way - by words or by a symbolic code. For example, to attempt to categorise a colour by calling it "blue" is imprecise. On the other hand, we can then describe this standard as "blue", "7-079" or "\+%=" since these names and symbols merely refer us to the standard and do not attempt to describe the colour

It is important to remember that a classification identifies ideas or concepts and not particular objects. For example, it can identify "windows", "aluminium windows" or even "anodised aluminium

vertical sliding sash windows 6ft 2in high by 3ft 4in wide ......"
but it will not identify "the kitchen window at 42 Claremont Road,
Surbiton." or "that window in the warehouse with a scratch on the
sill". To identify particular objects such as these, some
additional numbering (such as serial numbering) is necessary

Analysis of data

The third function of a classification is to make possible the
analysis and comparison of data. The simple classification in
which documents on the same subject are gathered together on to one
shelf does this in a primitive way. A faceted classification
enables us to perform more complex analysis, such as that of
dwellings quoted on page 4, or the analysis of subject matter from
many different viewpoints

CRITERIA

The choice of classification method depends on the relative
importance of the functions (organisation, identification,
analysis) it is required to perform. To some extent these
functions are cumulative: a classification which is capable of
analysing information will also identify, but one which organises
or identifies will not necessarily analyse except in inflexible
groups or classes

There is much to be said for choosing a system capable of use for
analysis even if this function is not immediately required, as it
does not necessarily require a more complicated notation. For
example, if it was required to identify 100000 parts or products,
these could be identified uniquely by a simple sequential
numbering 00000 to 99999, using five digits. It has, however,
already been shown that a faceted classification of five
concepts, each with 10 characteristics, can also identify 100000
items using five digits and this is also capable of analysis under
any combination of the five concepts. Such a classification would
therefore provide opportunities for detailed analysis and sortation
without increasing the complexity of notation

In a product classification the primary requirement is to identify
each item, but a necessary function is also to enable product
information to be analysed. A form of faceted classification
therefore appears appropriate. The following criteria are
suggested

a) notation should be as short as possible compatible with the
   desired degree of analysis

b) facets should be chosen to <u>identify</u> the product and <u>describe</u> significant characteristics

c) the classification shoud accommodate all identifiable separate parts, whether these are marketed as products or not. Parts not marketed as products should be related in the classification to the marketed product which contains them. For example, if a door with ironmongery is sold as a single product, the ironmongery should be capable of being coded both as a separate component and as part of the door. This will also apply to components which are marketed both separately and as parts of more complex products

d) the number and scope of facets should be chosen on the basis of:

   i)   the information required from the customer

   ii) the information required internally to process an order

   iii) the selection of information from i) and ii) required as feedback for purposes such as forecasting and market investigation

   iv) information required for outside purchasing

INFORMATION RETRIEVAL

The problems of finding stored information are essentially different from those involved in classifying ideas, although classifications are frequently used for information retrieval. A classification may be likened to a series of drawers or boxes, each labelled with a particular idea or concept. Items of information may be placed in appropriate drawers and a search for a specific item will consequently be limited to one drawer. A search, however limited, will still have to be made, since it is the ideas or concepts which are listed (classified), rather than individual items of information

One shortcoming of conventional classification for retrieval of information has been illustrated where consideration of aluminium alloys was limited by the classes chosen. It is evident that to try to accommodate rapidly changing knowledge in predetermined groups and categories is artificial and fundamentally wrong. Classification, storage and retrieval of information will inevitably depend on the viewpoint of the person performing these activities and any method used must take this into account

At first sight a faceted classification method appears to overcome
the latter problem, but the difficulties of choosing and defining
the concepts represented by each facet are far more severe when
dealing with diffuse general information than with products which
are more clearly defined. A faceted classification would also
isolate specific concepts rather than specific items of information

It is apparent that any method which takes account of specific
items must be an index, rather than a classification, and that the
index must be so arranged that all items of information on a chosen
concept or group of concepts are retrieved and those items which
are not relevant are not retrieved. These requirements are
satisfied by a post-coordinate type of index known as a 'keyword
index'

KEYWORDS

By careful selection it is possible to choose a limited number of
words (keywords) which, singly or in combination will describe any
item of information in a particular field. These words are usually
assembled in a controlled list called a thesaurus from which they
are selected to suit the item concerned. Thesauri can themselves
become quite elaborate with loose hierarchical structures relating
synonyms; broader, narrower and related terms; and often with a
form of faceted notation. A typical example is the BSI ROOT
Thesaurus which covers the terminology relevant to subjects covered
by standards

It has been found that the number of keywords varies between 300
and 800 for any technical application limited to one field or
industry. Shell Petroleum, for instance, whose products vary from
nuclear power installations to lipsticks, were able to use a
vocabulary of about 500 keywords to describe the content of the
technical information with which they are concerned. It was found
that between 17 and 25 keywords were necessary to describe a
particular technical article

For retrieval of information the process works in reverse. The
enquirer frames his request as a series of keywords describing the
information he requires. These may be given Boolean relationships
to refine the search, the combination resulting, via the retrieval
mechanism, in the addresses of items matching (or nearly matching)
the description. The address may, for example, represent the
number of the required document. In practice it has been found
that only four or five keywords are necessary for retrieval,
compared with the 17 to 25 needed for entries; larger numbers may
result in 'silence'

The method possesses many advantages. Grouping of ideas does not occur until the search is carried out (in contrast to a pre-coordinated classification) and ideas can be grouped by the individual requiring the information. Thus his personal assessment of the information needed (which may be different from that of another enquirer) is accommodated by the system. Secondly, the system does not govern the way in which documents are stored. Each document has an accession order, they can be equally well stored in any order convenient to other needs (eg browsing, date order for journals, numerical order for BSS etc) and located by means of an accession register which gives their "address"

It is not even necessary to possess documents in order to index them, since the "address" may be a library some distance away from the index centre

Finally, the keyword method is not closed and can accommodate both new keywords and new documents without limit and without disturbance to documents already indexed, and can be used in combination with classifications

Before embarking on a keyword index, the following information is required:

a) the number of existing items of information to be indexed

b) the rate (number per year) at which new items of information will be added

c) the type of documents to be indexed

d) who will be responsible for allocating keywords to existing and new documents

The main technical problems involved in the creation and use of a keyword index are the compilation of the list of keywords, the method of dealing with synonyms and homonyms and the avoidance of "false drops" or retrieval of unwanted information

There is a relationship between the number of available keywords and the number used to index a document. Suppose 500 keywords are available and only one is used for indexing, there would obviously only be 500 different available indexing positions. As the number of keywords used for indexing is increased the number of available indexing positions increases very greatly. Using two keywords for indexing from a list of 500 makes available 124750 indexing positions and using three keywords produces over 20 million positions

These numbers used by Shell Petroleum (500 keywords available and about 20 used for indexing) make available descriptions of ideas totalling over 26×10^{34} or 260 thousand million million million million million positions. This is, of course, a very large number, but it should be seen as a proportion (probably a very small proportion of <u>all</u> ideas on all subjects)

If it is accepted that this large number is sufficient for indexing purposes, there are many ways it can be achieved. 20 keywords selected from 500, 8 keywords selected from 100,000 and 4 keywords selected from 1,580 million all provide about 26×10^{34} combinations

It is apparent therefore that the keyword list can be of any convenient size, but the smaller the number of available keywords, the larger the number which must be used for indexing. There are, however, other criteria for determining the size of the keyword list. Ideally the indexer should be able to remember the range of available keywords and this points to a short list. On the other hand, the list should be of sufficient size to describe adequately the content of all documents to be indexed. The keyword list should therefore be as small as is compatible with the latter requirement

A small keyword list requires a comparatively large number of keywords to be used for indexing, but this is also an advantage, if we assume that an average of 20 keywords is used for indexing and an average of 4 keywords for retrieval in 4,845 different ways. If, on the other hand only 10 keywords had been used for indexing and 4 for retrieval, the number of ways available for retrieval would only be 210. Because different enquirers will ask for the same item of information in many different ways, the larger the number of keyboards used for indexing the better, and this is a direct consequence of a small keyword list

When compiling the keyword list, care must be taken with synonyms (the same item or concept denoted by different words) and homonyms (one word representing different concepts). Because a keyword is merely a label for a concept (or even a group of similar concepts) synonyms must be collected together as a single keyword. For example, it is likely that heat, cold, heating, cooling, refrigeration, temperature, thermal, caloric and so on would be represented by a single keyword, which would be the label for the concept of the thermal manifestation of energy

Homonyms must be dealt with in a converse way. Aggregate (= broken stone) represents a different concept from aggregate (= collect into a body), plastic (= synthetic material) is different from plastic (= capable of being moulded) and each of these must be identified by different keywords. Each keyword must, by adequate description, make clear in which sense it is to be used

A "false drop" is a reference to an unwanted item of information and these may be of two kinds. If, for example, keywords existed for the concept of "house" and for the concept of "boat", combining the two keywords to retrieve information on boat houses would also retrieve unwanted information on house boats. The second type is similar and results from unwanted combinations of keywords. Suppose the keywords:

> strength
> steel
> bolts
> timber
> structural frames

were combined in a search for information on "the strength of steel bolts used in timber frames". Data (if it existed) would also be retrived on "steel frames", "strength of steel frames", "strength of timber" as well as such unlikely items as "timber bolts"

It has been found in practice that false drops are not as great a hindrance as might be supposed, providing keywords are intelligently chosen. In the boathouse example, for instance, "house" is a homonym and should therefore be represented by two keywords, say "dwelling" and "store". Secondly, wherever possible adjectival keywords should be avoided. "Structural frame" is a single concept and should therefore be represented by a single keyword "structural frame" and not by two keywords "structural" and "frame". Finally, the occurrence of false drops is obviously diminished by retrieving on as many keywords as possible, or, expressed differently, by defining the information needed as precisely as possible. No indexing system would provide precise information on, say, "the cost of oil-fired central heating of multi-storey flats in Siberia" if the request was for information on "heating" and in such a case the number of false drops would be great. The number of false drops diminishes rapidly as the number of keywords used for retrieval is increased

HUTTON + ROSTRON KEYCODES

Hutton + Rostron have developed a type of keyword system (Keycodes) for use in the broad retrieval of reference material. This is machine-readable and can be used as an interlexicon to cross-reference natural language keywords in English and other languages. Keycodes have been in use since 1968 for coordinate indexes and computer generation of synonyms, and as a supplementary index language. Keycodes have been applied to products, computer programs, test methods, standard details and general information. Because the system is concerned with identifying ideas and not words it is particularly suitable for indexing ideographic scripts and a study is in hand for the extension of the Keycode system to Chinese

The objectives of Keycodes are:

1   Consistency of indexing and retrieval
2   Low skill operation
3   Multi-language facility
4   Broad retrieval on initial enquiry capable of refinement
5   Compact feature list for convenience in computer systems and revision
6   Controlled feature list
7   Possibility of computer-aided indexing
8   Compatibility with other systems
9   Aid in technical translation

The basis of the system is a dictionary of natural language words used in building and related fields. There are currently about 6000 words in the dictionary, but additions are continually made. Each natural language word in the dictionary has been analysed into the basic concepts it represents. There are in all 318 basic concepts to cover design, building, planning, environmental and related subjects. New terms are regularly added to the Keycode Dictionary as a result of indexing but it is relatively rare for a new concept code to be introduced. Each of these is represented by a four-letter code. For example, the word 'abbey' has been analysed into the concepts:

    building
    dwelling
    religion

and these have been given the codes:

    BAUL
    DWOL
    ROLU

The dictionary entry for 'abbey' is, therefore:

    abbey   BAUL+DWOL+ROLU

There are a number of advantages in this dictionary approach over the more conventional thesaurus. Because the indexer is not involved in conceptual analysis, both indexing and retrieving is more consistent. For the same reason, unskilled staff or machines

may be used for indexing. The Keycodes are independent of the
language used, as the four-letter codes are only labels and can
represent concepts whatever the language. The dictionary is
currently available in English, French and German, enabling
indexing and retrieval to be carried out in any combination of
these languages. The conceptual basis of the Keycode system is of
particular relevance when converting the European languages to
Chinese and vice versa

DATA STRUCTURES

Classifications and keyword systems are not sufficiently specific
when particular items have to be selected from a large collection.
The attributes used in the selection of a particular product may run
to many hundreds and each of these may involve descriptive text,
characteristics expressed in semantic and numerical scales, codes
and values related, for example, to source of supply, physical
properties and performance. Thus, although the classification may
take one to the generality of records, to compare and select within
the group it is necessary for the record to be subdivided,
structured and indentified so that the data itself can be used to
create indexes

Highly structured data of this type requires careful analysis
before collection but is not necessarily more time consuming to
collect or enter if the work is carefully planned and the
appropriate method of data capture used. This involves the choice
of criteria, the standards and methods of test used to define them
and the units in which they are expressed. Text may be coded to
economise in data preparation and permit substitution eg
translation into other languages, and controlled terminologi or
keywords may be used in the descriptive text

The data should, as far as possible, be neutral. That is not
dedicated to any particular computer system or form of output

MAINTAINING THE UNDERWEAR

Classification, terminologies, coding and data structures require
regular review and revision. Unfortunately, some of the major
classifications have become discredited to some extent because
revision and republication has been too slow to cater for the
changes in the use of language and the rate of technical
development. This has lead to a proliferation of ad hoc systems

developed by individuals and special interest groups, these in turn, tend to be poorly controlled and limited in scope to the data collection or organisation concerned. Ultimately these systems will have to be recombined by reference to a major classification or interlexicon

The Universal Decimal Classification, the BSI ROOT Thesaurus, the ISONET Thesaurus and the H+R Keycodes are now maintained in machine readable form using data bases devised by the author. These provide for management information, cross referencing within and between systems, the automatic generation of schedules, alphabetical listing, concordances, and output of various types. The most important feature is, of course, the ability to produce tools for the intellectual work in maintaining the classification or thesaurus and providing regular revisions for users

The increasing use of communications will require common means of access and the ability to carry out searches across data bases, between disciplines and in many languages. Already there is a study in hand by UNESCO to merge some thirty machine readable thesaur in the social sciences to create an intergrated, multi-lingual system. The 'underwear' is being developed

The construction of a thesaurus, ASLIB Proceedings, Vol 20, No 3, p181

The construction of a thesaurus, Building, 215(43), 25 October 1968, pp111-112

'The thesaurus in retrieval', Gilchrist (ASLIB, 1971, pp83-86)

INFORMATION FOR DESIGN DECISION-MAKING

S B Mathe
Research Fellow
ABACUS, University of Strathclyde
UK

Computer based appraisal techniques allow rapid, accurate and explicit prediction of the cost and performance characteristics of alternative design proposals. This wealth of new information can now be analysed by the program GLOSS to provide:

i)   comparative evaluation and ranking of design alternatives;

ii)   insight in the way in which design decisions affect cost and performance, and

iii) the basis for performance specifications.

The use of GLOSS is exemplified by a parametric study of school buildings in Nepal.

Sri Mathe, a qualified architect, has recently completed his doctorate study of which this paper is a short summary. He is returning to Katmandu to resume his teaching post in the Institute of Engineering.

Introduction

The new generation of design appraisal techniques not only permit the designers a free reign of their intuitive and creative powers but also provide them with an immediate evaluation of the costs and effects of their design decisions. These techniques have developed largely to satisfy the growing demand of an increasingly cost-conscious society for greater accountability for the design decisions taken by the design profession.

Many of these techniques are computer-based. As these techniques become increasingly sophisticated and comprehensive, the predictive performance results, obtained by the use of these techniques to appraise a large number of design hypotheses in various design situations, can so overwhelm the investigators that design decisions cannot easily be made. Therefore, there is a need for an analytical tool that processes the output not only to facilitate the comparison of the different competitive designs but also to increase the understanding of the causal relationships between design decisions and their consequences. It is only when the interrelationships are adequately understood can designers control the consequences of their decisions.

The program GLOSS (GOAL Output Solution Schemes) is one such analytical tool. It is seen to have the following three principal uses:

-       to facilitate the comparative evaluation of the different
        competitive designs;

-       to enhance the understanding of the causal relationships
        so as to control the consequences of design decisions, and

-       to help formulate performance specifications applicable to
        different design types.

Clearly, the more often GLOSS is used in conjunction with appraisal programs such as the ABACUS developed program GOAL, to explore different design alternatives, the richer will be the data base on which analyses can be performed to get a clearer perception of design.

In this paper, the program is explained within a broad framework of a decision-making strategy, which can be used for research and education, as well as in practice. The proposed decision-making strategy is explained with reference to a school study in Nepal.

The Design Process

The use of GLOSS in a decision-making strategy may be seen by those who still believe exclusively in the Intuitive Design Method, and as such consider the design process as sacrosanct and inviolable, as

one more overt attempt at the externalisation of the design process.
They may well construe this as stemming from the design methods
movement, which has continuously strived to externalise and system-
atise the design process.

However, even these designers concede that modern design is complex
and goes beyond the designer's intuitive evaluative abilities. In a
world of depleting and finite resources, where there is a moral and
economic case for making the best use of the resources, they understand the need for pertinent information from many disciplines that
can point out the strengths and weaknesses of each aspect of the
propsoed design. If objection there is, it is to the means used to
satisfy this need.

This continuing debate about the externalisation of the design process
is reflective of the background debate about creativity and ration-
ality. In the design morphological context which is seen as a sequential progression from the general strategic stages to the detailed
tactical stages, it is evident that careful planning and the right
decisions in the early stages can yield disproportionately high
savings over the life span of the proposed buildings. It is, therefore, important to be able to appraise the design hypotheses in the
very early stages of design. GLOSS in conjunction with programs like
GOAL enables the appraisal exercise to be undertaken quite effectively
in the early stages of design.

Design Appraisal

Computer-aided appraisal involves the testing of a design solution on
a computer-based model of the hypothesised design. The model allows
the prediction to be made of the quantitative and qualitative attributes which will characterise the real building. Computer-aided
appraisal essentially consists of three aspects as shown in Figure 1.

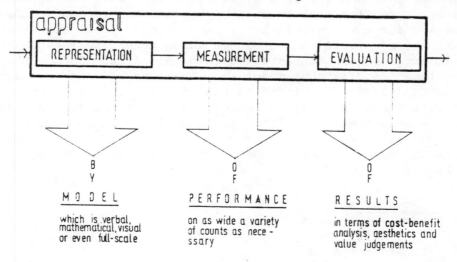

FIGURE 1: The Three Aspects of Computer-Aided Appraisal

Thus, the proposed layout derived by a traditional or intuitive design process or any generative mechanism must be suitably represented by a model. The performance can then be measured and the results evaluated. Computer assistance allows the exploration of a much wider range of design solutions and permits the assessment of quantitative aspects that would not normally be provided at all or might be provided much later. Based on the simulation results, the designer can modify the design hypotheses iteratively to converge on the optimal solutions (Figure 2).

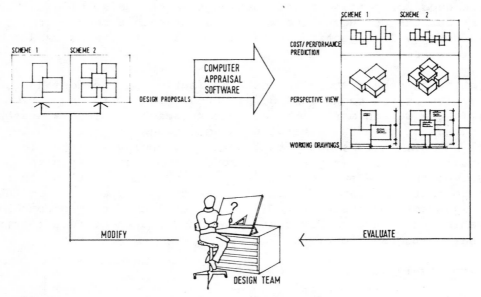

FIGURE 2: Computer for Iterative Modification of Design Hypotheses

Analysis of Appraisal Results

Before the designer can effect modifications to his design hypotheses, the performance results have to be analysed and understood. GLOSS should aid the designer in this task. At present, it is structured to handle the various significant measures which summarise the design and its cost and performance characteristics obtained from GOAL - the ABACUS developed program that model the behaviour and characteristics of the building, as if it existed in reality, and outputs predictions as to the cost - both capital and recurring - performance (spatial, functional, environmental) and the visual quality of the design.

The significant measures that GLOSS is presently structured to handle are as follows:

a   Geometrical Data
    -     Total Floor Area
    -     Total Wall Area
    -     Total Roof Area
    -     Total Volume
    -     Wall to Floor Ratio

    -    Volume Compactness
    -    Standard Deviation of Scheme

b   **Design Data**
    -    Amount of Glazing in Walls
    -    Amount of Glazing in Roofs
    -    Angle of Orientation of Scheme
    -    Fuel Type Used

c   **Environmental Performance**
    -    Heat Loss in Winter
    -    Heat Gain in Summer
    -    Peak Energy Required for Cooling
    -    Peak Energy Required for Heating
    -    Annual Energy Required for Heating
    -    Annual Energy Required for Cooling
    -    Total Annual Energy Required
    -    Lighting Requirement (in kW)
    -    Lighting Energy Requirement

d   **Cost Data**
    -    Running Costs
    -    Capital Costs
    -    Annual Equivalent Cost-In-Use

It should be stressed that even though GLOSS is presently structured to handle the output from GOAL, it can be used equally well with other appraisal programs. All that GLOSS requires is a data bank from which it can retrieve the relevant data so that a variety of analyses can be performed (Figure 3).

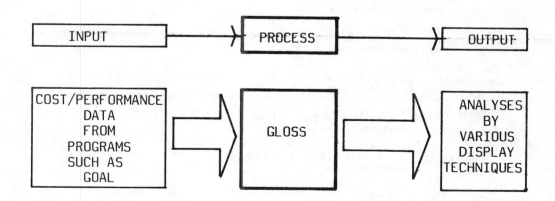

FIGURE 3: The Input-Process-Output Mechanism in the Use of GLOSS

The analyses undertaken by GLOSS can take a number of forms. The choice may well depend on the evaluation stage at which comparison is required, the type of comparison to be made and/or the preference of the investigator.

a   TABLES: Various performance data of a number of design hypotheses can be analysed with the help of tabular display format (Figure 4). This format can be extremely useful for a general overview of performance so that those performance aspects which the designer wishes to investigate in greater detail (using other options in GLOSS) can be identified.

SCHEME/VARIABLES	HEAT LOSSW	HEAT GAINS	LIGHT ENE
GEOMETRY HIGH SCHOOL 3 SCHOOL PROJECT CONSTRUCTION 1B SCHOOL PROJECT ENVIRONMENT 2A	25.00	20.00	41920.00
GEOMETRY HIGH SCHOOL 3 SCHOOL PROJECT CONSTRUCTION 3B SCHOOL PROJECT ENVIRONMENT 2A	17.00	21.00	41920.00
GEOMETRY HIGH SCHOOL 3 SCHOOL PROJECT CONSTRUCTION 4B SCHOOL PROJECT ENVIRONMENT 2A	17.00	22.00	41920.00
GEOMETRY HIGH SCHOOL 4 SCHOOL PROJECT CONSTRUCTION 1B SCHOOL PROJECT ENVIRONMENT 2A	24.00	17.00	49563.00
GEOMETRY HIGH SCHOOL 4 SCHOOL PROJECT CONSTRUCTION 3B SCHOOL PROJECT ENVIRONMENT 2A	16.00	19.00	49563.00
GEOMETRY HIGH SCHOOL 4 SCHOOL PROJECT CONSTRUCTION 4B SCHOOL PROJECT ENVIRONMENT 2A	16.00	19.00	49563.00
GEOMETRY HIGH SCHOOL 7 SCHOOL PROJECT CONSTRUCTION 1B SCHOOL PROJECT ENVIRONMENT 2A	20.00	28.00	39418.00
GEOMETRY HIGH SCHOOL 7 SCHOOL PROJECT CONSTRUCTION 3B SCHOOL PROJECT ENVIRONMENT 2A	14.00	29.00	39418.00
GEOMETRY HIGH SCHOOL 7 SCHOOL PROJECT CONSTRUCTION 4B SCHOOL PROJECT ENVIRONMENT 2A	15.00	29.00	39418.00
GEOMETRY HIGH SCHOOL 8 SCHOOL PROJECT CONSTRUCTION 1B SCHOOL PROJECT ENVIRONMENT 2A	19.00	22.00	45694.00
GEOMETRY HIGH SCHOOL 8 SCHOOL PROJECT CONSTRUCTION 3B SCHOOL PROJECT ENVIRONMENT 2A	13.00	23.00	45694.00
GEOMETRY HIGH SCHOOL 8 SCHOOL PROJECT CONSTRUCTION 4B SCHOOL PROJECT ENVIRONMENT 2A	14.00	22.00	45694.00

FIGURE 4: An example of tabular display giving various performance results of a number of design hypotheses.

b   GRAPHS: Graphs are useful in identifying the causal relation-ships between design and performance variables, e.g. the change in environmental performance with respect to the change in the percentage of glazing (Figure 5).

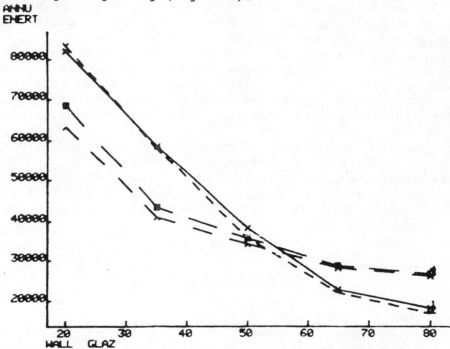

FIGURE 5:   Graph showing the change in heat loss in winter due to the change in the % of glazing in walls for different schemes.

c   HISTOGRAMS: Histograms can be used to study how well the different design hypotheses perform with respect to a particular performance variable (Figure 6).

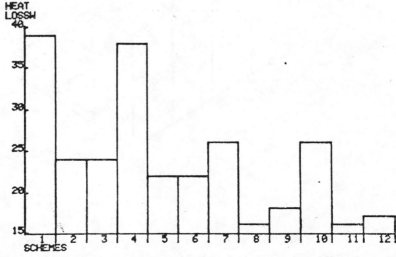

FIGURE 6:   Histograms showing a particular performance variable of a number of schemes.

d   COLOURED GRIDS: The performance data of the different design
         hypotheses can also be depicted by coloured grids where the
         colour and intensity corresponds to a particular value as given
         in the colour scale.   This technique can be used to study the
         trends or patterns in performance.   Thus, if the rows were to
         depict the alternative schemes, the columns the different
         construction systems, then the colour pattern resulting from the
         use of GLOSS to examine a particular performance variable
         should help the designer draw relevant conclusions on the
         relative merits of the different schemes and the construction
         systems.   The colour patterns may even help the designer fathom
         the interrelationships between design and performance variables.

e   3-D BLOCKS: In the case of depiction by 3-D blocks (in conjunc-
         tion with another ABACUS developed program BIBLE), the height of
         the blocks indicate the performance value of the different
         design-construction configurations.   This technique also permits
         the study of trends/patterns in performance of a large number of
         configurations (Figure 7).

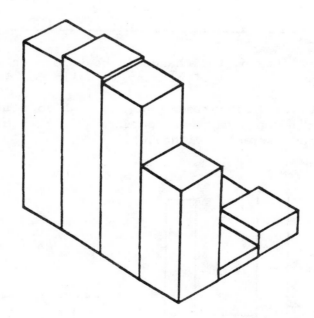

FIGURE 7:   An example of 3-D display of a performance variable of a
            number of design-construction configurations.

f   PERFORMANCE PROFILES: Performance profiles permit the analysis
     of a number of performance variables of a number of schemes
     (Figure 8).   The profiles are drawn against a standard set of
     values which are contained in a file or specified on-line. If
     the standard set of values are not available, the profiles are
     drawn against the average values of the schemes being compared.

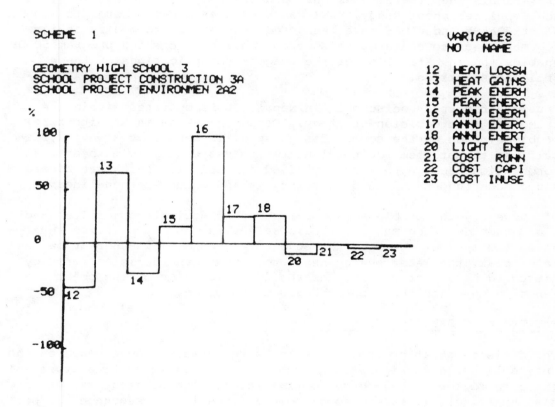

FIGURE 8: An example of a performance profile of a number of per-
           formance variables of one scheme.

Gloss In Education

To increase the perception of design amongst students, GLOSS is
curently being used in the Department of Architecture at the
Technical University of Delft; it is also being implemented at the
Technical University of Eindhoven. Reaction from both the students
and the staff has been very encouraging. From the feedback received,
improvements are being made to make GLOSS an even better analytical
tool.

Gloss In Research

GLOSS has been used in a study on school design for Nepal, in conjunction with a number of CAD programes - GOALSM (a synopsised version of
GOAL), RANK and SCOOP. The main appraisal program GOALSM allows the
appraisal results to be stored in solution files. When an unusually
high number of solution files are involved it may be necessary to
reduce the number of files to only those that meet a predetermined
criterion. The program RANK has been created to do this. Thus, in
the Nepalese school study, RANK was used as a pre-processor to GLOSS.
After GOALSM and GLOSS have been used tentatively to modify design
schemes so as to converge on some optimal solutions the program SCOOP
enables the investigation of the budgetary implications of these
optional solutions.

Thus, in the study on schools in Nepal, GLOSS operated within the
framework of a decision-strategy. Decision-making in architectural
problems, such as the school design study in Nepal, is always difficult, as the problems do not lend themselves easily to mathematical
formulation because they are typified by variables which are discrete
and discontinuous and involve relationships which are non-linear.

If, however, the problems can be reduced to a single objective function, then decision-making entails selection of that solution that
gives the optimal value of the objective function, whether it be the
least cost, the least energy use, etc. Thus, the decision-strategy
discussed hereunder presupposes the identification of the objective
function on which the decisions are to be based.

The Proposed Decision-Strategy

The decision strategy proposed entails the gradual convergence on the
optional design configurations, subsequent to an exhaustive appraisal
exercise followed by informal optimisation. The strategy may be
disconcertingly linear to some; however, the linear sequence has been
adopted to establish the degree of correlation at each successive
stage so that desirable guidelines can be formulated to optimise the
performance at the subsequent stage. As the understanding of design
increases, the linear strategy can be modified or replaced by more
sophisticated and sensitive techniques.

The decision-strategy is explained with reference to the school design
study for Nepal. The strategy envisages the following four phases:

a   First Phase: The first phase covers the representation and
     measurement stages of the appraisal paradigm shown in Figure 9.
     In this phase, a standard design data file is created. The
     different alternative schemes, along with different construction
     systems and environmental locations, which combine to form
     various 'configurations', are appraised by GOALSM. The perform-
     ance results are stored in solution files.

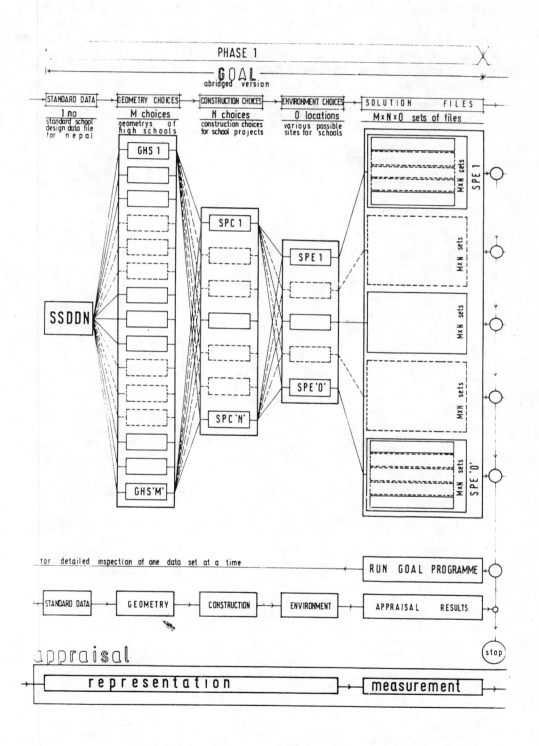

FIGURE 9: PHASE 1 of the Decision-Strategy as applied to the Nepalese School Study

b   Second Phase: This phase covers the evaluation aspect of the appraisal paradigm. The primary objective of this phase is to identify some configurations to be carried forward to the next phase for performance improvement or 'optimisation' tests. The evaluation is done in two stages. In the primary evaluation, the total number of configurations is reduced to only those desirable, with the help of the program RANK.

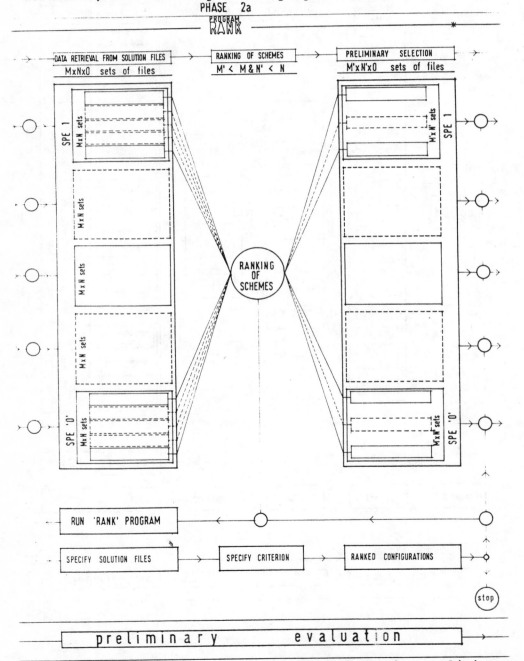

FIGURE 10:   PHASE 2A of the Decision-Strategy involving preliminary evaluation of the schemes using the program RANK.

In the secondary evaluation, the selected configurations are studied
in detail, using the program GLOSS, in order to identify the inter-
relationships and to investigate aberrations, if any, in performance.
The secondary evaluation should help to converge on a select number of
schemes, which will be subjected to performance optimisation tests.

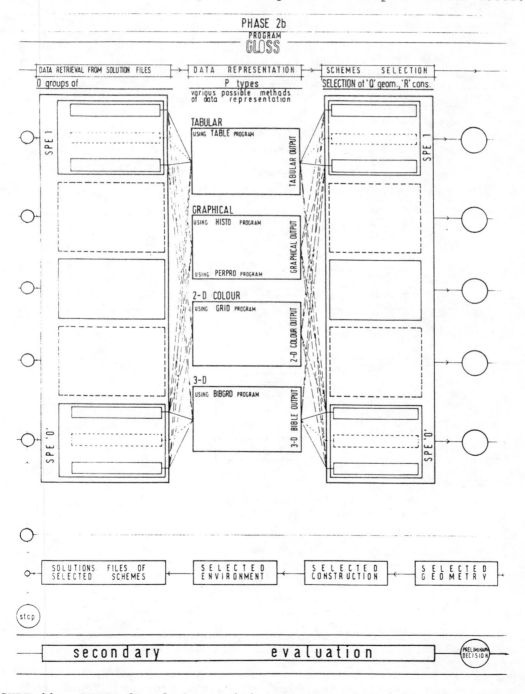

FIGURE 11:   PHASE 2B of the Decision-Strategy involving secondary
             evaluation of the selected configurations, using GLOSS

c   Third Phase: The configurations selected at the end of the second phase are subjected to sensitivity and stability analyses to determine how minor design decisions such as incremental changes in the amount of glazing affects performance. During this phase, the programs GOALSM and GLOSS are used.

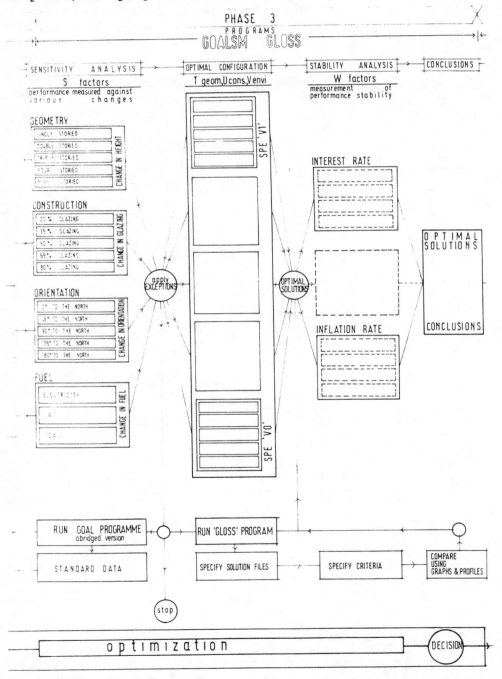

FIGURE 12: PHASE 3 of the Decision-Strategy, comprising sensitivity and stability Analyses, using the programs GOALSM and GLOSS.

d   Fourth Phase: In this phase, the budgetary implications of a
flow competitve configuration identified at the end of Phase 3
are investigated over a predefined plan period so that a final
decision can be made. Obviously, in the Napalese school study,
this phase entailed an assessment of school requirements so that
the implications over the whole period could be assessed.
SCOOP could be easily altered to deal with other design situations.

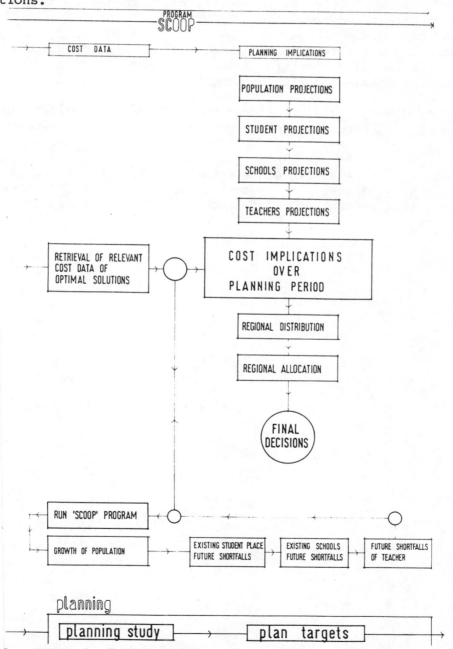

FIGURE 13: PHASE 4 of the Decision-Strategy entailing the investigation of budgetary requirements using the program SCOOP.

Conclusions

From the discussion in the preceding pages, GLOSS may be seen as a design aid which promotes decision-making. The analyses that GLOSS is capable of performing are such as to guide the design towards those design modifications which bring about significant improvements in some aspects of costs and/or performance without significant deterioration in others. Initially, the degree of improvement or deterioration might have to be judged against arbitrarily set upper or lower limits of cost and performance. However, as an increasing number of design alternatives are explored, insights are provided into the complex relationship which translate the change in one variable into corresponding changes in all the other variables.

With enhanced understanding of design, performance specifications can be drawn up to ensure that design undertaken subsequently perform well.

Consequently, programs like GLOSS open up a whole new vista of research, the findings of which should greatly aid the designers so as to help them in controlling the complex design process to produce better designs.

VALIDITY OF THERMAL CALCULATION METHODS

D Bloomfield
Building Research Establishment
UK

SUMMARY

This paper gives a summary of the work on validation of thermal
calculation methods being performed at the Building Research
Establishment (BRE) and of a collaborative project to be undertaken with the Science and Engineering Research Council (SERC). The
current work being conducted within the International Energy Agency
is also discussed briefly.

The BRE and SERC work encompasses examination of the theoretical
basis of the physical model, numerical analysis aspects of the
solution techniques employed, inter-model comparisons, sensitivity
analyses and comparisons with experimentally derived results.
Emphasis is placed upon a modular approach, building up from simple
test conditions.

The comparisons with experiments is the final and essential stage
in the process, and emphasis is placed upon the need to establish
levels of accuracy in the data obtained and to identify the
consequences of these on the parameters being compared. Some
preliminary comparisons will be presented.

Dave Bloomfield is Head of Thermal Models
Section at BRE. Since joining in 1970, he has
been involved in development of calculation
methods to assess transient room surface
temperatures, development of multi-zone,
network computer model of building thermal
behaviour and investigation of optimal
intermittent heating strategies. Current work
includes comparison of software for modelling
building thermal behaviour and investigations
into methods of improving solution speed and
availability of appropriate methods for
architects/designers.

INTRODUCTION

There is a large number of thermal calculation methods in existence ranging in complexity from manual methods at one extreme to very large computer packages at the other. They utilise a variety of different techniques leading to very different speeds of solution and ease of use. They are intended to be used not for a single purpose, but rather to answer a number of different questions, of which the calculation of annual energy is only one. Other important problems which can be treated include the sizing of plant, assessment of the need for air conditioning equipment and the prediction of comfort conditions. It is important to bear this in mind when selecting a method.

Comparison of results produced by different people using different methods and, indeed, different people using the same method, have shown wide discrepancies. There is, therefore, currently an urgent need for an objective assessment of what accuracy can be expected. Without this, results cannot be used with any confidence, especially when the problem involves a once only decision such as 'Should air conditioning be installed or not?' It would be preferable to re-phrase this question as 'What is the risk of failing to meet desired comfort conditions without this type of plant?'

The word 'validation' is used in this paper to mean the testing of the theoretical (physical) correctness of a calculation method and of the numerical and mathematical procedures used to solve the resulting 'model'.

The primary aim of a 'validation' programme of work is to develop techniques to quantify the confidence with which a method can be used and hence to aid in the selection of appropriate methods to use in solving a particular problem.

Programme of work at BRE

BRE has been involved in calculating and measuring the thermal performance of buildings since the 1950's. More recently emphasis has shifted away from development of models to the examination and assessment of available programs.

Much of the work on validation to date has been inconclusive. Comparison with experimental data by a program author poses particular difficulties. It is only natural that a model/compare/ refine loop is performed with the process terminating when 'reasonable' agreement is obtained. All too often, there are many unknowns remaining even in a carefully controlled experiment. The vagaries of the weather, the building process and occupants all combine to allow many degrees of freedom to the modeller. This process is perhaps what is commonly understood by the word 'validation' and it does, after all, answer the question 'how well does program X predict the actual performance of a particular building under real conditions?'

BRE takes the view that although comparison with buildings operated under real conditions is an essential part of 'validation', this should be the final step in a much more detailed process.

A calculation method can be split into two separate parts:

(a) a model of the physical processes combining to produce an effect on the thermal environment within a building and the formulation of a set of equations describing these processes,

(b) a manipulation of these equations to allow the explicit determination of variables of interest.

Process (a) will certainly involve many approximations and some components may be very incompletely understood (eg air movement within and between spaces, the consequent effect on convection coefficients; ventilation etc.)

Process (b) is not straightforward either. Again many approximations are made (eg linearisation of non-linear dependencies, replacement of partial differential equations by difference equations, use of past-time values to decouple large sets of equations etc.) apart from errors introduced by the finite representations of numbers in the computer itself.

It is therefore desirable to treat these two aspects separately.

The range of techniques which are available and can contribute to validation can be summarised as follows:

  i) a theoretical examination of the components (or sub-models) of the overall package, which presupposes a high standard of documentation. It would incorporate an examination of the original source material, experimental data, etc., and cover both the physical models and the numerical solution aspects

 ii) evaluation and comparison of models and sub-models with analytic solutions

iii) inter-model comparisons

 iv) sensitivity analyses

  v) comparison with measured data (empirical verification)

BRE's programme of work incorporates all of these techniques which are described in the following sections.

(i)   Theoretical

An examination of the models for long wave radiation exchange is currently being conducted. This is virtually always linearised over the temperature range assumed to be applicable. Models differ in how (or if) multiple reflections are treated and in whether a detailed model or a simple 'mean radiant temperature' one is used. The use of the latter has important consequences on the complexity of the eventual equation set obtained. The heat loss through ground floors is at present very crudely modelled in what are essentially one dimensional models. The BRE programme includes an examination of more realistic 3-dimensional models of ground floor heat loss based on finite element methods and analytic solutions. A paper describing the analytical approach is to be published shortly.

It seems probable that insufficient attention has been paid to the accuracy of the purely numerical solution techniques used in solving the equation set resulting from the physical model assumed. Current topics being addressed at BRE are:

(a) the number of nodes used in finite difference methods

(b) methods of finding roots in the calculation of response
    factors (for finding poles of Laplace Transformed variables)

(c) the need for iteration, particularly to ensure convergence
    in multi-room models.

Problems with (b) have been encountered in most of the response factor methods. BRE has devised an improved procedure.

(ii) Analytic solutions

It is only possible to derive analytic solutions for very simple cases or for sub-systems of the whole model. Analytic solutions should have been used by the modeller during development for checking the accuracy of the numerical solution technique employed. The set of excitations for which solutions can be developed are:

> steady state conditions
> steady cyclic conditions
> step change in temperature
> step change in heat input

Tests of this sort have been conducted (eg by SERI) and have been found useful in identifying program errors. They have, however, shown not to be a sufficient guarantee of validity when operating with more general inputs.

It is important to realise that it is not enough to carry out tests on a single building type or design, operating under a particular set of conditions. Rather, it is necessary to establish validity for a number of cases covering as large a range in the important model parameters as is justified by the intended use of the model. In other words, once validity is established for a number of cases, inferring validity for a given run should ideally involve interpolation not extrapolation. BRE has prepared a set of house designs thought to be appropriate to current, past and future building practice in the UK which will be used as a standard set of houses for the validation work.

(iii)   Inter-model comparisons

Any two models will differ in many respects, so that it may be difficult to identify the source of any discrepancy between the results obtained from them. To obtain much value from such studies it is felt essential to have access to good quality documentation and to be able to examine the code. Without this, inter-model comparisons can, at best, give an idea of the order of magnitude of accuracy to be obtained from any model. If the documentation does spell out what assumptions and methods have been used, inter-model comparisons may help to indicate the relative importance of varying assumptions.

Although different models may produce differing absolute results it is often stated that they will give better agreement on the effect of changing design decisions (eg single versus double glazing).

BRE has been obtaining and implementing a number of models on a PRIME 550 computer at BRS, Garston. Currently, of the larger packages, the following are available:

   DEROB4, ESP, NBSLD and TAS on the PRIME

and BLAST3 via a bureau. SERIRES will be implemented in the near future.

(iv)   Sensitivity analyses

A sensitivity analysis consists of multiple runs of a single model with the value of one or a few parameter(s) varying between runs. This allows the 'sensitivity' of some quantity of interest (energy, temperature, etc.) to a change in the parameter(s) to be studied.

This technique is useful in:

(a) determining the appropriate degree of sophistication in physical models,

(b) assessing the uncertainties introduced by essentially unknown quantities (eg the way in which a building will be used, weather, ventilation, etc.) or by inaccurately known quantities (materials properties etc),

(c) assessing the usefulness of a given experimental dataset for validation,

(d) calibrating simplified models applicable to a restricted range of building types (eg residential buildings).

(v) <u>Comparison with measured data</u>

Comparison with real building performance represents the ultimate test of the validity of a model. Empirical validation studies can only be of value, however, if the experimental datasets are sufficiently detailed, and in addition cover a suitably wide range of building types, operating conditions and weather patterns.

Detailed, well documented datasets are required in order that the many assumptions embodied in a simulation relating to building construction and boundary conditions can be checked and any uncertainties connected with them quantified. When, as will invariably be the case, differences are observed between measured and predicted behaviour, it is essential that an estimate is available of the degree to which these differences may be due to measurement error or uncertainty in construction parameters, so that meaningful inferences can be drawn concerning the implications of the observed discrepancies for the validity (or otherwise) of the model.

BRE has monitored one unoccupied house under the following conditions:

(a) unheated
(b) constant temperature throughout
(c) intermittently heated, once per day
(d)   "   "   , twice "   "

In addition a pair of semi-detached houses have been extensively monitored for some years operating both unoccupied and with two very detailed simulated occupancy schedules. One of the pair was used to act as a 'control' for the other which had changes made to it (eg different heating controls, insulation etc.). The suitability of these datasets for validation studies will be investigated. Further experiments of this type in eight houses are currently being conducted.

SERC/BRE Collaborative Work

The Science and Engineering Research Committee has funded a number of university groups in the UK to develop thermal models and to study related topics. After considerable discussions within the research community it was decided that funding should be devoted to validation of existing models rather than to development of further ones. In accord with the comments made previously, it was decided that the initial need was for better and fuller documentation to be produced and accordingly a number of grants have been awarded.

The SERC and BRE have agreed upon a joint collaborative venture on validation which should commence in October 1983. The main groups involved in this work will be:

    (a)   BRE
    (b)   Leicester Polytechnic
    (c)   Nottingham University

The work will be coordinated by BRE and a small steering group will oversee progress. The various other groups within the research community will be encouraged to participate and information will be made available to all concerned. It is envisaged that program authors will be commissioned to undertake specific pieces of work in connection with the validation programme.

The objective of the study is generally to improve confidence in thermal modelling procedures with specific goals being:

(a)   improvements in the ease of use and accessibility to current modelling programs

(b)   guidance on the conditions for which algorithms/programs are valid and the errors and risks associated with their use

(c)   recommendations, where necessary, for the improvement of the accuracy and documentation of existing algorithms/programs

(d)   recommendations on numerical solution methods for some sub-models

(e)   guidance on the development of future algorithms/programs

(f)   an improved appreciation of how fundamental decisions on, say, the treatment of particular sub-models and/or the adoption of particular numerical methods affect the architecture of a model

(g)   the provision of procedures and identification of data sets for testing models

(h)   identification of requirements for future monitoring experiments

The major effort will be directed towards the development of verification techniques to examine the theoretical basis of each model and its components. The remaining resources will be devoted to a study of empirical validation, with particular emphasis being paid to assessing the current situation and assembling existing data sets.

A structured approach will be adopted, developing from simple to more complex building configurations. Initially the goal will be to understand the relatively simple hermetically sealed box not in contact with the ground before the intricacies of internal air movement and systems are introduced.

All groups will have access to ESP and will commence by performing some relatively simple runs using it. This will help to ensure that common definitions are used by all groups and should yield information on the human problems of interpreting building specifications and documentation.

Work will proceed both on a selected number of models, and on the study of sub-systems and algorithms across a wide range of models. These two activities will proceed in parallel, with each group taking responsibility for:

(a) one or more different models in addition to ESP; these will be studied in detail and, in collaboration with the program authors, summary descriptions of their workings and assumptions prepared; among possible models in addition to ESP are SUNCODE/ SERIRES : DEROB : BLAST : HTB2 (UWIST) : PASOLE : HOUSE

(b) an in-depth examination of particular sub-topics (solar, ventilation etc.); this examination would deal with the adequacy of the physical model, numerical methods and not least a study of the errors associated with particular solutions.

One group will pay particular attention to the technique of empirical validation and will:

(a) determine the requirements of test data for validation purposes

(b) assess the suitability of existing data sets

(c) document and make such data sets available.

In carrying out (b) particular attention will be paid to the inherent errors and limitation of the studies and, not least, the consequence of instrumentation inaccuracies on derived parameters.

If necessary, specifications for new data sets will be drawn up to meet the particular needs of 'validation'. The use of a model to perform sensitivity analyses is envisaged as an important part of this work.

It is hoped subsequently to proceed to further stages of 'validation' with a much greater measure of agreement and on a sounder basis, particularly with regard to some of the numerical aspects of thermal modelling.

IEA Annex IV

The International Energy Agency was set up in 1974 within OECD. It sponsors research and development in a number of areas related to energy.

Annex I was set up to address the area of validation of thermal models. Its main interest was in air-conditioned buildings. Some useful progress was made and the reasons for the initial huge differences between results generated by the participating programs was partially resolved.

Subsequently Annex IV was set up and a large air-conditioned building in Glasgow was selected for monitoring. This has been heavily instrumented and despite initial problems, data has been collected for some nine months. This is currently being analysed by the five participating countries and a final report should be prepared by December 1983.

This activity represents an example of the final stage validation technique in that it is a real, occupied building with complicated plant and controls. It is expected that these results will help to answer some of the problems associated with modelling buildings of its type.

IEA Task VIII

This task is aimed at the production of a handbook for the design of passive and hybrid solar buildings. It has been running for 18 months and does comprise elements of 'validation' in that experimental data sets are being used to check the 'correctness' of large computer models, which are, in turn, used to perform spot checks on simpler 'design tools'. The latter will be used to provide information for the handbook itself. BRE is likely to participate in Task VIII on behalf of the UK Department of Energy.

COMPARISON OF PASSIVE SOLAR DESIGN METHODS

John G F Littler
Reader in Building
Polytechnic of Central London
UK

Participants from eight European countries gathered details
of models and calculated methods for the prediction of
passive solar performance.
Practical constraints reduced the large number of models to
a small number which were subjected to various kinds of
test, each carried out on one model by more than one participant.
A comparison is presented of manual simulations on a 1 cm
cell and a Los Alamos cell, and of the response following
an external temperature jump.

JOHN LITTLER is Reader in Building at the Polytechnic of
Central London. He currently controls nine major research
contracts - including two concerned with the use of
computers for the thermal simulation of buildings. He is
leader of the Research in Building Group at the
Polytechnic, and also a consultant to Energy Design Group.
Prior to joining the Polytechnic in 1979 he was a Senior
Research Fellow at the Martin Centre for Architecture,
Cambridge University.

Introduction

In 1981 the Passive Solar Modelling Group of the Commission of European Communities was formed to make a comparison of main frame, mini, micro, calculator and manual methods for estimating the thermal performance of passive solar houses. This Report is a personal view of the UK participant and does not necessarily reflect the opinions of the Group.

Dupagne has reported on some of the principles governing the choice of models, and some of the Group's general conclusions, in the Draft Passive Solar Handbook (CEC 1983).

The aim of the Modelling Group was not to make firm recommendations concerning the choice of models, but rather to eliminate from the large list those which could not at the time be strongly recommended. In the end choices were made at either end of the scale of complexity. A manual method was selected so that a complete technique could be reprinted in the CEC Passive Solar Handbook since some manual methods are excellent vehicles for conveying principles of design to the architectural profession. A particular main frame method (ESP) was selected because it was European and thus more easily serviced than those from the U.S. because it is the subject of continuing investment, and because it is a priori one of the world leaders in assessing building thermal response.

The participants are listed in Table 1 so that interested readers may consult further with a participant from their own country.

Model Elimination

In January 1982, Littler summarised conclusions about main frame models available in 1981. It was suggested that the short list of large programs which should be considered was limited to BLAST, DEROB, ESP, SUNCODE and their future developments.

As a result partly of this study, the UK Department of Energy elected to use SUNCODE within its Passive Solar Programme, primarily for its intermediate size (which reduced the costs of repeated use): because it contains treatment of all the passive solar techniques suitable for the UK (i.e. direct gain, mass walls, Trombe walls, conservatories and thermosiphon systems); and because it was written with these techniques constantly, in mind, as opposed to models such as DOE-2 written mainly for heavily serviced commercial buildings.

TABLE 1	European Commission Modelling Group	
DENMARK		
H Lund	Thermal Insulation Laboratory	Lyngby
FRANCE		
M Raoust	Claux-Pesso-Raoust	Paris
WEST GERMANY		
C Kupke	Fraunhofer Institute	Stuttgart
IRELAND		
J Cash	Dublin Institute of Technology	Dublin
ITALY		
F Rubini	Advanced Consulting Technologies	Torino
NETHERLANDS		
C Pernot	Samenwerkingsverband FAGO/TPD	Eindhoven
BELGIUM		
A Dupagne	Lab.Phys.Batiment Univ.Liege	Liege
UK		
J Clarke	University of Strathclyde	Glasgow
J Littler	Polytechnic of Central London	London
CEC		
T Steemers	The European Commission	Brussels
R Lebens	Ralph Lebens Associates	London

Each participant in the CEC study was asked to list all the
models available in his country (large, small and manual).
Many models were eliminated because they were not readily
available (i.e. they could be used only via a bureau
service or their codes were not open to inspection or they
could not be transported to other host machines; or because
they were not clearly documented, or because software
support in the event of problems was not likely to be
provided. If participants had already experienced
difficulty in mounting a model from elsewhere on their own
(apparently suitable) computing facilities, the model was
not considered further. Table 2 indicates the list of
'large' models considered.

When the constraints outlined above had been applied, only
five large programs survived: LPB-1, MORE, ESP, SUNCODE and
DEROB. In depth investigation suggested that the first two
were not completely documented and were not ready for
transportation to other host machines. Some problems had
been reported in the use of DEROB by Hastings (1981) and
thus the two models used for subsequent examination were
ESP and SUNCODE.

Table 3 lists the models reported by participants and which
fit micros, together with the passive designs which they
address.

TABLE 2 Large Models considered initially

Program	Author	Country
LPB-1	Lab.Phys.Bat.Liege	Belgium
CEN	Vandenplas	Belgium
Masuch	Masuch	West Germany
Philips	Philips	West Germany
BA4	Lund	Denmark
OPT	Gilles	France
Lyons	Lyons	Ireland
Admittance	Cowan	Ireland
MORE	Alpa	Italy
KLIMASIN	Seeleman	Netherlands
DYWON	Van Dijk	Netherlands
KLIPAS	Pernot	Netherlands
ATKOOL	Atkins	UK
BEEP	CEGB	UK
THERM	Sharman	UK
BUILD	Jones	UK
ESP	Clarke	UK
HOUSE	Basnett	UK
PASOLE	Balcomb	US
DEROB	Arumi-Noe	US
DOE2	LBL	US
BLAST	Hittel	US
SUNCODE	PALMITOR	US

TABLE 3   Micro-computer models

		DIRECT GAIN	SUN SPACE	TROMBE WALL	MASS WALL	WATER WALL	THERMOSIPHON	ROOF POND
LPB2-3-4	Lab.Phys.Liege	*	*					
SOLPA	Gratia	*						
BA4	Lund	*						
EFP 1-2-3	Nielsen	*						
CASAMO	Ecole des Mines	*	*	*	*	*		
Cash	Cash				*			
Fuller	Fuller	*						
FRED 10	Baker	*	*	*	*	*		*
SPIEL	Green	*	*	*	*	*	*	*
SUNPAS	Balcomb	*	*	*	*			

When constraints similar to those mentioned above were
applied, the micro-models selected for further comparison
were SPIEL, CASANO and SUNPAS.

Thirteen potentially useful methods were located running on
calculators, however, given their purchase cost and the
falling price of micros, it was felt that such tools might
become quickly redundant and what was needed was a
transparent manual method. The only manual methods which
passed the "constraints" test were Los Alamos III and
Method 5000 (from the Los Alamos Laboratories, US, and
Claux-Pesso-Raoust, Paris, respectively). The main
objection to LASL III was that students using it had great
difficulty in seeing through the equations and understanding what was actually being calculated, and thus Method
5000 was chosen for further study.

Model Comparison
The tests shown in Table 4 were applied by at least two
participants to each model.

TABLE 4   Tests applied to the Models

Ambient temperature jump, applied to the lightweight Liege
1 cm cell.
Monthly values of auxiliary heating for the lightweight
Liege cell.
Monthly values of auxiliary heating of a heavyweight LASL
test cell.
Monthly internal temperatures for 10 days in January and
June for the Liege cell.
Monthly internal temperatures for 10 days in January and
June for the LASL cell.

The models under consideration are ESP, SUNCODE, SPIEL,
CASAMO, SUNPAS and Method 5000. Figure 1 indicates the
behaviour of those which aim to predict hourly temperatures. For this test, the window in the lightweight Liege
cube (detailed in Table 5) was assumed to be insulated as
the walls. After equilibration without sun at 0 degrees C,
the ambient temperature was assumed suddenly to rise to 10
degrees C. The results were taken as an indication that
ESP, SUNCODE and SPIEL handle dynamic heat loss acceptably.

TABLE 5   Outline of the Liege cube

External length 1m: height 1m: width 1m
Walls U=0.76: Floor U=0.37; roof U=0.76 w/sqm.K
South window double glazed 0.36 sqm.
Raised off ground
Thermal mass restricted to plasterboard (total=50 Wh/K)

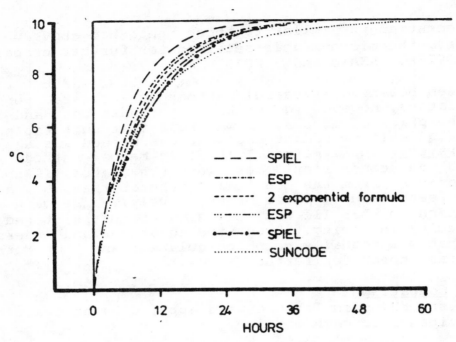

Figure 1. Model response to an external temperature jump.

Table 6 summarises the annual auxiliary energy required to heat the Liege cell to 18.3 degrees C(24 hrs/day, no venting and no internal gains with the window exposed to the sun.

TABLE 6   Annual Auxiliary Heating Demand for the Liege cube in kWh

5000	Lebens	347
5000	Pernot	313
5000	Raoust	339
5000	Rubini	338
5000	Dupagne	366
5000	Cash	348
LASL III	Rubini	322
LASL III	Kupke	439
LASL III	Pernot	327
LASL III	Lebens	408
ESP	Clarke	241
CASAMO	Raoust	311
CASAMO	Dupagne	357
SPIEL	Cash	377
SPIEL	Littler	371
SPIEL	Dupagne	416
SUNCODE	Littler	325
SUNCODE	Kupke	325
SUNCODE	Lebens	380

It was very encouraging to find such self consistency amongst users of Method 5000. On the other hand the direct gain system is the most easy to calculate using this procedure. Subsequent work by the author with a group of architects has shown that at least 4 hours is needed for a calculation using "5000" on a realistic house with buffer spaces and a conservatory, and it is not clear how to deal with ventilation preheating in a sunspace.

It was discouraging to find an overall lack of agreement, However, the internal consistency of the ESP and SUNCODE results show that for these models different users on different computers obtained similar results with the same model, in other words the fault is not with the implementation on alien machines. Similar data for the heavyweight Los Alamos cell (summary description in Table 7) are shown in Table 8.

TABLE 7   Outline of the Los Alamos Cell

Internal length 2.3m; height 2.8m; width 1.4m.
Walls U=0.34(north); 0.34(EAST); 0.0.(WEST); 0.39 (South
    opaque)
Roof U=0.27; floor U=0.21 W/sq m.K
South window double glazed 4.1 sq.m.
Cell in contact with the ground
Thermal mass 1230 Wh/K

TABLE 8 Annual Auxiliary Heating Demand for the
LASL Cell

Model	Participant	Energy
5000	Cash	1393
5000	Lebens	803
5000	Pernot	1024
5000	Raoust	835
5000	Dupagne	833
LASL III	Kupke	1505
LASL III	Lebens	1208
LASL III	Pernot	1109
ESP	Clarke	1100
ESP	Littler	1157
CASAMO	Raoust	1074
CASAMO	Dupagne	1014
SPIEL	Cash	1132
SPIEL	Littler	873
SPIEL	Raoust	1146
SUNCODE	Lebens	922
SUNCODE	Littler	867
ESP	Lebens	1100

The results of Table 8 are more indicative of how models
respond to a real house with appreciable thermal mass.
Data for ESP and SUNCODE are expanded in Figure 2. It
should be noted that the values quoted are "first round"
ones, and much of the disparity may be due to differences
in the assumptions made by participants when inputting
building descriptions. Except for ESP the models require
the specification of surface heat transfer coefficients,
and the data chosen can greatly affect the output.

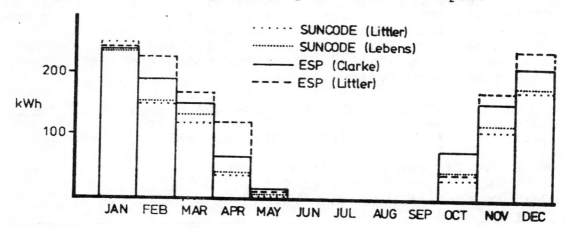

Figure 2.   Monthly prdicted auxillary energy consumption of
            direct gain LASL test cell, set point 18.3 deg C
            driven with Danish TRY hourly weather data.

Conclusions
- On light weight structures the manual method showed good
self consistency amongst various users.

- On both light and heavy weight cells, the large models
SUNCODE and ESP showed good self consistency amongst
various users, but did not compare very well one with
another.

- Such "round robin" tests need very careful attention to
input detail.

- Comparisons of this type warn us dramatically about user
induced errors and should persuade modellers to make input
simpler and less prone to mistakes.

Such intermodel comparisons are in the end not very useful.
They lead to confusion in the absence of comparison with
good experimental data. Such comparisons are the subject
of work at SERI (the U.S. Solar Energy Research Institute)
where Judkoff, Wortman et al have clearly shown excellent
agreement between class A monitored data and the models
SERIRES(=SUNCODE) and BLAST.

References

CEC (1983/4). To be published in the series "Solar Energy R and D in the European Community" as the "CEC Passive Solar Handbook, document 8588.

Littler, J.G.F. (1982). "Overview of Some Available Models for Passive Solar Design", Computer Aided Design, 14, 15-18.

Hastings, S.A., (1981). "Analysis of an Attached Greenhouse in a Low Insolation Northern Climate", Proceedings Sixth National Passive Solar Conference, American Solar Energy Society, 251-255.

CALCULATION METHODS FOR ENERGY SAVING IN RESIDENTIAL BUILDINGS

K G Kallblad
Department of Building Science
University of Lund
Sweden

The international Energy Agency (IEA) encourages research and development in a number of areas related to energy. In one of these areas energy conservation in buildings, the IEA is encouraging various exercises to predict more accurately the energy use of buildings, including comparison of calculation methods etc. The present state of these activities and some major conclusions from different tasks are reviewed.

Kurt Källblad is since 1968 research scientist at the Department of Building Science, University of Lund, Sweden. His research has been focused on energy use in buildings, including field experiments, development of calculation methods and computer programs. From 1976 he has participated in IEA-projects and was from 1979 operating as the Lead Country in an IEA-task concerning calculation methods.

Introduction

Around two decades have passed since the first computer programs on energy requirements of buildings were developed. At that time calculation of heating and especially cooling loads were of interest e.g. problems with high temperatures in office buildings with large glassed areas. Most of these programs were built either on differential methods or on ASHRAE's response factor method. The common parts for all were detailed thermal models of the building and the use of big main frame computers.

The energy crisis in 1973 focused the problem to predict energy consumption in buildings. Using the elaborate main frame computer programs was in many situations too expensive for this type of calculations. To meet this problem, a lot of simplified hand calculation methods were developed and with the introduction of the small personal computers some of the methods were transformed into simplified computer programs. The growing size of the personal computers made it possible to increase the complexity of the models and we have ended up in a state of confusion, particularly as many of the program originators only document the input and output parts of their programs. For the consulting architects and engineers this situation is, of course, more pronounced than for the scientists. A careful examination of the limitations and accuracy of the used models and computer programs has to be carried out.

Within the IEA's executive committee on Energy Conservation in Building and Community Systems have thus far two tasks concerning calculation methods and computer programs been carried out. The committee on Solar Heating and Cooling has encouraged some work which partly covers the same area. Some of this work will be reviewed below and further details can be found in the given references.

Methodologies for Load/Energy Determination of Buildings

This was the very first task within IEA - Energy Conservation in Building and Community Systems program and was initiated in 1977. The objective of this task was surveying, collecting and evaluating analytical methods used for predicting loads and energy consumption for buildings. The work was divided into two separate parts, comparison of some existing computer programs followed up with the Avonbank Energy Analysis Project.

Comparison of computer programs

A total of 23 computer programs from nine countries were used to predict thermal loads and energy consumption of one commercial building located in Wethersfield, U.K. The programs were arbitrarily selected and represented a wide range of different methodologies.

Results of the first simulations varied widely, mainly because of varying interpretations of the building specifications, differing assumptions about incomplete specified parameters, built-in default values and even program errors.

To identify specific areas where programs differed a hypothetical building without windows or internal load was specified. The participants simulated this building hour-by-hour for an entire year, allowing comparison of the programs according to heat transfer and solar gains through opaque surfaces. The next step was to add windows to the building. This allowed the analysts to compare methods for solar gains and losses through glass. Finally, internal load was added.

Also the results of simulations on the simplified buildings varied. For the third version the predicted annual heating and cooling loads are shown in Figure 1.

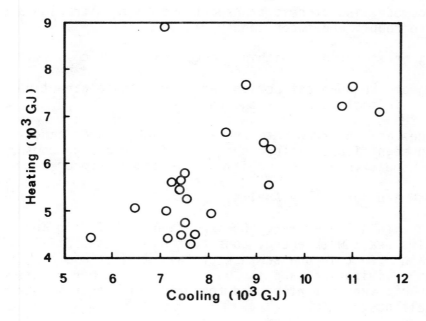

Figure 1 Estimates of annual heating and cooling loads.

Some conclusions about the consistency of results were reached by analyses of the results from the simulations on the three simplified buildings. Differences in the results arise because of differences in the methodologies used, particularly methodologies for handling internal thermal balances, storage and utilization of solar heat gain. Even programs that use similar methodologies can predict different loads due to program assumptions about key parameters, such as indoor convective and radiative film coefficients.

These comparisons did not consider the effects of infiltration, ventilation systems, plans or effects of floating temperatures. Recommendations were suggested for further development of energy analyses programs and research efforts in these areas as well as validations of programs by field experiments on buildings.

Avonbank Building Simulation

Some of the participants in the first project used eleven of the programs to predict the energy flows within the Avonbank office building near Bristol, U.K. Detailed specifications of the building were prepared and used by the participants in their simulations of the building. The results were compared with monitored data from the real building.

The summary and conclusions from this project strengthen the conclusions from the first project and point out the following areas of importance:

- Realistic modelling of heat transport due to infiltration and convective coupling between zones

- Modelling of stored heat within the building fabric

- Modelling of the heat extraction rates from space cannot be considered in isolation from the equipment.

- Differences arising from interpretations of the specification can cause significant differences in predicted energy consumption, irrespective of the quality of the computer program.

Residential Buildings Energy Analysis

This project within IEA - Energy Conservation in Building and Community Systems dealt with energy conservation in residential buildings. The main effort in one subtask of this project has been made at finding the limitations and the best use of a number of calculation models that are currently used for predicting energy consumptions of dwellings.

The methods were selected among those in use among the participants and in order to cover the scale from the simple degree-day method to the most complex computer programs. The included simulation methods were

Method	Size of thermal model	Main mathematical method	Includes air conditioning system
BA-4	Simple	Finite differences	No
NBSLD	Complex	Response factors	Yes
DYWON-2	Simple	Finite differences	No
KLIMASIM	Complex	Response factors	No
JULOTTA	Variable	Finite differences	No
DOE-II	Complex	Weighting factors	Yes

Following correlation methods were also examined:

Method	Required calculation equipment	Time-base for weather data
LPB-4	Computer	Week
EFB-1	Pocket-calculator	Month
SMECC	Pocket-calculator	Month
NEVACA	Pocket-calculator	Month
Degree-Day	-	Year
BKL	Pocket-calculator	Month
JAENV	Computer	Day

The participants simulated in this task a low energy one-family house in the town of Vetlanda, Sweden and an 8-storey residential building situated in Stockholm, Sweden. For the one-family house a rather detailed specification was given to allow comparisons with measured data. In this case the weather data were monitored at site. In addition to the original specifications, five parametric cases were defined in order to study how the methods predict energy conservation by different retrofits. The 8-storey building was more schematically specified and weather data from a meteorelogical station were used.

For the 8-storey building, the predicted energy consumptions are shown in Figure 2. Most of the results are rather close to each other, but the degree-day method shows an unacceptable deviation. This is clearly caused by the fact that this method cannot take into account the relative high level of free heat in this example.

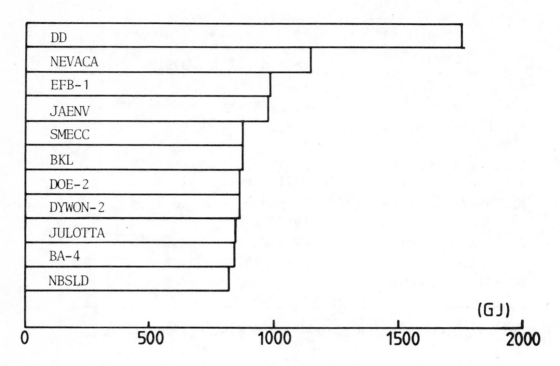

Figure 2   Estimated heating loads for an 8-storey apartment build-
          ing.

The results from the simulations of the original case of the one-
family house are, together with the measured heat consumption, shown
in Figure 3. The results from the parametric studies also showed
similar deviations which required a more detailed examination in
order to find the reasons. Only in the **simplest**   case, change of
ventilation rate, the methods predicted relatively consistent results.

The further examination gave the following conclusions:

Although a detailed description of the building envelope was given,
the analysis ended up with a 15% variation in the loss calculation.
A much bigger spread would be expected if each analyst was to extract the building data from drawings and other basic sources.

The different estimations of the solar gain cause a variation of 10%
in the total energy consumption of the building, a spread which
seems caused by different calculation algorithms rather than by the
analyst's interpretation of data.

The utilization of free heat shows variation of 40% which also results in another 10% variation in the total energy consumption. This
variation is normally caused entirely by the mathematical model and
cannot be influenced by the user.

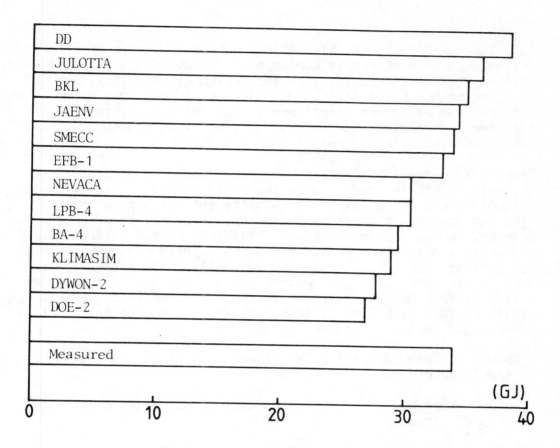

Figure 3 Five month's heat consumption for the one-family house.

Energy conservation effects are often smaller than the variation reaulting from a use of different calculation methods. This under-lines the fact that analyses of different conservation measures must be based on estimations using the same calculation method. The analyst must in each case make his own choice.

Solar Heating and Cooling Program

Within this IEA-program both active and passive solar systems are investigated. Relevant to this paper is the task on Passive and Hybrid Solar Low Energy Buildings which was initiated in 1982. The task is designed to contribute to the state-of-the-art in three areas - performance measurement, computer modeling and design tools. Especially the last area is of interest as the interaction between the designer and the calculation method is analyzed by architects with small or none experience in this field. The task is still under-way and no public reports are yet available.

Conclusions

The state-of-the-art of calculation methods and computer programs designed to predict energy consumptions of buildings are still rather unsatisfactory. The work inside IEA has primarily been of great value to the participating scientists, sometimes by pointing out problems or errors in different methodologies to model heat transfer in buildings and sometimes by relating his work to the users' need of accurate calculation methods.

Some work inside the IEA-tasks and other research projects have shown that detailed modeling of the building and carefully chosen parameters can bring results from different calculation methods close to each other or close to measured performance of buildings. However, in the design stage of a building, no measurements are available and the predictions are to be carried out by architects and designers who do not have the possibility to start a research project for each case. The designer also often meets the problem that complex computer programs are too expensive to use before the final design of a building. Thus further research efforts in this field ought to be focused on

- how different parameters in a thermal model of a building should be chosen

- how thermal models of buildings could be simplified without loss of accuracy

Finally, one must remember that the Art of Architecture and engineering always must include a good knowledge of the methods and tools used, their advantages, disadvantages and limitations.

References

Comparisons of Load Determination Methodologies for Building Energy Analysis Programs, Prepared for IEA by U.S. Department of Energy, 1981, DOE/CE/20184-1.

Result and analyses of Avonbank Building Simulation, Prepared for IEA by Oscar Faber and Partners, St. Albans, U.K., 1980.

Calculation Methods to Predict Energy Saving in Residential Buildings, Prepared for IEA by Kurt Källblad and published by the Swedish Council for Building Research, Document D4:1983, ISBN-91-540-3885-5.

THE DATA STATION:
AN INTEGRATED GRAPHIC INFORMATION FACILITY

Patrick A Purcell
Visiting Associate Professor
of Computer Graphics
Architecture Machine Group
Massachusetts Institute of Technology
USA

Currently, many of the most significant developments in information technology are directed at providing the user with facilities to engage directly with an increasingly varied and complex information environment. A further feature of current development is the capacity of information systems to incorporate visual data as an integral element in the data base. Both these developments are of particular significance to applications in architecture and allied professions.

The paper describes a system for a graphic data station which acts as a user oriented interface to an information facilities, namely an image data base, an electronic mail editor, and an information facility which combines an interactive query system, an image archive, and access to electronic mail.

Patrick Purcell is presently Visiting Associate Professor of Computer Graphics at the Architecture Machine Group of MIT. Previously he has been Senior Research Fellow and Tutor in Design Research at the Royal College of Art. He has written and lectured extensively on the application of information technology in design, architecture, and the graphic arts.

Introduction

In general, information technology has favoured text as the medium
of communication with the user. The interface with the technology
may be generally characterized as an alpha numeric keyboard terminal. The representation of information graphically has consistently been less favoured on the basis that it has been an expensive, technically difficult and generally esoteric medium for the
representation and communication of information.

Yet for many professions, the graphic image is the dominant element in their information environment. A variety of hardware and
software techniques have been evolved, to cater for the special
needs of this specialist community of users, for example in design,
architecture, and the graphic arts. Perhaps it is timely to look
at the technical achievements of these graphic information systems
and assess the implications and the opportunities for a wider
population of users.

Graphics and the Architect

The information context in which the architect works, continues
to expand both in scale and in complexity. This modern challenge
to professional competence is by no means unique to the design professions, but in this paper it is the special needs of the architectural designer and how they are being catered for by current
developments in information technology, which constitutes the
prime concern.

Amongst the growth points in the architect's information base can
be listed the literature of energy conservation, and the associated topic of environmental engineering. Advances in materials
technology and new fabrication methods add considerably to the body
of relevant knowledge. In general, keeping abreast of trends
and developments in the state-of-the-art of his subject is possibly
the architect's major information need whether it be in notable
examples of new building or in the literature of statutory regulations.

The ways in which the designer receives or construes his source
data are many and varied, so it is apposite to review the data
forms in which he generates design solutions and the forms which he
employs to transmit descriptions of the design projects to clients,
to consultants and to construction or fabrication agencies.

Alphanumeric data is handled by the designer as design briefs, as
performance specifications, design specifications, schedules of
equipment or as bills of quentities. Externally generated documents

include building codes, BSI standards, component catalogues, professional journals, and reports. Today's designer may also include computer program listings and output amongst his documentation forms.

However, that which distinguishes a designer's data base from most other professions is the scope and variety of the graphic analogues which the designer employs to represent the artifacts, the buildings or the complex of buildings which he has produced. These graphic data forms include the orthographic projections (plans, sections, and elevations) of working drawings. They also include the sketches, the formal perspectives, the isometric and axonometric projections of presentation drawings.

The graphic character of these data forms varies greatly. They range from the symbolic coding of the cross-section on a working drawing to the refinements of colour, texture, and shading of the presentation perspective.

Information processing in building design and construction has been one of the longest standing applications of computing, originating in the sorting and scheduling packages of quantity surveying and progressively extending to each phase of the design process including the designer's brief, sketch design, scheme design, working drawings, and post-contract documentation. This span of applications now aggregates to some fifty discrete subject areas.

The systems employed, vary in scale from "in house" structured data base management systems for the control of specific design projects to large "free-text" bibliographic reference systems providing state-of-the-art information on individual applications topics. Viewdata-type systems such as the CONTEL data base in PRESTEL provide information services catering for building design and construction.

The main concern of this paper is to assess the place of the visual image in current information technology and to review some of the techniques being employed, which accommodate the need for graphic facilities in information systems which purport to cater for architectural and associated design and graphic arts professions. Two examples are based on architecture and one based on the work of a particular artist are presented.

Archfile: An Interactive Architectural Data Base

The hardware installation for both systems is a Perkin-Elmer 3230 Mega-mini computer driving a Discovision optical video disc unit. A touch-sensitive display completes the installation (Fig. 4)

The video images are displayed on a Panasonic monitor (Figs. 1, 2). An interactive color graphic display is activated by a touch-sensitive screen (Fig. 1,3).

The architectural data base of the project is comprised of approximately 5,500 building records. Each record in the file is divided into 9 fields in the following manner. Fields 1 and 2 define the location of the building. Field 3 defines the building type of which there are eight types. Field 5 gives the data of construction. Field 6 lists the title of the building in question. Field 7 describes the view presented of the building (for example, interior, exterior, or detail). Field 8 gives the index of the building in the architectural archive and finally, field 9 holds the five digit code, which is transmitted by the computer to the Discovision Unit to locate and display the relevant frame on the optical disc.

The user accessing the architectural data base may opt to view the records in the data base selected by building type, by designer, by location, by period or by one or more combinations of these parameters.

The principal building types offered by the data base include the following examples:

1. Religious, Funerary
2. Residential
3. Medical
4. Public, Amusement & Recreation, Museums
5. Governmental & Military
6. Educational: Schools & Libraries
7. Communications & Transportation
8. Commercial & Industrial

The search procedure locates and presents successively, the records specified by the search command, for example "Schools by Gropius after 1950". As each example of the reference requested is found and displayed on the graphics monitor, the corresponding visual images are projected on the video monitor of the workstation (Figs. 1, 2).

Picassofile

Picassofile is the name given to an interactive graphic information system focused on the work of a single artist, namely Pablo Picasso. Over eight hundred images with associated text provide a comprehensive account of the painter's 'oeuvre'.

For the system, a data record was chosen which consisted of some 13 fields (excluding the name of the artist and other extraneous factors). These fields are respectively:

1. Title
2. Date
3. Location
4. Accession no.
5. Video disc frame no.
6. Material of the given art work
7. Period or style
8. Subject of the particular art work
9. Related art works (to the work in question)
10. Master works.
11. Series (sequences of works on a common theme)
12. Remarks (explanatory remarks or comments on a given work)
13. Background (contextual information on a given work)

"Material" refers to the physical identity of the work and has two fields, one naming the type of artwork, (painting, sculpture, collage, etc), the second specifying its medium (oil on canvas, bronze, pastel on paper, etc). The two fields, "period" or "style" (7) and "subject" (8), are each subdived into three additional fields, which allows one to deal with works that straddle several periods or styles, and to specify up to three of the subjects or themes of any one work. Related works (9), three fields of four subfields each, allow one to note and identify completely (title, date, location) up to three works related to the main work whose data file this record happens to be "Masterworks" are works that are important either in Picasso's oeuvre and/or in the history of modern art, "Series" refer to Picasso's variations on some other artist's image, Delacroix's Women of Algiers, for instance. It provides for the identification of a slide as belonging to a series as well as for giving the whole series a common title. "Remarks" leaves room for any comments that may be necessary. "Background" consists of some 60 images, (each identified only by artist and title) of works that influenced Picasso in his early career.

Altogether, each record can hold 32 distinct fields of information about each slide. The program that creates the data base, allows one to skip any irrelevant field and most records do in fact hold fewer than the possible maximum number of fields.

Any one of the Picasso images on the disc can be accessed, the information about it printed out on the monitor, and the image itself shown, through any one of the fields, each of which is unique. Thus, slides can be accessed through their subject, the museum, the city, or even the country where the work is located; the style or the period of the work, or even through the name of an artist who influenced Picasso.

Work in Progress

Both the architectural query system (Archfile) and Picassofile are under active development. The main thrust of these developments are directed towards a more versatile query system and a faster response time to search commands.

The Picassofile is being developed further, not only to offer the user the complete range of fields to access, but also to give him some control over the direction or order in which he sees the images (i.e. forward, reverse), and possibly also in choosing, or not choosing, to print out verbal information about the images. This may involve several menu pages, where the user is offered a very general series of choices on the first page, which are then narrowed down in the succeeding pages, to finally become as specific as a title. Anywhere along this process the user could, of course, request to see an image or images.

The whole project can be made purely graphic by having the touch sensitive control "buttons" on the pages identified not verbally, but pictorially, with graphic symbols, icons, or logos. A further extension of the project will be to record Picasso images on a write-once disc.

On the Archfile system, work in progress is aimed at extending the user interface. To this end, a voice recognition and voice synthesis input/output has been implemented. Experiments have been carried out with a large back-projection screen on which to present the images. Access to an electronic mail system has been implemented.

Finally, it may be said that the linking of the video disc with the computer-based information system has created a new type of graphic information system which will be used for a variety of applications in design, architecture and the graphic arts and for a variety of purposes by the student, by the professional designer, and perhaps most significantly by the lay person.

Acknowledgement

Acknowledgement is unreservedly made to the contribution to both projects by Henry Okun, Carter Pfaelzer, John Lewis, Morissa Miller and Paul Paternoster, and to colleagues at the Architecture Machine Group, to Eric Hulteen and Mike Naimark, and to the staff of the MIT Rotch Visual Collection. The project has been supported in part by a grant from the MIT Council for the Arts.

References

1. Miller, M. "Archfile: A System for Slide Retrieval". MIT Architecture Machine: Internal Paper. 1983.

2. Okun, Henry. "Picassofile". MIT Architecture Machine Group: Internal Paper. 1983.

3. Paternoster, Paul. "The Archfile Project". MIT Architecture Machine Group: Internal Paper. 1983.

4. Pfaelzer, Carter. "An Interactive Keyboardless Access and Display System for a Database with both Videodisc and Magnetic Disc Storage". MIT Architecture Machine Group: Internal Paper. 1983.

5. Purcell, P.A. "Information Systems: The Visual Dimension". Proceedings: EEC--Conference, "The Information Society", Dublin, Ireland. 1980.

6. Purcell, P.A. "Information Systems for Design, Architecture and the Graphic Arts". Proceedings: National Computer Graphic Association Conference, Anaheim, CA. 1982.

(1) The graphic information system work station

(2) Close up of the video monitor

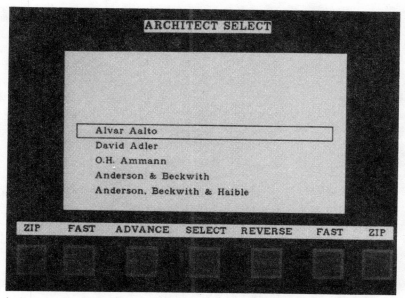

(3) The architects register on the touch sensitive screen

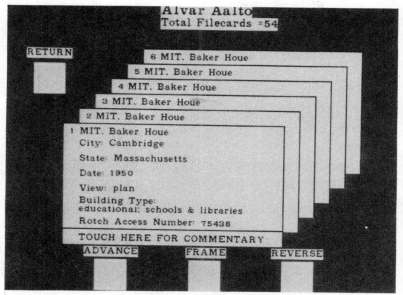

(4) Detail of the touch sensitive display

A GRAPHICS INTERFACE TO COMPLEMENT
TRADITIONAL TECHNIQUES

B G Hammond
D Leifer
Research Students
Scott Sutherland School of Architecture
UK

Noting the reluctance of architects in small private practices to adopt CAAD aids, the crudity of existing graphic interfaces is identified as an inhibiting factor.

A suite of computer programmes currently under development are described which are designed to permit the input of geometric plan forms by traditional pencil and paper techniques, whilst utilising the computers processing power to edit and manipulate the data so 'captured'.

Brian Hammond is currently undertaking an SERC funded Research Degree at Scott Sutherland School of Architecture, Aberdeen, from which he graduated with B.Sc (Hons) in 1981. A short period (81-82) with a small London based practice gave insight into the problems of practical architecture.

Dave Leifer is a Registered Architect having been employed in private practice in London. His introduction to computers came through thermal modelling whilst a student at the Welsh School of Architecture. He is currently undertaking an SERC funded Research Degree at Scott Sutherland School of Architecture.

INTRODUCTION

Many reasons have been offered to explain why architects have failed to utilise computers more fully than they have done[1]. Despite the promise of the micro-chip revolution, most architects' design work is still carried out by manual methods; computer aids being viewed as a specialised adjunct applicable to a few atypical projects. This is perhaps understandable in a profession where some 85% of all registered architects work in practices employing 10 or less architectural staff[2], and where the stability of workload is sufficiently uncertain to make large capital investment precarious[3].

To most architectural practitioners who are accustomed to, and moreover enjoy using, drawing board and set-square, computers represent an alien technology requiring unfamiliar and sometimes inappropriate languages and working methods. The relative magnitude of the capital investment that computers represent to the small architectural practice requires extremely efficient and close management of the system to ensure that it is run cost-effectively. Not only is this expertise expensive, but it is at present rarely available. More insidiously, principals in small practices may feel a potential loss of overall control posed by the inherent complexity of such systems. Such fears cannot be easily allayed.

It has been argued elsewhere that one of the most positive ways with which to promote CAAD would be to utilise the computers processing power to take on more of the burden of man-machine communication[4]. The machines must become more approachable by the non-computer literate user, leaving him free to devote his energies to designing rather than on communicating with, and operating the system.

THE ARCHITECTS ROLE

The architects task may be construed as the conception and communication of a hypothetical building model. In fact, the design process is one in which the designer compiles ever increasingly accurate data pertaining to the hypothetical model until such time as it is sufficiently complete and consistent to allow the client to 'experience' it and the builder to build it. (This pragmatic description does not belittle the implicit importance attached to the role of the architect as an aesthete). The common feature underlying all of the various architect generated data sets is the building models geometry; whilst the materials specifications state 'what' it is and the performance specifications state what 'it' is to do, the drawings state where all of this other information is to apply, and how it is interrelated.

The corollary to this process is constant appraisal to ensure that the sub-systems do what they are supposed to, be it the adequacy of the structural system or that the project may be built within the budget.

DATA MANIPULATION

The magnitude and complexity of the data generated for any one building project, not least of which is the project drawings, can only be 'guesstimated' in advance. This puts extraordinary demands on any computer system which would handle such a large and various data-set. Although some data-basing systems have been evolved and utilised by the profession[5], none have been sufficiently effective for machine implementation. Perhaps one of the most significant developments in data-manipulating techniques has been the development of logical programming languages such as PROLOG[6] which offer a powerful means for interogating large data-structures. The application of these languages to graphic data is currently under investigation elsewhere[7].

COMPUTER GRAPHICS

Within the overall CAAD context, one area of concern is the machines data-aquisition rather than its data-manipulation. This is particularly relevant to drawn information, since it is at this level that architects 'experience' computer systems. Current systems require inhibiting draughting conventions and crude levels of communication.

Drawings represent simultaneously many different levels of significance to the user[8]. Each level is 'distilled' from its contextural relationship to other parts of the drawing. Thus the fundamental problem with computer graphics is the radical difference between man's and machine's perception of drawings. Whilst the human can relate parts of a 'picture' to the whole, the machine is simply a collection of registers which can only cope with one data item at a time. The only 'context' the machine has for construing a drawing is the artificial one implicit in the structure of the data-base. To illustrate this, consider the example – Diagram 1.

Consider a simple CAAD graphics input system where drawings are created as combinations of squares. The user wishes to input a picture shown in 1a. The picture comprises of three squares A,B and C. Ignoring the interrelationship of the squares with each other, the machine must be given sufficient information about each geometric primitive not only to carry out the calculations that might be required in the subsequent applications programme, but simply to draw them on the screen. In the case illustrated the necessary input data includes the coordinate position of a point of reference for each square (here taken as the lower left-hand corner), and a scaling factor for each square. (This input data is shown in the table, Diagram 1d.). In order to draw these squares, the machine must convert this input data such that the drawing routines may be enacted. (These drawing routines are shown in Diagram 1e.)

It will be seen that in such a system it is necessary to refer to the lower levels of the data-structure if the user wants to address any particular line. This level is of course different to the 'vocabulary' used to create the picture in the first place. This cumbersome method of dealing with drawings does not bear comparison to the ease of paper and pencil techniques.

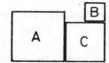

a) Picture to be created

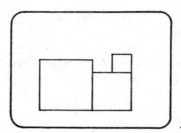

b) Association of Graphic Primitives

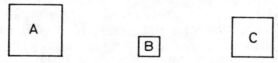

c) Primitives

Primitive	A	B	C
scale factor	S_a	S_b	S_c
reference point x	x_a	x_b	x_c
y	y_a	y_b	y_c

d) Input Data

move pen to	(x_a, y_a)	(x_b, y_b)	(x_c, y_c)
draw line to	$(x_a + S_a, y_a)$	$(x_b + S_b, y_b)$	$(x_c + S_c, y_c)$
draw line to	$(x_a + S_a, y_a + S_a)$	$(x_b + S_b, y_b + S_b)$	$(x_c + S_c, y_c + S_c)$
draw line to	$(x_a, y_a + S_a)$	$(x_b, y_b + S_b)$	$(x_c, y_c + S_c)$
draw line to	(x_a, y_a)	(x_b, y_b)	(x_c, y_c)

e) Machine Draughting Commands

Diagram 1 Example Of A Data Structure

THE PROPOSED GRAPHICS INTERFACE

To overcome the disincentive outlined above, an opposite route may be considered. Accepting the premise that architects generally design in the initial stages by 'toying' with freehand sketches, it is legitimate to place the onus on the computer to derive higher levels of significance (ie. recognition of graphic primitives), from the lowest level of input data (ie. the continuous digitisation of architects sketches); in effect to deduce the data-structure from the act of drawing.

The system being developed is summarised in Diagram 2. Architectural sketches are digitised on a graphics tablet (Tektronix 4954) which is connected via a Tektronix 4010 interface to a micro-computer with graphics display screen (Tektronix 4054).

Sketch Input   Dynamic Editing   Applications
                      and Manipulation   software.

Diagram 2   Configuration Of Proposed Interface

SYSTEM DESCRIPTION

The proposed system operates in five sections.

1. As described the designer sketches his intentions on the digitising tablet, an example of which is shown in Diagram 3. The rate of data capture by the machine will depend upon the speed at which the user draws and the cycle time of the digitiser.

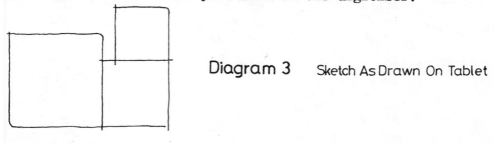

Diagram 3   Sketch As Drawn On Tablet

The drawing is echoed on the screen of the graphics terminal
to confirm to the user that the drawing has been captured. The
echo on the screen resulting from the sketch shown in Diagram 3,
and the format that the digitised data takes is shown in Diagram 4.

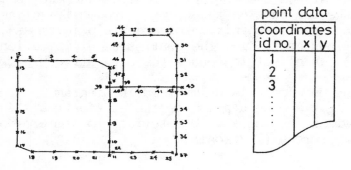

Diagram 4 Digitised Information Echoed On Screen

2.   The digitised tablet data is processed, and the data is sorted
into discrete lines by comparing the gradient of each successive
line element to the line of closest fit through the preceeding data
points. If the deviation is greater than a user defined tolerance a
new line is deemed to have been encountered.
    Moreover the 'image' is enhanced: Not only are freehand lines
straightened, but overlapping lines are removed, clipped corners
reconstructed, and almost touching lines made to touch. The information about the lines composing the drawing are stored in an array
for further processing, and the enhanced image displayed on the
screen as shown in Diagram 5.

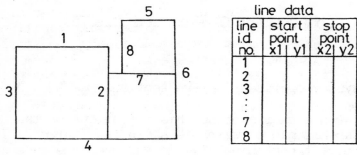

Diagram 5   Computer Interpretation Of Lines

3.   The user may wish to edit the interpretation the computer has generated. Using the dynamic graphic facilities of the terminal, he may delete or add lines by means of the cross-hair cursor, or indeed add information via the tablet.

Manipulation via the terminal has the advantage that the user can, if he wishes, make the drawing orthogonal, or place the lines in a range of sectors (ie. 0,15,30,45,60,75 or 90 degrees). With this editing process via the terminal, the dynamic feedback technique mentioned earlier is available to ensure the accurate placing of lines on the screen.

4.   The line data generated at the completion of the above editing process is then disassociated into discrete single line sections. Thus a line disected by another is split into two individual lines. The result of this disassociation is shown in Diagram 6.

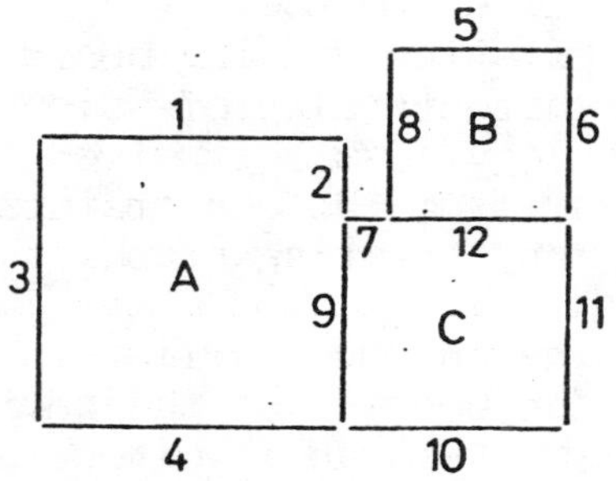

graphic primitive data

shape ref.	no. of edges	line i.d's				
A	5	1	2	3	4	9
B	4	5	6	8	12	
C	5	7	9	10	11	12

Diagram 6 Line Disassociation And Primitive Identification

By envoking a search algorithm, the perimeter of each enclosed space is traced and the line identifiers for the boundaries stored in an array. The system has thus abstracted geometric primitives from the data in a form which may be used directly by the advanced graphics capabilities of the graphics terminal.

Utilising the terminals capabilities, the user can manipulate complete primitives. He may repeat, move, mirror, rotate, and scale. An indication of these facilities is demonstrated in Diagram 7.

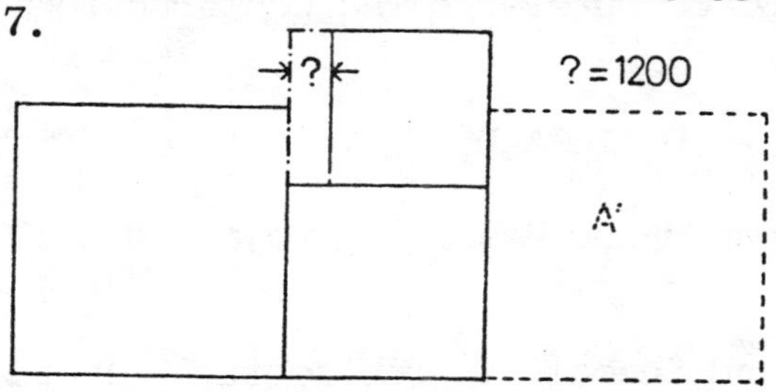

? = 1200

Diagram 7   Graphic Manipulation Option Utilising Dynamic Graphics Offering Instant Feedback And Rubber Banding

5.   The final step for the system is to reformat the graphic
data into structures suitable for input into other applications
programs. Since most applications software deals with polyhedral
geometries the data-structure produced by the above system contains
the necessary information for transmutation to other forms.

SUMMARY

The development project described above is intended to ease
the communication of drawings between the architectural user and the
machine in the following ways:
1.   By placing the onus of interpretation on the machine, the
designer can devote his time more fully to the task of
designing.
2.   By automating the interpretation system the machine is
made accessible to the non-computer literate user.
3.   Such a system supplements the existing drawing board
techniques generally used by the architectural profession at
present, and can make the new technology less obtrusive.
4.   Such a system frees the designer from the constraints of
draughting conventions common with many existing graphics
handling applications programmes.
5.   Appraisal programs may be instigated much earlier in the
design process, which can maximise the benefit of the advice
thus rendered. Moreover there is less overhead involved in the
time consuming task of 'digitising' drawings done in advance
by manual methods.

REFERENCES

1.   Standing Committee On Computing And Data Coordination
"Computing And Communication In The Building Industry"
D.o.E.   March 1979

2.   CICA
"Fact Sheet On The Use Of Computers In The Construction
Industry" CICA Bulletin   March 1982

3.   Bijl.A, Stone.D, Rosenthal.D EdCAAD, University of Edinburgh
"Integrated CAAD Systems"
Final Report To D.o.E. On Funded Research Project DRG 470/12
                                                      March 1979

4.   Leifer.D Scott Sutherland School of Architecture, Aberdeen
'Man Before The Machine : An Issue In CAAD"
BoCAAD University Of Strathclyde, Glasgow Vol 43-46 Feb. 1983

5.   Ray-Jones.A.R, Clegg.D   SfB Agency
     "CI/SfB Construction Indexing Manual"
     RIBA Publications   1976

6.   Clocksin.W.F, Mellish.C.S
     "Programming In PROLOG"
     Springer-Verlag   1981

7.   Work currently being undertaken at EdCAAD, Edinburgh University.

8.   Willey.D.S   University of Liverpool
     "Approaches To Computer-Aided Architectural Sketch Design"
     Computer Aided Design   Vol 8 No. 3   July 1976

A BETTER MAN-MACHINE INTERFACE
TO REPLACE THE KEYBOARD

Simon Ruffle
Architect
David Ruffle Associates
UK

This paper outlines techniques for improving interaction in computer-aided design programs. It discusses the concept of the User Model and demonstrates the effectiveness of the new breed of 'continuous' input devices. Programs based on these techniques, used by Architects and other designers, are proving exceptionally easy to use in practice.

Simon Ruffle trained as an Architect at Cambridge University and is now working on several Computer-aided design software projects. He is the author of two Architectural design programs that are available commercially.

It seems astonishing that despite the local processing power
that is available on microcomputers and intelligent terminals
today that so many Computer-aided Design programs are
still based on slow-response ('batch') computing techniques.
Just because users can type their own data at the computer
keyboard, and receive output in seconds rather than hours,
such systems are labelled 'interactive'. This paper will
show that to achieve interaction, and thereby become useful
design tools, programs must be designed to simulate the
user's view of the problem being solved, presented in familiar
terms and manipulated by appropriate input devices.

How important interaction is in design - aid computer programs
depends somewhat on one's definition of design itself, but
there would seem to be agreement that certain classes of
design problems, particularly in building design, consist
of a variety of conflicting, changing requirements. These
design problems are described by Mitchell (1977) as 'ill-
defined' and '... The existence of open constraints indicates
the use of highly interactive computer-aided design systems'.

It is characteristic of ill-defined problems that at the outset
no-one knows what form the solution will take, whether
there are many solutions or none. It is possible that the
solution will be missed either by wrongly formulated
constraints or by not recognising solutions when they manifest
themselves.

The Architect or Engineering designer's particular skill
in this situation is the ability to try out ideas and test
them to see whether they lead to solutions; possibly altering
the solution criteria as they pin down the problem, weighing
the importance of the various constraints. I would propose
that good designers are always watching for solutions and
are experts in knowing when they appear. Consequently,
when using computer models of parts of the design process,
they are interested in how the outputs vary in terms of
inputs, not in generating the inputs as ends in themselves
which then produce a fixed output from the computer.

'Batch' input to design programs seems to involve the designer
in an absurd guessing-game with the machine; the designer
entering alternative sets of input variables until the program
produces the answer that meets the solution criteria.

The designer needs a program that is genuinely interactive, where the outputs are directly linked to the inputs and the act of adjusting an input becomes synonymous with adjusting an output, the only difference being that the input is varying linearly and the output as a result of the model algorithms. In this way the output of the program can be watched for solutions to appear while inputs are varied through a variety of values and in many combinations.

ELEMENTS OF A GOOD INTERFACE : The User Model

The algorithms + data structure program model (figure 1) is a usual starting point for a good structured computer program but it must be realised that for the program to be interactive further fundamental software concepts are needed. Underpinning these is the User's Model (Newman & Sproull, 1979).

The User's Model is the conceptual model formed in the user's mind of the information he manipulates and of the process he applies to this information. It is not a flow chart of the program's process, but what the user imagines the program to be, so it must be imaginable given his training and experience. The user only reaches fluency, as with a foreign language, when he ceases to be conscious of the model as a guiding influence. A good model can be so close to the User's real-life view of the problem that he is never aware of it at all, on the other hand, '...without this model the user can do little more than blindly follow instructions like an inexperienced cook following a recipe.'

A User Model has to be designed, therefore it is subject to critical examination. The same program could have a number of different user models, each appropriate to the ways that users conceive the problem. Programs with similar algorithms and data structures can be clearly compared by their user models, and a user can choose a program accordingly.

We conclude that the user models of computer-aided design programs must follow closely the Architect or Engineer designer's views of design problems.

ELEMENTS OF A GOOD INTERFACE : Input Devices

The digitiser tablet is well established as an input device for two-dimensional graphical information and Newman & Sproull give clear guidance on designing tablet-based interactive systems. Less established are methods for passing numerical variables to design programs.

We can distinguish between discrete and continuous input
devices: Discrete devices such as keyboards, keypads and
to an extent user-buttons, pass data to the program in
discrete packets often with heading and terminating characters.
A user attempting to meet a given output target value from
a computer model by adjusting an input by keyboard needs
to repeatedly enter numbers which approach, and meet the
necessary input value. A speedy typist could well do this
fairly quickly though there are additional pitfalls: It is
possible to enter values outside the maximum and minimum
limits for the variable, or more 'accurately' than the variable's
resolution; there are a variety of 'wrong keys' that can
be pressed; it is possible to make a mistake and enter
the wrong number. Many of these conditions will produce
the unfortunate 'user-error message' from the bemused software.

A continuous input device is one in which numerical values
are produced on an arbitary scale selected by some kind
of tool, usually a knob or pointer. The actual value itself
is fairly irrelevant because the software can convert it
into an input value. If this value is fed back to the user,
he will feel that this is his input value - even though
it is the result of some software processing. This step of
taking the actual numerical input out of the user's hands
is important and can be extended beyond input to the output
of the model too.

Continuous input devices can be further categorised as restricted
and unrestricted, and can be assigned a dimensionality
(figure 2). Restricted input devices have a disadvantage
of producing variables from a defined, finite range with
built-in resolution, though they have the advantage of
repeatability. Unrestricted input devices do not have any
associated absolute value range or inherent resolution;
they merely pass 'up' or 'down' pulses to the computer,
allowing input variables and command system to exist entirely
within software and therefore fully under the programmer's
control. The user merely 'updates' in an almost entirely
predictable manner, removing a whole host of the disadvantages
of keyboard input, whilst adding the power of software
to the input process. Figure 3 shows a typical software
model for an input variable under control of a rotary encoder.
Notice that as the variable value is held in software, several
variables can be controlled by one rotary encoder with
suitable switching; and indeed the switching can be provided
by the same rotary encoder.

INTERACTIVE PROGRAMS

We have developed Pascal programs based on the techniques
outlined above using our own rotary encoder input device
and the results have been encouraging. Architects and designers
find the programs very easy to learn, to use, and to re-
approach after periods of time. Figure 4 shows a typical
program structure.

There are two kinds of information passed back to the user
by the program:

Confirming Feedback which confirms the current values of
input variables and the current state of the database, and
Output which is the results of the program's algorithms
processing the input data. Whenever the user adjusts any
of his inputs – altering a parameter or modifying the database
– both confirming feedback and output will be revised by
the program. In fact as both feedback and output are integrated
into a single consistent screen display they simply become
feedback.

We now have an interactive design program. The user can
'play' with inputs seeing what effect they have on outputs
and how they are interdependent. He can simply set the
output to a required value and read off what inputs caused
it. The continuous input will result in continuous output;
their respective rates of change will be a function of the
program's algorithms. The user has immediate access to
all program information, and can adjust any input at any
time, in any order. Thus, in addition to being immune
to errors in input, the program does not have a sequence
of operations which the user can break. The program need
not issue error messages.

REFERENCES

1 – Mitchell, W J, 1977, Computer-aided Architectural Design.
Van Nostrand Reinhold Company.

2 – Newman, W M, and Sproull, R F, 1979, Principles of
Interactive Computer Graphics, Second Edition, McGraw Hill.

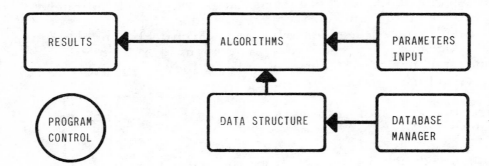

FIGURE 1 : Algorithms + Data Structure program model :
Typical starting point for program design.

	1D	2D	3D
RESTRICTED	POTENTIOMETER	TABLET LIGHT PEN JOYSTICK	DIGITISING ARM
UNRESTRICTED	ROTARY ENCODER	MOUSE TRACKER BALL	

FIGURE 2 : Types of continuous input devices

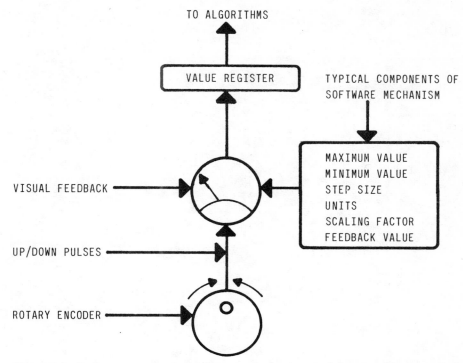

FIGURE 3 : Software model for input variable under control of a rotary encoder.

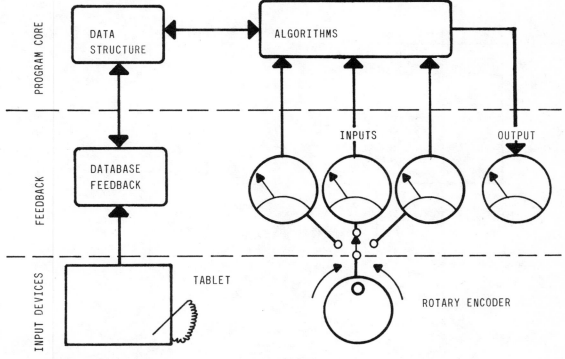

FIGURE 4 : Structure of an interactive program.

A FRAMEWORK FOR EUROPEAN CAAD EDUCATION

Richard Foque
Professor
National Higher Institute of Architecture
& Town Planning
Belgium

Rifka Hashimshony
Senior Lecturer
Israel Institute of Technology

Rik Schijf
Lecturer
Architectural Department
Technical University Delft
Netherlands

Richard Foqué is professor at the
National Higher Institute of Archi-
tecture and Town Planning, Antwerp,
Belgium. His teaching includes
Design Methods, project analysis and
CAAD. He was and still is a visiting
lecturer at different schools of
Architecture throughout Europe among
them, the Technical University Delft.
Besides he runs a private architec-
tural practice in the Antwerp Region.

Rifka Hashimshony is senior lecturer at the Faculty
of Architecture and Town Planning, Technion, Israel
Institute of Technology, Haifa, Israel. She was a visiting research fellow at the Technical University Delft
in 1982-'83, dealing with CAAD-research. During that
same period she was acting as secretary of the ECAADE project.

Rik Schijf is lecturer at the Architectural Department
of the Technical University Delft. In that position he
is responsible for the coördination of the CAAD-curricu-
lum. He is one of the co-responsibles of the ECAADE-
project.

A Framework for European CAAD education.

Given the fact that CAAD will dramatically change the entire structure, including working methods, of the traditional architectural office within this decade, the responsibility of the schools of architecture in these matters is enormous.

They not only should introduce the students to the concepts underlying the new generation of computer-based design aids and to their application in design project work, but they also should intensively deal with research and development within the CAAD-field. It would be a mistake indeed to limit the commitment of the architectural schools to the use of existing programs only.

This means that at least a selection of schools of Architecture should offer the opportunity to students and professionals to become "expert" in the theory and practice of CAAD as Maver and Schijf (1982) put it. It seems the only reasonable way for the development of new software and of new hardware-specifications appropriate to the architectural profession and the building industry.

However, introductions both at the undergraduate and at the graduate level, of CAAD into the curriculum of the traditional school of Architecture throughout Europe seems difficult for several reasons.

First of all there are a number of practical difficulties: overloaded time-tables, lack of information regarding appropriate hardware and existing software, budgetary problems and very often the absence of qualified or even just interested staff-members.

Secondly and even more important is the dislike of a great majority of faculty-members of what they see as a threat for their creativity leading to the decline of the architectural environment in general.

It is typical that over the last years a lot of schools promote again this traditional "beaux-arts-vision" of the architect-artist, whose task it is to create primarily aesthetic environmental form rather than function.

However signals from the profession show the absolute necessity for the implementation of a CAAD-course as an integrated part of the entire curriculum of a school of architecture.

With the modestly funding from the European Cultural Committee, the Technical University of Delft, has been

working jointly on a pilot project, trying to establish
a structure for CAAD education, within Architecture
schools in Europe.

Such a co-operation was felt worthwhile to overcome the
difficulties mentioned above. Moreover as the number
of teachers dealing with the subject of CAAD-education
in most of the schools is very limited, economising
seemed possible by forming a common frame for exchange
of teaching materials between various schools. The
common use and exchange of existing software on the
other hand could save time and effort and be an excellent
stimulus for the development of new software.

Although this European CAAD Education project (shortly
called ECAADE) started officially October 1982 with an
international seminar at the Delft University, its
origins go back a few years.
It started with an informal cooperation between the
Delft Faculty of Architecture and ABACUS of the
Strathclyde university. Delft borrowed the ABACUS
programs (Goal, Bible, Spaces, Magic, Air-q.) and
reported back on their use.
Additionally Delft tried out some other programs within
a student context: GABLE from Sheffield University
and CEDAR from PSA. (Schijf,1980)

From these experiences Delft started to develop its own
program, IVOGAR, which is intended to provide an appropriate interface between GOAL, BIBLE, GABLE and other
packages.

It is obvious that from these small experiments of
international collaboration emerged the idea to share
these experiences with other schools of architecture
throughout Europe:

1. Pilot work was done with the help of a number of
   other schools: notably the schools of Architecture
   in Antwerp, Tilburg, Sheffield and Aberdeen.

2. Contact by correspondence was sought with a large
   number of other schools from Finland to Portugal.

3. A case for cooperation was presented at two major
   conferences in 1982 (Schijf, 1982; Maver and Schijf,
   1982): CAD 82 in Brighton and CAD-ED 82 in Manchester.
   These papers advocated a first structure for a
   modular CAAD-course on the basis of a number of
   8-hour units divided into 5 categories :

1. <u>Exposition</u>: The concepts underlying CAAD, survey of
the state of the art, and demonstrations

2. <u>Inspection</u>: Hands-on experience of a range of programs and discussion of their form,
content and inferfaces. Exploration
of specific programs, without learning
a computer language first.

3. <u>Application</u>: Using one or more programs in a studio
design project.

4. <u>Instruction</u>: Acquiring programming skills and knowledge of hardware and software systems.

5. <u>Development</u>: Specifying implementing and maintaining
hardware and software systems.

Units 1, 2 and 3 are sufficient to prepare students for
CAAD use; units 4 and 5 are needed if the student
wishes to go on to develop CAAD expertise.

From the pilot work it turned up that the concept of
an 8-hour unit never worked. Such units seemed too
long on the exposition and inspection level and too
short on the other ones. Nevertheless the concept of
specific categories or levels of education seems to
be more relevant. This emerged not only from the
pilot projects but also from the correspondence with
other european schools and from the discussions at the
October seminar attended by about 50 participants of
30 different schools of architecture coming from 10
different countries.

In 1983 an enquiry was carried out regarding software,
in teaching curricula and hardware at use in these different schools. This investigation distinguishes 3 levels
which cover to a great extent the 5 categories mentioned:

1. Introductory lectures, mainly giving a general background and state of the art of CAAD: (Exposition
and inspection categories.)

2. Exercises, or projects, making use of existing CAAD
programs, developed in the schools themselves, or
purchased from other educational institutes:Applica-
tion-category.

3. Expert courses in which students are taught to develop their own programs: the Instruction and development categories.

The answers (27 respondants) show that the third level exists only in very few schools, and even the second level is mostly at a very experimental stage, not only for the students, but also for the teachers.

1. 16 schools reported on having an introductory course in CAAD, which is either compulsory or free choice.

   The main topics of such a course unit are:
   . History of computer use - roles and capacity of computers.
   . State of the art of CAAD.
   . Different types of computers & peripherals.
   . Flow-charts-Algorithms - From a problem to a program.
   . 2 D & 3 D graphic systems.
   . Evaluation programs: 5 schools, include the teaching of Basic in this introductory course, 3 other schools include hands-on experience as well.

2. In 10 schools out of the 16, the introductory course is then followed by an exercise, or project, in which students may have a practical experience with using an existing program for developing or remodelling an Architectural project.
   This course is usually not a compulsory one (while the introduction course usually is) and is given to a smaller number of students.
   In some schools this hands-on experience is an integral part of the design studio work. Typical is that 6 out the above 10 schools are making use of the programs developed by ABACUS, mainly GOAL & BIBLE for the design appraisal stage.

3. Expert courses following the two introductory levels, exist only in very few schools. Examples here are a course that will be given on a Master's level in Strathclyde University starting 1983/4 and another one which is given in Edinburgh on a Postgraduate level.

Some schools who did answer the enquiry do not have any formal CAAD education at all, but are interested in it, starting one, and therefore are very interested in the collaboration project, to speed up their development.

Conclusions to take out of this enquiry are very difficult and premature. Some points may attract more attention and further investigation:

1. Many schools do start with <u>exposition course-units</u>,
   which are mostly compulsory:
   It could be significant to compare the contents of
   these lectures and seminars. A tool for comparison
   could be the Lecture-Note-Book which recently became
   available in English and Dutch as part of the ECAADE
   project.

2. Many schools have application courses, and also here
   a comparison would be of great significance. Hopefully the ECAADE seminars, which now may become a
   yearly event, could serve as a forum for such an
   exchange.

3. The Inspection category suffers from being rather
   In -defined. If the Application category is
   primarily concerned with design and secondly with
   computer aids, with the objective of testing the
   influence of such aids on design. In the Inspection
   category it is the other way around: computers come
   first and the design project is rather the vehicle
   which enables students to explore certain computer
   tools. It seems important that exercises are followed by an Application Project using the same computer
   program(s). Such exercises have been run in Delft
   (Schijf, 1980; Foqué and Hashimshony, 1983) and are
   an integral part of this year's teaching in Delft
   as well as in Eindhoven. Although there is little
   experience to draw on yet, the Inspection category
   must have great potential for CAAD-education, probably going as far as Computer-Assisted-Instruction-
   Packages. (A detailed evalutation of such an
   inspection-exercise is to be found in Foqué and
   Hashimshony 1983).

4. The Instruction and development category do not belong
   to the normal architectural students curriculum.
   This aspect of CAAD-education and research should
   be part of a post-graduate level meant for those,
   who will become CAAD-systems developers but on a
   solid foundation of architectural training to ensure
   the emergence of "architect-friendly" and "architect-
   relevant" systems.

5. An additional 6th category could be thought of:
    packages to teach and instruct the CAAD-teacher.

Years ago in 1971, on one of the first European CAAD-
seminars in Rotterdam I put forward the emergence of
a new type of architect in developing 3 steps towards
an integrated evolutionary CAAD-system (Foqué, 1971
and 1975). At that moment as a consequence I pleaded
for a drastical review of architectural education.

One must admit that since then very little has been
done on the training and education of such type of
architects. The experience of many architectural
offices prove that there is a considerable need for
such architects-systems-managers.
Unfortunately the schools of architecture cannot cope
with this new situation as they suffer from an inadequate and old-fashioned curriculum.
Especially in a time , that there are more architectural students than vacant positions in practice,
the architectural educational world would be well
advised to broaden their insight by not only providing
the necessary undergraduate courses but also by creating
new options with a variety of computer specialisations.

e.g. A Systems-Management-Category before or after
instruction would be a most useful addition to the
CAAD-education framework.

References :

Foqué, Rich. 1971, "Towards an evolutionary
          Integrated CAAD" in DARU, M. 'ED.)
          CAAD, Bouwcentrum, Rotterdam.

Foqué, Rich., 1975, Ontwerpsystemen, Het Spectrum,
          Utrecht - Antwerpen.

Foqué, Rich. and Hashimshony R., 1983,
          "Experience of a design exercise,
          making use of the programs: Goal,
          Bible and Gloss." Proceedings of the
          ECAADE - Seminar '83, V.U.B. Brussels.

Maver T.W. and Schijf R., 1982, "International
          Implementation of a CAAD project
          in Schools of Architecture" in
          Proceedings CAD - ED 82, Manchester.

Schijf, R. 1980, CAADD 80, Evaluatie van 7 komputer-
          programma's;
          TH.Delft, Afd. der Bouwkunde.

Schijf, R. 1982, "Modular CAAD Courses" in Proceedings
          CAD 82, Brighton.

CAAD FOR UNDERGRADUATE STUDENTS
OF ARCHITECTURE
'TEACH WHAT, AND WHEN, AND TO WHOM - AND WHY?'

Dr L W W Laing
Lecturer
Scott Sutherland School of Architecture
Robert Gordon's Institute of Technology
UK

The role of Computer Aided Architectural Design in the education of architecture students is discussed and a possible strategy for how this may be integrated within the curriculum is described. This includes identification of the relevance of the related disciplines of mathematics and design methods and it is proposed that all three be presented under the umbrella of Empirical Methods in Design.

Lamond Laing has been involved with the teaching of CAAD methods in Architectural Education since 1973. Over the last 4 years he has developed CAAD as a regular element in the B.Sc (Hons) architecture course at Aberdeen and is active in the promotion of collaborative links with other schools of architecture in Europe through eCAADe. Since 1963 he has held various posts in architectural practice and it was in 1971, while Assistant Principal Architect at Cumbernauld New Town, that his interest in Design Methods (and subsequently CAAD) led him to take a degree in Mathematics and a MSc in Architectural Science. After a period as Research Fellow at the University of Strathclyde (ABACUS) he joined the Scottish Office as a Research Architect prior to his current commitment as a lecturer and studio master in the Scott Sutherland School of Architecture.

INTRODUCTION

Despite the underlying technological push implicit in the Oxford Conference as early as 1958, it is really only in the last ten years or so that 'many' schools of Architecture in Europe have acquired access to computing facilities (though this probably applies now to 'most' schools). The (once ubiquitous) Jeremiahs, who tried so hard to keep CAAD out of the design studios, have largely been persuaded (with not a little help from the profession and society at large) to accept that, at the very least, students have the right to gain some familiarity with computing. However, the issues surrounding the teaching of CAAD are deep and go to the core of architectural education. Indeed, it is a temptation, in discussing the teaching and uses of CAAD in schools of architecture, to be diverted into consideration of the whole structure of education for designers. To isolate CAAD as yet another specialism is dangerous - after all, isn't that what has gone wrong with the teaching of structures, environmental science, history and so on? The need for an integrated approach is essential with CAAD since it involves presentation of a design philosophy ...

Design activity has to be seen as an iterative process within which the role of the computer may be identified (]

a design method ...

Abstract or mathematical analogues must first be isolated and constructed

and through which the rules of designing can be learned by doing ...

Giving the naive designer instant feedback on the consequences of his design decisions

Rather than debate these wider issues of design education I will attempt a more pragmatic approach concentrating on the structured teaching of CAAD. By considering "what" topics need to be taught and at what stage in the student's development these need to be introduced ie "when" and "to whom" - perhaps the "why" of CAAD in architecture schools may become self-evident.

DESIGN SYSTEMS OR DRAUGHTING SYSTEMS

Before going on it has to be recognised that, at this point in time,
there is an apparent dichotomy in CAAD made manifest by the various
software systems available (2). I refer of course to the division
between draughting systems and design systems. The former represent
the use of the computer as a labour-saving device and are based on
fast information retrieval. Since this is the aspect of computing
most readily amenable to cost-benefit analysis - ideal for smoothing
out the cash flow problems of an irregular client market - it is not
surprising that architectural practice has opted almost exclusively
for draughting systems. Design systems, on the other hand, are
concerned with helping the architect to produce better, more
efficient design solutions, mainly by providing fast and reliable
feedback on the consequences of his current design proposals (either
by visual display of building geometries or by calculation of costs,
energy performance, daylighting analysis etc).

Within schools of architecture I do not see draughting systems as
having much immediate relevance for the following reasons

   (i)   The diversity of draughting systems, their dependency
        on sophisticated hardware devices and the high cost
        of these devices make it very difficult to opt for
        any one system as being representative of the whole -
        and few schools of architecture could afford any one
        of these systems let alone a representative cross-
        section of systems for comparison.

  (ii)   With currently available systems, the time required
        to create the necessary data-files of geometry
        elements is disproportionate to the likely benefit
        to students who may have to produce several design
        studies in any one year of the course.

 (iii)   We cannot and should not deny the real pleasure there
        is in the art of drawing using traditional techniques.
        Indeed many would argue that this tactile process is
        essential in developing a student's sense of proportion
        and form.

Design systems, on the other hand, must inevitably become an
indispensable part of architectural practice (if only in response
to the demands of an increasingly perceptive, well-educated and
more demanding clientelle) while in the context of architectural
education they provide, in themselves, a vehicle for the better
understanding of design problems. This point will be exemplified
in what follows.

GENERAL STRATEGY

Educating potential architects for the efficient use of the
computer as a design tool can be seen to fall into three broad
areas of study

1. Learning to Use Existing Software

    This involves learning how to communicate with the machine
    and, initially, using the computer as an educative device
    to explore the consequences of simple design decisions
    involving a few discrete variables (eg the effects of
    window location on daylighting and heat loss) building up
    to more complex applications whereby a wider range of
    design options can be explored than is feasible using
    manual techniques. For this process, the only computing
    skills required are those of data file creation and
    editing including learning how to make use of the hard-
    ware (terminals, digitisers, plotters and other hard-copy
    devices). The main thrust of CAAD in this context
    becomes using the machine as a device through which
    knowledge and experience of designing is acquired by
    forcing the student to be aware of the complex interrela-
    tionships which exist among the design variables which
    he has to manipulate while, incidentally, providing
    the student with an awareness of what computers can do –
    or cannot do perhaps.

2. Program Specification and Design

    This requires learning how to analyse design problems
    so as to produce a specification or heuristic whereby
    the problem may be explored (or even solved) using the
    computer. This is essentially the architect as systems
    analyst producing a flow-chart from which a programmer
    might produce the necessary software. Note that this
    does require knowledge of how computers work (binary
    logic) and, helpful but not essential, at least an
    elementary knowledge of a high-level programming
    language (eg BASIC or FORTRAN). I do not subscribe
    to the school of thought which requires program
    specifiers to be themselves competent programmers
    and hence the need for this additional skill is
    debatable.

    However, producing a logical brief from which a
    programmer can work does invoke two further areas of
    study. Firstly, techniques of design problem solving
    using logical methods are the bread and butter of
    'Design Methods' – a subject which has met with mixed
    reactions in schools of architecture but which must
    be revived if the architect is to assume control of

program specification, Indeed it can be argued that
the whole relevance of CAAD to architectural design
should be presented within the context of Design
Methodology, since that isindeed what it is.

Secondly, and of lesser significance, defining a
logical problem-solving technique must inevitably
involve some element of mathematical modelling and,
until we can be sure that all entrants to schools
of architecture have at least a good, 'O-level'
knowledge of maths, some remedial tuition will be
required.

3.   Computer Programming

There is no more need for architects to become skilled
programmers than there is for them to become skilled
joiners or bricklayers or plasterers. That is not to
say therefore that an understanding of this craft can
be ignored. Indeed, many (and very soon most) students
entering higher education already have a working knowledge of programming (usually BASIC) and this may
eventually lead to architects accepting more responsibility for this task. What I have found in my
experience however is that it is at this level of
activity that a sound knowledge of certain branches
of mathematics becomes essential if only in the
interests of programming efficiency.

As a general strategy, therefore, there is surely no longer any
dispute about the need for 1 above (learning to use existing s'ware).
This should however be introduced at an early stage in the syllabus
with students encouraged to look upon the computer as an educational
aid. In this I am aware of contradicting Bryan Lawson (3) who
argues that ".. (first year) students need to understand more about
architecture before starting on architectural computing " but in
this he is underestimating the relevance of the machine as an
educational aid.

The second learning process (Program Specification and Design) is
an equally essential part of architectural education if we are to
produce the "right software" for the "right job" - quite apart from
the fact that the skills of systems analysis are (to me at any rate)
fundamental to design problem solving and are skills which must be
developed anyway.

As I have already said, the need for all architects to acquire
programming skills (Computer Programming) is debatable and I therefore see this as an optional choice subject - but in the hope that
sufficient student numbers do opt to acquire this knowledge because,
without this, the objectives of 1 and 2 above become more difficult

to secure.

A POSSIBLE STRUCTURE

Having identified the three main areas of study and the two
associated disciplines of Mathematics and Design Methods I will
attempt to describe how this might be formulated within the school
curriculum. However, before doing so I must first dispose of the
notion that Design Methods and Mathematics are a separate part of
the process, instead I will group ALL of the ideas and techniques
of CAAD under one general heading - "Empirical Methods in Design".

Empirical Methods - Year 1

Design is presented as a "... goal directed problem solving activity"
(4) by reference to the theories of the design methodologists and
ways of looking at the design process are discussed including the
Markus/Maver sequential model (5) and its refutation by Lawson (6).
Possible modelling techniques are offered for the analysis and/or
appraisal of design problems which draw largely on the mathematics
of Set Theory (Boolean Algebra) and Graph Theory. For this purpose
it is necessary to review Mathematics as a 'Language of discourse'
through which relationships of design variables may be explored.

Having established the existance and relevance of numerical methods,
students are then more amenable to accept the computer as a friendly
aid which avoids the trauma of number crunching. At this stage,
students are shown how to switch on and communicate with the machine,
using it to perform simple operations such as calculation of U-values,
condensation prediction and daylighting analysis (this assumes a
parallel course in Environmental Science having already introduced
these subjects). Problems are then set up which explore the inter-
relationships which exist among these three variables and through
which students not only gain confidence and expertise in the use of
the computer but also gain insight into the nature of trade-offs in
design.

For such small-scale applications, the use of micro-computers is
generally adequate and, by dealing with limited input requirements
the need for sophisticated editing skills is obviated.

Empirical Methods - Year 2

More advanced modelling techniques are introduced with particular
emphasis on geometry modelling (the ultimate interface between
designers and computers). For this purpose students require some
intensive teaching of the mathematics of vector spaces, including
their representation in matrix form with matrix arithmetic manipulation being seen to provide the perfect language for communicating
with the computer. Consolidation of this knowledge is achieved
through study of geometry transformations which give rise to, firstly,
the wallpaper and freeze groups, and secondly, linear programming

as a powerful tool in solving design problems involving unequalities. For this part of the course March & Steadmans book provides an excellent source (7).

Again the computer is presented as a device through which these complex modelling techniques can be applied with emphasis being given to the application of techniques (eg the simplex algorithm for linear programming) which would be impractical if attempted manually.

By this time the student is ready to develop his own algorithms for design modelling and techniques for computer program specification are applied to typical projects.

Use of applications programs is continued but with a shift in emphasis to more sophisticated software mounted on the mainframe computer. This requires students having to acquire knowledge of more advance editing procedures as an aid to the management of the necessarily larger data file structures required by these programs.

Empirical Methods - Year 3

Based on their experiences during the first two years, students are now equipped to make decisions affecting how much further they wish to expand their computing skills. It is at this stage therefore that options are offered within three sub-courses as follows.

  (i)   Systems Analysis/Operations Research
 (ii)   Statistical techniques and their applications
(iii)   Computer programming.

Whatever option(s) is chosen, all students continue with the application of CAAD but within the context of normal studio activity. This requires a commitment on the part of studio masters to helping students to identify those aspects of their studio projects which can make good use of the computer and, for one major project at least, using the computer as a highly integrated part of the design process (culminating in a full economic and environmental appraisal of the student's scheme).

Empirical Methods - Subsequent Years

Further use of CAAD techniques must now be left to the individual motivation of the student. If the lessons learned in the first three years are of any merit then a willingness to continue using the computer as a necessary part of design should be automatic and further instruction should only arise in response to specific requests.

However, in saying so, it has to be acknowledged that studio instructors can do much to either promote CAAD, or, indeed, to kill it stone dead. However, where students have acquired a sound

POSSIBLE COURSE STRUCTURE

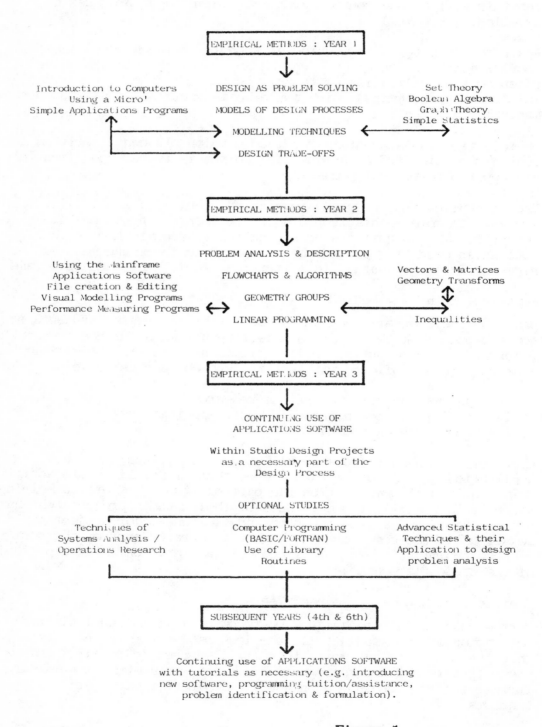

Figure 1

knowledge of the role of CAAD in design, those who continue to lobby against its use in the studio will find themselves in a position of growing weakness and unable to argue with a body of student knowledge which outstrips their own.

CONCLUSION

The structure outlined in the foregoing chapter is presented for easier reference and assimilation in Figure 1 . There is however one major issue remaining and I have already introduced this in my last paragraph. As Brian Lawson (3) has stated ...

"Computer evaluations ... could present a challenge to the staff since, as technical factors move more into the studio, students are likely to encounter staff who understand neither the building technology nor computing."

This problem within schools of architecture cannot be ignored and it follows that, where it exists, parallel courses are required in staff development without which any attempt at integrating CAAD within course structures falls flat on its face and the subject is, like so many others in the past, relegated to the level of 'subject specialism' and not to be taken too seriously by aspiring 'designers'!

REFERENCES

1. MAVER, T.W., "A Theory of Architectural Design in which the Role of the Computer is Identified", Building Science 4, (1970), (pp 199-207)

2. —————— , "Draughting and Design", Report of the RIBA/ CICA Conference on 'Buildings Designed by Computers', Architects Journal (No 3, Vol 177), (Jan 1983), (pp 69-75)

3. —————— , "Know your Building - Modelling and Education", Architects Journal, (No 25, Vol 175), (June 1982), (pp 81-84)

4. ARCHER, L.B., "The Structure of Design Processes", RCA, School of Industrial Design (Engineering) (Research), (1969)

5. MARKUS, T.A. et al, "Building Performance", Applied Science Ltd., (London), (1972)

6. LAWSON, B., "How Designers Think", The Architectural Press Ltd., (London), (1980)

7. MARCH, L. and STEADMAN, P., "The Geometry of Environment", Methun & Co., (London), (1974).

356

A STRATEGY FOR COMPUTER EDUCATION
IN A SCHOOL OF ARCHITECTURE

Patrick A Purcell
Visiting Associate Professor
of Computer Graphics
Architecture Machine Group
Massachusetts Institute of Technology
USA

abstract

Prior to discussing the provision of computer courses in a school
of architecture the paper sketches out a framework within which a
scheme of computer training and education for architecture students
might be formulated. The principal facets of such a scheme are
discussed in the context of recent references in the literature.

The paper concludes with an account of a major new initiative on
the MIT campus linking computers and education, namely the Athena
Project. It speculates the impact this project will have on
computer training and education not just on the teaching of computer
techniques to architects but on the role of the computer in higher
education generally.

Patrick Purcell is presently visiting
Associate Professor of Computer Graphics
at the Architecture Machine Group of
MIT. Previously he has been Senior
Research Fellow and Tutor in Design
Research at the Royal College of Art.
He has written and lectured extensively
on the application of information
technology in design, architecture,
and the graphic arts.

introduction

As an application topic the role of computers in architecture has been the subject of very extensive research and development. However, the degree of computer usage by architects has not been commensurate with the scale of the original research or with the variety of facilities now available.

The quality (or lack of quality) of computer courses being provided in schools of architecture may be a significant factor in this disparity between the facilities now available and their use by the practising architect. This paper looks at computer training and education in architecture and its relationship to the use of computers in the design and construction of the built environment.

As an application area architectural computing has become a very broad topic indeed, covering a wide spectrum of technical, aesthetic and social issues from participatory planning to the simulation of color and texture.

Any system of computer training and education has to acknowledge the extensiveness of the "state-of-the-art" in architectural computing if it purports to be a viable preparatory experience for the architect engaging in the technology. Applications touch every phase of the design process. Modelling software effectively represents the most complex and detailed building geometry.

Checking programs assist in establishing the feasibility of the design brief. Other programs aid in the development of the 'bubble diagram' of the initial design concept into a sketch design. Analysis software tests the proposed design for structural stability, for environmental performance or for cost. Synthesis programs help to generate design solutions for specific criteria such as the location of facilities, or the layout of spatial accommodation. In the design realization phase, production systems generate working drawings and associated documentation, based on the scheme design.

The progressive enhancement of the range and scope of computer-based design aids has led to the implementation of integrated systems. The effective utilization of such systems demands special insights and skills on the part of the designer using them. Such facilities now exist to serve each of the major building types (housing, schools and hospitals for example). A question for computer training and education is how effectively can it provide the requisite insights and skills for designers employing such design aids?

Personal computing now makes computing in the studio an increasingly feasible proposition, both technically and economically. Refinements in display technology both in raster-scan tonal images and line-based calligraphic techniques have significantly extended the graphic capabilities of computer application in architecture.

Computer-based information technology is a further relevant factor in the reassessment of computer education for the designer. Automatic bank tellers, airline reservation systems, and the public viewdata systems are examples of general applications of this technology. Examples, specific to design practice are being developed for design and construction. Apart from practical application in architectural practice there is the theoretical potential of using the information processing capabilities of the computer as a basis for the study of design itself, literally as a metaphor for design activity. This contribution to elucidating the complexities of the design process also has implications for the development of future computer-based design aids.

As the information load on the designer increases, for example in the area of statutory regulations or in revised energy codes, the principles and techniques of information processing are becoming a significant part of the syllabus of the computer course for the architect.

framework for computer education

While 'computer education in architecture' may be specifically focused as a topic for investigation, the contextual issues pertinent to the study are varied and wide ranging. Taken together they represent a comprehensive basis for making an assessment of current provision of computer education available to the architectural designer today.

In the context of architecture, computer education has several roles to play. It provides the practising architect with training in computer methods. It also acts as the vehicle by which advanced techniques emerging from research are tested in 'real world' applications. In this respect computer education could be seen as having a triadic relationship with architectural practice on one hand and with research in architectural computing on the other.

The usual rationale offered for the introduction of computer education in architectural schools has been based on the need for professionally relevant techniques and for tuition in programming to enable designers to develop and apply these methods in their individual design practices. However, there is evidence of a growing awareness of the potential of the computer as a learning resource in architectural education which serve educational objectives, other than simply anticipating the needs of design practice.

A major new initiative at MIT, the Athena project (discussed later in the paper) focuses on just this potential.

When comparing the various topics that may constitute a framework for complete education in architecture, the primary issue is the syllabus. The syllabus is discussed in two complementary areas, the technology of computation and the application of this technology in architecture.

The effectiveness of the architectural computing course hinges on the scale and the quality of resources available to it, namely hardware, software and staffing. Miniaturization and the economics of microprocessors have combined to make hardware the most tractable of the resource issues.

The view of software as a resource and recognition of the need to provide for the maintenance of an adequate repertoire of supported programs is a relatively recent development.

Staffing, the most important resource issue, anticipates a teaching function at once both academically and professionally relevant and which affords effective user support in the studio.

In order to provide a basis for discussing comprehensively the functions of the computer in relation to the practice of architecture the concept of computing modes is adopted as follows:

a the mode of calculation (the longest standing application topic in design)

b computer modelling (an application of computing, closely associated with the design process)

c information processing (a computing mode of more recent origin in the syllabus of architectural computing)

Architectural design represents a web of interlocking design roles (vocational, managerial and professional). Each of these roles involves a distinctly different mode of computer usage and consequently a distinctly different computer training require-ment. As the final element in the framework for discussing computer education in architecture the levels of computer education acknowledges the differing requirements of users and relates these requirements to the academic grades of under-graduate, post-graduate, mid-career and technician.

The four elements then (proferred as a framework for architectural computing) may be listed as follows - the syllabus, the resources available, the modes of computing and finally the educational levels at which courses are presented.

the syllabus: scope and content

An appraisal of syllabus design (1) indicates a very broad spectrum of approaches to the design of computer courses ranging from the most 'ad hoc' assemblage of topics centered on the provision of instruction in programming to formal curriculum design. The latter, while representing a minority of cases, reflects a need to adopt a more deliberate pedagogic approach if computer studies are to achieve their full potential in the individual 'host' discipline of architecture. Courtieux (5) proposes an academically oriented approach to computer course design. David (4) also, discussing computing courses for architectural students, proposes a clear definition of pedagogic goals as a pre-requisite to designing and teaching such courses.

Rzevski and Kaposi (7) report a most formally enunciated approach to the design of the computing curriculum. Their theoretical stance in general systems theory gives this application independent approach a relevance beyond the engineering disciplines in which it is presented. The approach requires a rigorous definition of educational objectives 'not least as a salutary exercise requiring hard thinking' and as a valuable prompt to course designers 'to expose their prejudices, search for new course structures and reconsider traditional teaching methods'.

the structure of the syllabus

The structure of the syllabus can be regarded as having two broad areas of emphasis, one concerned with computer technology and the other concerned with the application of computing techniques in architectural design.

Computing technology. The area of the syllabus concerned with
computing technology itself divides into topics concerned with
hardware and topics concerned with software. That part of the
syllabus concerned with hardware generally starts with an
introduction to the elements of hardware, the types of processing
units (main frames, minicomputers and microprocessors), storage
media (disks, tape units, drums and the newer storage technology),
input/output devices with an emphasis on graphic equipment such
as visual display units and plotting devices.

In the field of software, by far the greatest weight is often
given to that part of the syllabus which concerns the techniques
of writing and running ones own programs in a high-level language.
The emphasis given to learning the techniques of programming has
tended to militate against a balanced or comprehensive treatment
of the subject of software in the syllabus. The emphasis has also
produced a discernible reaction on the part of certain authors
in the literature.

For example, Blaauwendraad (8) says 'A computer-aided design
teacher ought to prevent his students as much as possible from
writing their own programs, . . . instead to use existing
software'. Commenting on the syllabus with excessive programming
content, Courtieux (5) warns 'one can easily tend to become a
computer programmer concerned with architecture, instead of a
designer using the best adapted techniques'. There is a need
to complement the experiential value of writing and running ones
own programs with some introduction to the operation of larger,
more complex 'real-world' systems. Lansdown (2) complains that
the large integrated systems for architectural design are grossly
under-used by the practising arthitect.

One plausible reason for this, is that the principles, techniques,
and above all the experience of using integrated systems are
entirely absent from the architectural computing course. Another
advocate (9) of the use of application software says 'Students
should be encouraged to use standard packages and should receive
training in the interpretation of results and should develop
methods of verifying computer output'.

The application of computing. The complementary aspect of the
syllabus is that which deals with the applications of computing
in architecture. The recent literature of architectural computing
shows what a varied repertoire of computing applications exist in
every phase of the architectural design process e.g. analysis,
synthesis, evaluation, communication and management. Yet the

day-to-day use of computing in the design office is hardly
commensurate with the scale and variety of facilities available.

In the feasibility stage of briefing the designer, facilities
exist for defining space needs, make predictive cost estimates,
and generating schedules of accommodation At the sketch design
stage, the computer may generate plan layouts or may perform
a series of environmental, structural or cost analyses on the
design proposals. To assist design realization and production,
computer drafting systems, scheduling programs, or other
documentation systems can be brought into play. For design
management, the architect may use critical path networks, PERT
techniques and other management and administration aids.

the provision of resources

Given the pace of development in hardware and the special needs
of architectural computing, securing adequate resources for
the computing course is a concise prerequisite.

Amongst the triad of resource issues – hardware, software and
staffing–hardware has become at once both eminently accessible
and cost effective. Recent advances in high definition graphics
and in frame buffers has enhanced the performance of the architectural work-station. Interface design has given the work
station access to a wide variety of remote information storage
and retrieval systems.

Provision of appropriate equipment, the proximity of terminals and
ease of access to computer facilities generally are major factors
in the effectiveness of the computer course. Gero (10) comments
that inadequate 'hands-on' facilities for the computer course
student produces 'a trained swimmer who has never been in the
water'.

software repertoire

Software as a resource has only recently been afforded adequate
recognition. This is due to a number of factors. With an
increasing repertoire of application programs now available, the
need to incorporate these as adequately documented application
packages into the computer course syllabus is becoming an
obvious requirement.

With the increasing capacity and processing power of current
technology, copies of even the largest integrated application
software packages are being 'shoe-horned' into minicomputer and

microcomputer systems. This proliferation of re-implemented
software has placed a new emphasis on the quality of documentation
(both system specification documentation and user manuals), and
emphasises a software virtue, that has been notably absent in the
past, given the academic provenance of most software in this
area. Pohl (6) comments 'there is a sizeable number of computer
programs in use today, particularly in educational institutions
which are of unknown origin, which have been subjected to
virtually no testing and which are based on unexplained or otherwise erroneous theories'.

Because of the dominance of programming techniques in the average
syllabus, the issue of providing good software support has been
greatly underestimated by organizers. Van Koetsveld (11)
comments 'good software is more than merely a set of statements.
It is also a manual, a support group, and enough computer capacity'.

staff resources: the human factor

The academic background and qualifications of course presenters
are important factors which determine the kinds of educational
objectives established for courses and the general orientation
of courses. With non-architect presenters there exists the
danger that the course becomes remote from the concerns of the
architectural studio and as a consequence students see little
relevance in them.

modes of computing in the syllabus

One of the more salient features of computer training has
been the 'ad hoc' and fortuitously contrived nature of many
computer course syllabuses based very often on a narrow group of
applications.

This section provides a framework for discussing the computer
syllabus in a more comprehensive way. It is based on the three
modes of computer operation (calculation, information processing
and modelling or simulation), referred to earlier.

Basing a discussion of the computer syllabus on the modes of
computing also offers an opportunity to draw together the many
heterogenous applications represented by the disciplines involved
in the design of the built environment. As well as drawing
together a variety of applications in architecture, this section
will also provide a perspective for relating both the theoretical
and practical aspects of computing in architecture. For example

in touching on the practical data processing applications in architectural practice and the potential of information processing as a theoretical basis for studying design behaviour.

role of calculation in the computer course

The longest standing if not the strongest association with architecture is in the sphere of calculation, especially in the relevant engineering subjects. Originally devised to solve very large systems of mathematical equations in science and engineering, applications in calculation are still closely associated with extended mathematical computation in applications in structural and environmental engineering, for example in the static and dynamic analysis of structures or in the calculation of energy flows. The calculation power of the large 'number crunching' systems have contributed distinctively to the design realization of many of the modern innovations in structural geometry including cable nets, shell geometry and geodesic domes.

Current concern with energy conservation and statutory obligations to comply with revised energy standards have given an enhanced significance and interest to the role of calculation in the sphere of energy and in environmental engineering generally. It has resulted in a rich repertoire of calculation software becoming accessible through the new generation of programmable calculators and desk-top computers. Relevant applications include calculations for heat loss, artificial lighting and daylighting, condensation risk, acoustic reverberation, peak temperatures.

information processing in the syllabus

Given the applications of information processing in design and construction, it is remarkable that the subject should figure so sparsely in the syllabus of courses in architectural schools, especially when compared to the incidence of computer modelling and calculation in such courses.

Pohl (6) complains the computer 'has been excessively represented as a high speed calculator rather than a powerful data-processing and simulation tool'. In this statement and similar statements based on US experience, there appears to be a new awareness of the significance of information processing in computer education. Mitchell (9) offers a relevant view of design, 'as an information processing activity and design organizations as information processing systems'. In application terms the subject is concerned with defining information flows in design or construction and with the application of computer techniques to meet defined information needs.

At MIT, Purcell (14) describes a graphic information system set as a class project. In the Department of Architecture at University of California at Los Angeles the course 'Information Systems' deals primarily 'with the way design information is stored and used; with computer information processing concepts and techniques . . . and how they apply to traditional techniques in planning, architecture and urban design'. The course includes a class project to build an information processing system as part of the study of the techniques of implementing 'real-world' information systems. The course on information systems has a complementary theoretical and practical structure.

modelling in the computer course

In the discussion of the modes of computing, it is the computer as modelling medium, which relates most closely with the typical form giving processes of architectural design. Consequently in those courses referring specifically to computer modelling, the references are almost entirely set in the context of the design studio, the design methods course or the study of design theory.

In the Department of Architecture at Strathclyde, the computers in architecture course is very closely involved in the main stream of the studio design projects. Maver (12) reports that special emphasis is given in the course 'to the concept of modelling, that is the development of the geometrical, behavioural and aesthetic character of design proposals which will allow prediction of how real buildings will perform in the real world'.

The computer course in the Department of Architecture at the University of Eindhoven (3) is introduced in the context of design methodology. The subject of computer-aided design modelling includes: 'concepts of systems and model theory; model sensitivity analysis; specifiying model parameters; mapping the design object on the model'.

Rogers (13) describes the development and operation of a dynamic 3D modelling system in the computer course at the School of Architecture in Zurich. The system acts as a vehicle for studying complex geometrical structures.

levels: computer education as a graded system

The previous paragraphs have focused on individual parameters for assessing computer courses, for example, on the scope and content of the syllabus or on the various resources which contribute to the effectiveness of the computer course.

The final issue to round off this discussion is that of levels. In this section the concern is with the variety of roles and skill that constitute the architectural design team and in particular the manner in which computer courses cater for each of these roles. For example the graduate architect, the technician or the project manager. Beyond these there are specialist roles related to the machine which do not concern us here but which conspectus of computer education ought to embrace (such as applicable programmer, system designer or hardware specialist).

While the whole area of computer courses in architecture contain a strong remedial character, it will be difficult to set up any rigorous system of prerequisites or scheme of ascending specializations.

on reflection

Apart from a lack of structure to accommodate the differing needs of generalist and specialist users of computer in architecture, other factors also inhibit progress. For example, in UK architectural circles the lack of formal assessment inhibits student commitment to the computer courses given. This contrasts with the credit system in the US or the 'unite' de valeur in France.

In general there is a lack of identity where computer courses in architecture are concerned. Very often computing courses are presented as an adjunct to other disciplines such as mathematics, statistics, design methods or energy studies. While computation will continue to contribute to these other disparate topics, the growing body of applications represented by architectural computing suggest that the subject should be more firmly con- solidated as a separate topic in its own right in the architectural syllabus.

computer courses in a school of arthitecture: current provision at MIT

The provision of computer courses in the School of Architecture at MIT reflects a wide spectrum of skills and interests which span the full gamut from computer specialist to the professional concerns of the architect or graphic artist. The following titles and outlines give the character and the orientation of each.

a Computers and Graphics:

A general introduction to computer graphics and its applications in design, architecture, and the graphic arts. Practical assignments provide experience in the use of 2-D and 3-D graphics in the extensive facilities of the Architecture Machine Group, including touch sensitive screens, color raster displays, and computer-linked video systems. PL1 is the programming language most in use. Programming experience not mandatory.

b Advanced Computer Graphics and Its Applications:

Main thrust is enhancement of human/machine communication at computer graphics interface. Formulation of individual projects within current research of the Architecture Machine Group: modeling of human form and gesture and integrating of text and visual images in development of graphic information systems. Presents a wide spectrum of interactive techniques, including gesture modeling systems, voice recognition, synthesis methods, and touch-sensitive displays.

c Computer Graphics Programming:

Overview of the techniques of computer image synthesis, including both hardware and software. Line drawing and color raster graphics. Homogeneous coordinates, hidden surface and smooth-shading algorithms. Programming problems and a term project. Limited enrollment. Previous programming experience required.

d Advanced Computer Graphics:

Treats in-depth current research in 3-D computer graphics. Readings from recent papers. Significant term projects including an implementation, written report, and classroom presentation.

e Computer Graphics Workshop:

Project-based survey introduces the computer as an expressive tool in image and word manipulation/synthesis. Graphical problem solving in PL1 and Magic6 using sample programs.

Connections to traditional and experimental print forms using the Visible Language Workshop's full-color computer graphics system, color graphic arts scanner, plotter, small hardware projects in digital markmaking. Requires final project produced on VLW system and a software or hardware tool which can be installed as part of that system.

f   Computers and Architecture:

General introduction to the history and development of computer applications in architecture. The full range of such applications will be discussed from briefing through design to construction. Applications will be grouped in two main headings, digital modeling and information processing.

Principles and practice of computer-aided design. An integrated design system will serve as a vehicle for a series of practical workshops. The Computervision system will be the working example of such a system being used on a range of studio-related design exercises.

The role of the microcomputer in the design process will also be featured in the program. The IBM PC will be used to illustrate the range of applications now available. Programming the IBM PC in a high level language gives experience of developing application programs.

The computer as an information or communications medium. Topics here include on-line information retrieval, local and remote networks, electronic mail, and graphic information systems.

Review of the future of computers and architecture. Appraisal of research in fields as diverse as 3-D displays, expert systems and adaptive environments. Particular attention to those contemporary issues in information technology which have a bearing on the design or construction of the built environment.

development in prospect

While the dynamics of course development will continue due to hardware changes and new applications being included (of the six courses listed two are entirely new and two are substantially modified).

However, the most fundamental change to the current program of courses in the foreseeable future will come from the Athena project referred to earlier.

The Athena project is a campus wide experimental program undertaken by MIT to integrate computers with the educational process.

The project is being carried out with the support of both
Digital Equipment Corporation and IBM, who are providing the
logistics of the project totalling some 50 million dollars
including equipment, software, service, maintenance support
and record grants over a 5 year period.

The brief for the project extends to all schools at MIT, Science,
Engineering, Architecture and Planning, Management and Humanities
and Social Sciences. Athena will be carried out in two phases,
an initial 2 year phase, just begun, followed by a 3 year
final phase. Athena will have a major effect on the future
provision of computer courses in the School of Architecture.

One effect will be to change the emphasis of how computers
will relate to architecture, so as to enhance the process
of architectural education rather than just imparting professional
computing skills.

Special topics already identified for research are the use of
graphics to communicate as many mathematical or scientific
concepts. Another project is concerned with the visualization
of dynamic models.

Digital Equipment Corporation and IBM are each independently
providing local area network technology to organize their
computers into clusters to be connected with an overall "spine"
network. New interface technology is being built to acheive
the necessary coherent distributed computing. In the final
phase of the program DEC will add about 1600 advanced personal
computers to the 300 alpha numeric display terminals, personal
computers, and advanced graphic work-stations already being
provided in phase one.

IBM's hardware contribution will consist of 500 high function
personal computers in phase one and an additional 500 advanced
single-user systems in the final phase.

Coherence is a key concept in the Athena program. Work on the
development of a single user-friendly system has begun which
will allow all machines to function with the same operating
system interface and use the same language.

The successful implementation of the Athena system will make a
very substantial contribution to the integration of computers and
education in many disciplines, not least those concerned with the
design and construction of the built environment.

References

1   PSA <u>Computer Education for Design and Construction</u>, Property
    Services Agency, Croydon, UK (1980)

2   Lansdown, RJ 'Waiting for the revolution' CAD 78 IPC
    Science and Technology Press, Guildford, UK (1978)

3   Amkreutz, J 'Educational Implications for Computer Aided
    Design' CADED IPC Science and Technology Press,
    Guildford, UK (1978)

4   David, B 'Teaching Computer-Aided Design in an architectural
    school with the SIGMA-ARCH1 system' CAD ED IPC Science and
    Technology Press, Guildford, UK (1978)

5   Courtieux, G and Guibert, D 'An experiment in teaching CAD
    and CAM in architecture' CADED IPC Science and Technology
    Press, Guildford, UK (1978)

6   Pohl, J 'Computers in Architectural Education' Proc.
    National Computer Conference, AFIPS Press, Montvale,
    New Jersey, USA (1975)

7   Rzevski, G and Kaposi, A A 'Education in Computer-Aided
    Design for Practising Engineers' CAD '74, IPC Science
    and Technology Press, Guildford, UK (1974)

8   Blaauwendraad, J 'Computer-Aided Design and the Educational
    System' CADED IPC Science and Technology Press, Guildford,
    UK (1978)

9   Mitchell, W 'Computer-aided arthitectural design', Petrocelli/
    Charter Inc., NY, USA (1977)

10 Gero, J S 'Computer-Aids in Architecture: Australia'
    Computer-Aids in Design and Architecture Negroponte N (ed.)
    Petrocelli/Charter NY, USA (1975)

11 Van Koetsveld, M 'CAD Education in RWS-DIV' CADED IPC
    Science and Technology Press, Guildford, UK (1978)

12 Maver, T W 'Methods and Models' Design Methods and Theories,
    Preuss Press, Obispo, CA, USA (1977)

13 Rogers, G 'Dynamic 3D Modelling for Architectural Design'
    Proc. ParC 79 Online, Uxbridge, UK (1979)

14 Purcell, P Computers & Architecture upubl. paper MIT (1983)

15 MIT Bulletin MIT Cambridge, MA 02139 (1983)

EDUCATION AND TRAINING IN CAAD

A H Bridges
Deputy Director
ABACUS, University of Strathclyde
UK

The teaching of computer-aided design in schools of architecture
raises a number of educational problems. Some of these difficulties
are reviewed and a postgraduate course in computer-aided building
design, developed to meet some of the requirements identified, is
described.

Alan Bridges is an architect who has been
involved in CAD research and teaching for
some ten years. He is currently a Deputy
Director of ABACUS, Course Director of the
University of Strathclyde MSc (CABD) course,
and an elected Director of the Construction
Industry Computer Association.

Introduction

It may be considered that there is sufficient debate about what constitutes the basic body of architectural knowledge to be imparted to students at schools of architecture without introducing further contention by adding another subject to the already overloaded curriculum. However, specialising in computing (in all fields) is now a relatively fashionable pastime, and its importance to architectural practice is likely to increase rather than diminish. All students should, therefore, be given the opportunity of developing some familiarity with the computer during their architectural education. Nevertheless, Schools of Architecture are still in the business of developing architects, and it should only be after the student has become an architect that, if appropriate, one could go on to develop a computer specialism.

Some problems

The additional load placed on the undergraduate curriculum is one of the most crucial factors affecting the teaching of CAAD. The volume of information related to architectural education has increased to such an extent that it is no longer realistic to expect that it can all be covered to the same depth in the course of the normal undergraduate training. Different schools lay emphasis on different parts of the curriculum, but, unfortunately, these differences are not readily perceived by the prospective students. All schools, therefore, to a greater or lesser degree, attempt to cover everything they can, and concentrate on specific areas according to their different educational aims or, more pragmatically, the strengths and interests of their staff members. Given (in Britain at any rate) the recent cutbacks in educational spending the specialist skills of the reduced staffs of many schools tends to distort the educational balance even further.

To find the time and the personnel to teach the emerging subject of CAD is a serious enough problem in many schools, even without considering the more fundamental educational issues involved. These issues may be broadly summarised in the philosophical question 'Are we promoting CAD education or architectural education using CAD?' Put the other way around, are students in schools of architecture learning how to use the computer in design, rather than how to design using the computer.

A number of factors may contribute to this state of affairs. The software available for use in teaching in schools of architecture is often limited to software developed within the school itself. Therefore its use is often for pragmatic rather than theoretical, educational, reasons. Very rarely is software available which was specifically developed to meet educational requirements: and the needs of education (as distinct from practice) are such that the use of "professional software" developed commercially for sale to architectural practices would be no better educationally.

This gap between education and practice is particularly sharply defined in CAD. Such software as is used in education tends to be for design analysis and ad hoc problem solving, whereas the software used in practice is mainly for production information and management. Production information plays a minimal part in most school courses, but can account for some 80% of a practices costs. Again, management is a relatively minor element of most courses, but, with the software industry able to sell accounting packages to a wider market than just architects, the software is relatively cheap to acquire and, therefore, often cost-effective for the user.

It is not even really possible to "train" students in the operation of the professional systems, as distinct from "educating" them in the underlying principles. There are a wide variety of draughting systems available, none of them easily within the available budget of a school of architecture but all so different in their operation that a 'training' on one is of very little use should one need to use a different system. Even the terminology varies. Different systems use different terms to describe similar (or, in some cases, identical) features. Or, more confusingly, the same term to describe different features. As a trivial example, what an architect would call a standard detail some systems call "components", whilst another divides them into "objects and blocks". What is important in all cases is not the mechanics of operation but the implications on the structuring of drawings and the requirements for the architect to become a "data-base manager".

Further considerations reinforce this gap between education and practice. Most programs currently available suffer from user inter-faces which are not easy for the casual or intermittent user to master; from onerous data preparation requirements; and concentration on specific (limited) aspects of design. These limitations can all be tolerated in practice because of the economic returns, but in education there is neither the time or the facilities to overcome the problems. The result is that rather than computer programs being adapted to suit educational requirements courses are adapted to suit the available programs.

Some Responses

All of these considerations make the task of integrating CAD education into the undergraduate curriculum increasingly difficult. At the moment CAAD education tends to be a special "block" inserted into the normal curriculum, rather than a natural part of the subject as a whole. "Computer-aided design" is taught as distinct from just "design" (which may or may not make use of computers). A typical course structure is described by Maver and Schijf [1]. The course consists of five modules as follows:

1. Exposition - the concepts   underlying CAAD, a survey of the state of the art, and demonstrations.

2. Preparation - practical experience using a range of programs, and discussion of their form, content and interfaces.

3. Application - using one or more programs in a studio design project.

4. Instruction - acquiring programming skills and knowledge of hardware and software systems.

5. Development - specifying, implementing and maintaining hardware and software systems.

Modules 1,2 and 3 are intended to give students a general awareness of CAD; units 4 and 5 are used for students wishing to develop special CAD expertise.

At the moment it is difficult to see any viable alternative to this pattern. The staff and facilities just do not exist, yet the value of much of the enterprise may still be questioned. The software used in the central application modules places severe restrictions on the permissable design forms; there are also difficulties associated with data input, and limitations on allowable building types and the data measured. The process of use is time consuming and frustrating. The benefits of its use are questionable. Students see only some of the worst aspects of CAD (not necessarily a bad thing) but learn nothing of the real potential. It is also quite remote from CAD use in practice. Until better software, written especially for teaching use, is available it is difficult to see this pattern of teaching improving.

The immediately available alternative is to make more use of quick, easy to use programs, made available on small computers, readily accessible in the design studios, and look at the complimentary 'professional' computing by visits to offices using computers or video instruction films. It is important that the current generation of students are made aware of computing methods and applications for it is sure to figure at some time during their professional career. However the long term solution to the problem lies in training more CAD specialists - both to become a more critical, demanding and selective client for commercial CAD systems, but also to provide the manpower to develop the next generation of software (or perhaps the first generation of specialist CAD teaching software) which is so desperately needed. This, obviously, cannot be done within the already overcrowded undergraduate course. The only answer is a specialist postgraduate course which would provide young architects wishing to specialise, or older architects wishing to retrain, with the opportunity to develop specialist CAD skills and then participate themselves in computer aided design, research and teaching; or act as interfaces between designers and computing specialists; or return to practice with the expertise to exploit the opportunities offered by computers and computing.

The remainder of this paper describes a one year, full time, post-graduate course in the techniques of computer-aided building design which aims to provide graduates from an architectural, engineering, surveying or other building related background with those particular CAD skills.

The Strathclyde MSc (CABD)

The course contains three main themes - Design Methods, Computing Methods and CABD Applications. The general framework is that the course consists of two thirds formal course work and one third dissertation. The course units themselves follow a two thirds to one third split between lectures and assignments specifically related to the project unit. The students are also required to write an essay over each of the Christmas and Easter 'vacations'.

The students are assessed upon their performance in the assignments and essays (approximately half of the total mark) and a formal dissertation which is written after the completion of the course work at Easter for submission in August. There are no formal examinations as such. The course units themselves are described in Appendix I. The type of work undertaken in the course is indicated by the follow-ing range of projects and dissertations, selected from the work done in the previous academic year.

Projects:

Design Methods Projects - application of a number of different techniques and critique of ease of use, effectiveness as design aid,etc.

Appraisal Project - use of program and critical appraisal of user interface, data required v. results obtained.

Computing Project - analysis of simple problem (eg checking of stair-case design against building regulations), structured English formulation, iterative refinement, coding.

Subsystem Evaluation Project - critical use of program for detailed design evaluation - eg dynamic thermal simulation.

User Interface Project - development of an improved user interface for an existing program, or specification for a user interface module.

Visual Impact Project - actual project preparing computer-generated photomontages or theoretical study of, eg colour variation under different types of lighting.

Dissertations:

Appraisal in CABD - a critical analysis of available software; a
discussion of techniques to meet the main criticism; the development
of a system of "fuzzy appraisal".

User Interface for Integrated CAAD Systems - analysis of 3-D modelling
systems and use of raster-op bit-map graphics techniques to develop a
sophisticated interface.

The Computer Based Building Model - Development of a specification for
a full 3-D modelling system.

Computer Aided Maintenance and Management - proposals for an automated
information system for maintenance engineers.

How the Use of Computing Draughting Systems by Architectural Practices
is Effecting the Design Process.

Computer Graphics Output in Architectural Practice.

Design and Implications of the Computer.

Resource Implications

A number of different types of resources are needed to support a
course of this type. The human resources are drawn from the ABACUS
research unit in the Department of Architecture, whose staff include
personnel with backgrounds in architecture, engineering, mathematics,
operations research and computer science. These resources are extended by research students in the department acting as part time tutors;
by visitors to the unit; and by visits to local offices already
using computers.

The physical resources required include a wide range of computing
hardware and software. The course provides computing experience
across a range of hardware from desktop microcomputers through minicomputers to large time-sharing mainframes. A range of terminal
equipment from simple alphanumeric terminals through storage tube and
raster scan graphics screens to sophisticated colour raster graphics
screens is available. Other peripherals include digitisers and
plotters, various hardcopy devices and video interface equipment.
The software available includes specially written teaching packages,
a wide range of application programs, and a wide range of system
software. Students are encouraged to investigate different high-
level languages and operating systems.

Beyond these obvious physical requirements are two other important
supportive resources. One is the presence of an active CAD research
unit which adds to the authority of the course and draws visiting
specialists to the Department. Following upon the presence of the

research unit is the availability of a good CAD library. The specialist books, conference proceedings and journals required to support a
course of this nature are not always available in most schools of
architecture.

Conclusion

The volume of information related to architectural education has
increased to such an extent that it is no longer realistic to expect
that it can all be covered to the same depth in the course of the
normal undergraduate training. Similarly, the rate of change in
theory, techniques and technology is such that the knowledge base
acquired cannot be expected to serve the graduate architect throughout
his professional life.

The field of computer-aided architectural design is an extreme example
of both the extension of the field of study and the fallibility of out-
dated information. Furthermore, many architects in practice have had
little or no contact with computers in their professional education.

The MSc course is designed to meet this need for postgraduate
education in CAD. To the extent that the students so far have been
a mix of younger architects wishing to specialise and older ones
wishing to retrain, the course appears to be succeeding. To the
further extent that two recent graduates have gone to teach in schools
of architecture, another has joined a CAD system vendor, and others
have gone into architectural practice,the quality of architectural CAD,
criticised at the beginning of the paper, may slowly begin to be
improved.

Reference

1.   Maver, T W and Schijf R, "International Implementation of a
     CAAD Project in Schools of Architecture". Bulletin of Computer
     Aided Architectural Design, no 47, February 1983, pp3-16.

APPENDIX 1 : MODULES OF THE MSc (CABD)

APPLICATIONS 1

Computational Methods in Building Design

An introduction to the application of computer methods in architecture and building science. Covers the following areas to provide information on the basic tools available to handle typical problems.

(a) general introduction to computer systems; (b) brief analysis; (c) generation of design proposals; (d) appraisal of design proposals; (e) building costing; (f) building structures; (g) energy usage; (h) building services; (i) daylight evaluation; (j) artificial lighting; (k) acoustics; (l) solar energy; (m) visualisation of design proposals; (n) visual impact analysis; (o) office management applications; (p) information retrieval; (q) specifications and bills of quantities; (r) computer draughting. Followed by 1 week project.

APPLICATIONS 2

Computer Applications in Architecture

Identifies those areas in architecture where, (i) significant use of computer techniques has been made, and (ii) future applications areas. Topics covered include the use of computers in the following areas:

(a) predesign decisions - economic studies, feasibility studies, brief development; (b) layout planning - representations of architectural spaces, representations of objectives and constraints, characteristics of different solution techniques, MAGIC; (c) integrated design appraisal - representation, measurement, evaluation, GOAL; (d) building subsystems appraisal - energy, lighting, visual aspects, ESP, BIBLE/VISTA; (e) specifications and bills of quantities - line and paragraph techniques, master bill techniques; (f) office management techniques - job and timesheet accounting, wordprocessing, CPM and forecasting; (g) automated draughting systems - devices and techniques, commercially available systems, integrated systems; (h) current research - ABACUS, elsewhere.

APPLICATIONS 3

Computer Applications in Visual Analysis and Modelling

The use of advanced computer graphics techniques in assessing the visual impact of proposed engineering and architectural developments.

(a) current visual modelling techniques; (b) evaluation of traditional methods of visual analysis; (c) computer potential in visual impact analysis; (d) photogrammetic techniques; (e) computer generated pictures and montages; (f) issues of accuracy. Followed by one week project.

APPLICATIONS 4

Computer Applications in Building Subsystem Evaluation

An advanced examination of computer applications in the detailed evaluation of building subsystem performance.

(a) detailed modelling of building interiors; (b) simulation of interior lighting effects; (c) colour rendering of different arti- ficial lighting schemes; (d) lighting systems; (e) acoustics evaluation; (f) energy modelling and energy resources; (g) numerical simulation energy models - harmonic response function, finite difference, computational methods; (h) numerical simulation techniques; (i) climatological data; (j) plant modelling; (k) examples using the ESP simulation system. Followed by one week project.

DESIGN METHODS 1

Introduction to Systems Theory and Design Methodology

An introduction to a systems approach to design, together with a number of formalised design methods.

(a) traditional methods of design; (b) the concepts of systems theory and its relevance to building design; (c) scientific methods; (d) new attitudes towards design - the concept of modelling; (e) formal design methods; (f) statistical design methods; (g) human science techniques; (h) problem solving techniques; (i) creative techniques; (j) development of design methodologies; (k) new design processes; (l) computer aided design. Followed by one week project.

DESIGN METHODS 2

Models in Building Design

To develop an appreciation of the role of architectural and environ- mental sciences in the overall field of design practice and education.

(a) new forms of building - problems posed by these new forms, growth of scientific methods of analysis, use of physical and mathe- matical models; (b) social changes - effects of legislation on built forms, impact of computing on design, changing role of building designers, the energy crises; (c) summary of role of designer in practice and society, and relevance of systems approach.

DESIGN METHODS 3

Brief Analysis and Layout Planning

An exploration of the computational aspects of the fundamental architectural planning problem.

(a) types of data - activity data analysis, quantitative, qualitative and dichotomous data, representations of data; (b) analysis of data - cluster analysis, multidimensional scaling; (c) relationship between brief analysis and layout planning/facilities planning; (d) representations of space - integer array, dimensionless vectors, point-vector, graph theoretic; (e) representation of objectives and constraints - adjacencies, constraint graph, dimensionless formulations, fit problems; (f) solution procedures - generate and test, hill climbing, heuristic search, implicit enumeration, linear and nonlinear programming, artifical intelligence approaches; (g) layout planning programs - CRAFT, GSP, IMAGE, CORELAP, SPS. Followed by one week project/essay.

DESIGN METHODS 4

Operations Research Applications in Design

An introduction to the techniques of operations research applicable to design.

(a) applied graph theory; (b) probability theory; (c) probability distributions; (d) algebraic and differential equations; (e) combinatorial programming; (f) Markov chains; (g) simulation modelling; (h) regression and correlation; (i) hypothesis testing. Following by one week project/essay.

COMPUTING METHODS 1

Introduction to computing.

An introduction to computer hardware and software.

(a) general concepts - analogue devices, digital computing; (b) computer hardware - mainframes, minis and micros, peripherals; (c) using computers - terminal connection, running a program; (d) software engineering - the concept of software engineering, software design methodologies, modularisation, portability of software; (e) software - systems software, machine independent operating systems, software libraries, software tools, applications software; (f) programming languages - review of different languages and their applications, FORTRAN language, writing FORTRAN programs, standards. Followed by project.

COMPUTING METHODS 2

Advanced Introduction to Computing

An opportunity to study advanced computing concepts and their application in architectural computing.

(a) advanced FORTRAN - file handling, data structures, interactive
computing, graphics; (b) special problem-oriented languages - GLIDE,
CECIL; (c) software tools - graphics libraries, utility libraries,
I/O conventions.

COMPUTING METHODS 3

Mathematical Methods

To thoroughly acquaint students with the mathematical techniques
necessary in computer graphics applications.

(a) Matrix methods - matrix algebra, diagonal matrics, submatrices,
determinants, etc, linear equations, mappings, projections, perspectives, etc, matrix inversion, tridiagonlisation, computer solutions
and further applications in computer graphics, numerical analysis -
accuracy and error propagation; (b) graph theory - introduction to
graphs and networks, planar/nonplanar graphs, trees and directed graphs,
computer representations, applications in data storage, etc.

COMPUTING METHODS 4

Computer Graphics in Design

Advanced consideration of computer graphics devices and techniques.

(a) display devices; (b) display files; (c) transformations;
(d) clipping and windowing; (e) interactive graphics techniques;
(f) graphical input techniques; (g) colour graphics techniques;
(h) graphics systems; (i) graphics languages; (j) general
applications; (k) special applications - video montage and mixing.

COMPUTING METHODS 5

Microcomputer Applications

A more detailed examination of microcomputer hardware and software.
Opportunity for hands-on experience with a wide range of micro-
computers is provided in association with the Microelectronics
Education Development Centre.

(a) central processor units; (b) memory devices; (c) mass storage;
(d) input and output peripherals; (e) system programs;
(f) application programs.

COMPUTING METHODS 6

Databases and Interfaces

A detailed discussion of information and databases in design
applications and a further consideration of aspects of the man-
machine interface.

Databases - (a) shape descriptions; (b) topology and geometry;
(c) component libraries; (d) conceptual models; (e) logical models;
(f) physical models; (g) data analysis; (h) functional analysis;
Interfaces - (i) conceptual design; (j) semantic design;
(k) syntatic design; (l) lexical design; (m) user interface models;
(n) user interface management systems.

CASE STUDIES IN DYNAMIC ENERGY MODELLING

D J McLean
Research Fellow
ABACUS, University of Strathclyde
UK

In recent years a number of building energy modelling systems have emerged. These systems differ considerably from the previous modelling generation because of their dynamic nature. This paper gives a summary description of these emerging models and based upon one particular model – the ESP system developed at the ABACUS research unit within the Department of Architecture and Building Science at the University of Strathclyde – a number of short case studies are given to demonstrate flexibility and technical potential.

Don McLean is a Research Fellow at ABACUS University of Strathclyde. He is involved in the development of building plant energy simulation models.

A graduate of Environmental Engineering, he obtained a PhD from the Department of Architecture at Strathclyde in 1982 for studies involving the dynamic modelling of active solar energy systems

Introduction

More than 25% of energy delivered in the U.K. is associated with maintaining the internal environment of commercial and domestic buildings.
It was suggested at the International Energy Agency Conference in West
Berlin (1) that - relative to 1973 figures - retofit measures in
buildings could produce energy savings of up to 50% with even greater
potential in the case of high technology energy saving features.
The concurrent need for rapid prediction techniques to assess the
implications of design features, has accelerated the development of
buildings energy models operating at the most fundamental first
principle level. These emerging simulation systems are substantially
different, in a number of respects, from the previous generation of
model they seek to replace: they are dunamic rather than static;
highly predictive in use; rigorous and flexible in analysis; and both
design- and research- orientated.

In essence these models are attempting to integrate all building energy
flowpaths (such as those illustrated in figure 1) over appropriate
time-increments (one hour or less). This implies the simultaneous
solution of:

- the transient conduction of heat through the enclosure envelope
  and therefore the associated lag and thermal storage effects

- the time dependent sensible and latent gains from occupants,
  lights, processing equipment, etc and the relative split of these
  gains into radiant and convective portions which will determine
  how they are lagged

- infiltration and natural or controlled ventilation

- the effects of shortwave solar radiation impinging on exposed
  external and internal surfaces

- the longwave radiation exchange between exposed external surfaces
  and the sky vault, ground and surrounding buildings

- the corresponding longwave radiation exchange between internal
  surfaces

- the shading of external opaque and transparent surfaces as caused
  by surrounding buildings as well as a variety of facade
  obstructions

- the mapping of insolation patch movement across internal surfaces

- time varying convection and other thermophysical system properties

- the essential link between control point location, system properties, plant interaction point location and the plant interaction medium

- condensation considerations

There are two principal techniques available to concatenate these flow-paths into a simulation model: response function and finite difference (2). Once assembled such a model will experience little difficulty in processing design problems which include the following variables: climate, occupancy, air flow, thermal properties, shading, shutter or blind operation, plant operation and control, lighting, insolation, changing geometry, and so on.

Table 1 lists a number of currently extant systems giving, in each case, their source organisation.

There is little doubt that simulation modelling leads to better insight into prevailing causal relationships (between design and performance parameters) and so offer considerable potential to improve the quality of the built environment. Some examples will serve to demonstrate the typical output potential of such systems. When properly used simulation models allow an investigation of:

- peak building loads and the various causal contributions

- energy requirements over any length of period

- environmental conditions in the absence of installed plant or under restricted capacity conditions

- the effects of geometrical or constructional design changes

- the influence of thermostatic type and position on energy requirements or consumption

- occupancy effects if behaviour patterns can be hypothesised

- zoning strategies for minimum energy demand

- likely savings if zone thermostates are set lower or if the installed system is deliberately undersized

- optimum plant start-times, optimum operating schedules and set-back temperatures, etc

- shading device performance or blind operational schemes to alleviate severe insolation problems

- load diversity, load levelling, energy sharing, etc.

Case Studies

The following short case studies are included to demonstrate the flexibility in use and the technical rigour of systems such as those of table 1. In each case study, the type of client is identified, technical aspects of the project are described and relevant issues are summarised.

One technical tool was common to each project; the ESP system developed at ABACUS at the University of Strathclyde. This model, based on an implicit finite difference simulation technique (3) is the outcome of an ongoing research project funded by the Science and Engineering Research Council.

Figure 2 shows the modules comprising ESP: an input management and database facility to allow the rapid definition of some target building for simulation against any real climatic collection selected on the basis of pre-simulation severity analysis. The results of each simulation are passed automatically to a results database which is subsequently accessed by the output module to achieve interrogation, graphical display and energy flow visualisation information.

Utility modules are available to enhance simulation rigour in those cases where the project has progressed to a stage where more detailed design data is available.

Case Study 1 : Retrofit design analysis

In one conventional design application, ESP was used by the design department of a large regional council to conduct a detailed analysis of various design possibilities in a proposed conversion of school promises to new office headquarters. The study involved an in-depth investigation of diversity of heating demand as affected by a variety of applied zoning strategies, plant operating schedules and building surface finishes.

The whole building data necessary for simulation - building geometry, fabric thermophysical properties, occupancy patterns, lighting levels and plant details - took approximately two days to enter into the computer with a further day spent on the essential data checking and validation process. Once entered, however, a number of simulation runs were performed, over a two day period, to investigate the various issues identified by the design team.

In tandem with the simulation exercise, and to test the feasibility of the modelling technique, the design team performed a range of traditional calculations and their final report raised the following points:

- the total cost incurred in the CAD exercise (including data preparation, computer charges, termninal usage and consultancy time)
  was estimated at half the cost which was incurred in the
  parallel manual exercise which involved only the straightforward
  calculation of individual zone heating loads.

- the results from the computer simulation allows a more detailed
  analysis of both building and plant performance than would otherwise have been possible. In particular, the ability to impose
  different plant operational regimes and interactively dictate
  design changes was deemed extremely useful.

- the ability to display the results graphically was conisdered
  invaluable as a mechanism for conveying information to the design
  team.

Case Study 2 : University Library

In another, not uncommon, application a multidisciplinary design
practice were involved as consulting engineers on an extension to a
university library comprising a reading room with an upper floor of
bookstacks. The external construction proposed was dense reinforced
concrete with double skin patent glazing angled back from cill to
ceiling. Concern for the environmental conditions focussed on the
maximum occupancy period of the reading room during May and the
mid-summer period June to August; the client also wished an appraisal
of the scheme under winter heating conditions.

An essential requirement of the project was that climatic information
relating to the actual site be used for all simulation work. Unfortunately climatic time-series data were not recorded locally and so an
alternative approach was adopted. Based on summary statistics
obtained from the Meteorological Office, the climate facility of ESP
was used to extract climatic data, corresponding to other UK locations,
but which conformed to the available statistics. In this way climatic
data was synthesised to represent the design site whilst preserving
the cross- and auto-correlations inherent in real climatic data.

The results of the ESP analysis revealed a 24 hour heating requirement
under the proposed ventilation scheme during May. Consequently the
ventilation rate was reduced to a level just sufficient to combat odours
and meet ventilation requirements. The higher ventilation rate was
required during summer for which a maximum temperature of 24 deg C.
was predicted. Given the slightly lower predicted resultant temperature and the possibility of occupants disposing themselves away from
the external wall this maximum air temperature was considered acceptable. A January analysis revealed acceptable comfort conditions.

It is important to note that dynamic energy models also provide a means for developing methods of assessing climatic suitability. ESP is currently being used in a project to establish a Climatic Severity Index which is building type specific and indicates, by a single dimensionless index, the stress placed on a buildings energy system by any given environment (4). Such an index would have many uses ranging from energy related decisions on building location to the determination of design climatic collections for simulation work.

Case Study 3 : Passive Solar Architecture

Increasing attention is being turned, worldwide, to the harnessing of solar energy to augment building requirements. The problems are often highly technical and require sophisticated modelling methods. In a number of projects ESP has been used to invesigate 'passive' solar design features. In each case the application has been research oriented or on behalf of a progressive architectural practice.

The studies usually focus on such issues as the performance of direct gain, attached sunspaces and mass Troube walls or attempt to optimise blind control, moveable insulation, shading devices or selective thin films applied to windows.

In one particular application ESP was employed by a specialised architectural practice who had been commissioned by a large housebuilder to investigate the feasibility of adding a low cost glass box (passive solar collector) to the south facade of an existing house. Louvres were controlled to vent the collector to the living space if the space required energy and the collector could supply it. The box was also used as a passive cooling device. If the living space overheated an external louvre would open to reduce collector temperature. The clients final design was simulated over an annual period and compared to an annual simulation of the original house design. It was established that the passive solar design would reduce annual energy consumption by some 30%. The simulation results compared favourably with a parallel monitoring project conducted by the client.

There is little doubt that the modelling of passive solar elements requires considerable technical rigour. Figure 3 for example shows the range of possible passive solar elements. Littler (5) has conducted a survey of over 50 models from the viewpoint of their suitability as passive solar analysis aids. Table 2 summarises the models which emerged as most suitable.

Case Study 4 : Low Energy Hospital

One interesting use of energy simulation systems is to apply them to a range of design variables, parametrically, to increase understanding of the compelx energy interrelationships. This was the strategy

adopted by a large design practice when commissioned by a government
agency to establish the base energy requirements for a low energy
hospital design. Once established, this base requirement would become
a reference standard against which altenative design proposals could
be assessed. By means of parametric analysis a range of design parameters were studied which were assumed to have a significant bearing
on energy usage - for example, different control temperatures, window
size and configuration, lighting levels, construction, ventialtion,
shading devices, etc.

Whilst parametric analysis is of fundamental importance to a more
complete understanding of the issues relating to energy efficient
building design it is important to constrain any exercise least the
combinatorial possibilities become too large for no appreciable benefit.
For this project three important constraints were invoked:

- an example zone was taken as representative of all similar zones
  thereby reducing the number of zones to be simulated

- monthly simulations were replaced by single week runs where the
  climatic data was selected as representative of the month

- and, most importantly, each parameter was not simulated in conjunction with every other design variable. Rather, the study was
  progressed employing an additive technique in which the best
  outcome from the study of parameter 'n' was used as the basis
  for the study of parameter 'n+1' - this ensures the required total
  number of simulations is considerably reduced for large parametric analyses.

As a result of this study the client concluded that parametric
studies could usefully employ similar constraints provided that the
design parameters can be ordered in terms of their likely energy and/
or cost consequences. However, the calculation techniques should
allow for data (eg occupant behaviour) which is probabalistic in
nature, with results ranging between agreed confidence limits.

Case Study 5 : Enclosed Shopping Centre with large Attria

Accompanying improved living standards is the increasing demand for
leisure and shopping facilities bringing new technical problems
requiring solution. In recent years a number of consultancies have
been required to develop solutions to the problems surrounding air
movement and temperature stratification in high roofed (usually glass)
shopping arcades. Typical designs have incorporated extensively
glazed roofs with large pedestrian malls and high attria domes.
Large air movements are associated with these designs and to predict
performance it is crucial to accurately model all air movement
induced by the stock effect (bouyancy forces) and pressure effects
due to the distributed leakage such as door, windows and smoke louvres.

In one particular application the client wished to model a large
enclosed shop and office development in a major city. The building
design involved a sloping glass 'skin' as an external construction
with a large central attria with courtyard below. A series of
internal walkways connected the offices and shops. The following
information was required for both 'typical' and 'design' periods
during summer and winter:

- the air flow patterns as affected by varying louvre openings and
  different external door arrangements

- the maximum and minimum air temperatures with uncontrolled court-
  yards and walkways and heated offices and shops.

- the effects of solar penetration and the best operation of a
  cloth blind arrangement inside the south facing glass 'skin'.

- the air velocity in the courtyard and walkways.

Appropriate climatic data was made ready, an equivalent air flow
network was established to represent the distributed leakage paths
and several areas, for example, the attria spaces were sub-divided
into a number of zones to model stack effect.

Based on detailed, and simultaneous, air flow and energy simulation,
it was possible to establish likely temperature gradients and
direction and magnitudes of all air movements. Variable venting
schemes, solar exclusion strategies and shop/mall heat sharing
options could be incorporated without difficulty.

Case Study 6 : Fan assisted electrical storage units

In many modelling applications it is crucial to treat the building
and its plant systems simultaneously to preserve the all important
temporal relationships. In one project it was required to simulate
the performance of fan-assisted electrical storage units in a building conversion to small factory workshop units. A detailed computer
description of the building was established, which included an
explicit representation of the electrical equipment, and a number
of simulations performed to investigate a range of issues such as:
comfort, unit controlability, charge/discharge ratios, weather
anticipator efficiency, running cost and so on.

It was shown that the current off-peak electrical storage technology
is technically capable of achieving satisfactory comfort conditions
provided a reasonable level of automatic output control is incorporated on each unit. On the other hand unit charge control is

often simplistic resulting in inefficient charge/discharge ratios.

Conclusion

There are a number of emergent energy models offering predictive capabilities hitherto unavailable. By means of a series of case studies these models have been shown to be cost effective in use as well as highly informative and flexible. As these models continue to develop they will occupy a central position in the design of new buildings and the re-design of existing buildings.

Acknowledgement

Many thanks to Dr Joe Clarke for his aid in assembling this paper.

References

1. International Energy Agency conference on New Conservation Technologies, Berlin, April 1981
2. Clarke, J A, 'Computer Applications in the Design of Energy Conscious Buildings', Computer-Aided Design, Vol 14 no 1 p3-9.
3. Clarke, J A, 'ESP System Documentation Set', ABACUS Publication University of Strathclyde, 1982
4. Markus, T A, Clarke, JA and Morris, E N 'Climatic Severity', Interim report, Department of architecture, University of Strathclyde, 1981
5. Littler, J G F, 'Overview of some available models for passive solar design', Computer-Aided Design, Vol 14 no 1 pp 15-18.

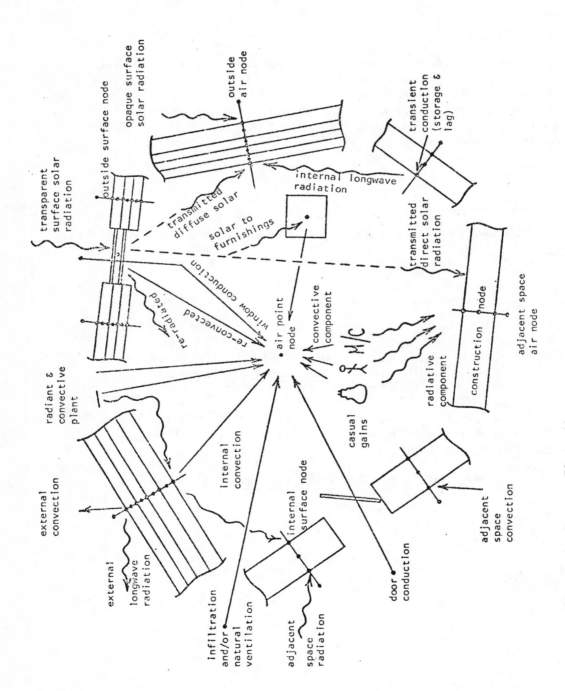

Figure 1 Energy Flowpaths

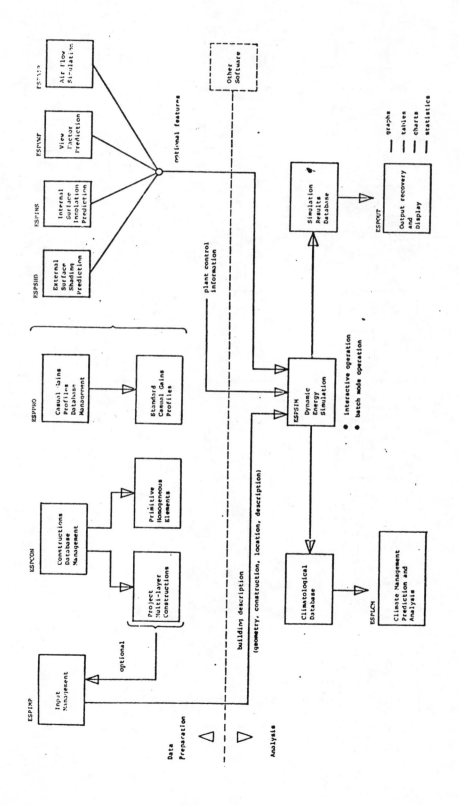

Figure 2   The ESP System

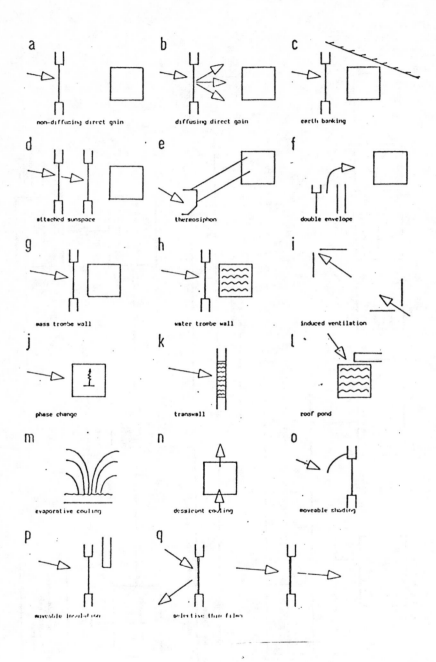

Figure 3   Architectural passive solar elements

Program Name	Organisation
ATKOOL	W S Atkins Group, UK
OFFICE	Electricity Council Research Centre, UK
THERM	British Gas Corporation, UK
HTM	UWIST, UK
AMBER	Faber Computer Operations, UK
ESP	University of Strathclyde, UK
ENCO2	Pilkington Bros., UK
SCOUT	Gard. Inc., US
DOE 11	Lawrence Berkeley Lab., US
ECUBE 111	American Gas Association, US
JULOTTA	Swedish Council for Building Research, SWEDEN
VENTAC	AB Svenska Flaktfabriken, SWEDEN
TEMPER	CSIRO, AUSTRALIA
WTE01	TPD-TNO, HOLLAND
LPB1	University of Liege, Belgium
BLAST	US Army Construction
DEROB	University of Austin, Texas, US
SUNCODE	Ecotape, Seattle, US
TRNSYS	University of Wisconsin, US
PASOLE	LASL, US
BUILD	Cranfield, UK
HOUSE	ECRC, UK

Table 1 List of dynamic energy programs and their source organisation

Topic handled		ESP	BLAST	DEROB	SUNCODE
Designs	Direct gain	✓	✓	✓	✓
	Attached sun space	✓	✓	✓	✓
	Thermosiphon	✓	✓	✓	✓
	Roof space collector	difficult	✓	✓	✓
	Double envelope	✓	✗	✓	✗
	Mass walls vented	✓	✓	✓	✗
	Mass walls unvented	✓	✓	✓	✓
	Under floor rock beds	✓	✓	✓	✓
Physical problems	Air/heat movement by convection/by fans	schedule	schedule	schedule	schedule
	Infiltration	schedule	schedule	✓	✗
	Solar radiation mapping round spaces	✗	✗	✓	✗
	Variable glass emissivity	✓	✓	✓	✓
	Variable room colour	difficult	difficult	difficult	✗
	Effect of furnishings	✗	✗	✓	✓
	Air/temperature/stratification	schedule	schedule	schedule	schedule
	Movable window insulation	✓	✓	✓	✓
	Isothermal and non-isothermal storage	✗	✗ †	✗	✗
	Phase change walls	✓	✓	✗	✓
	Isolated storage	✓	✓	✗	✗
	Adequate handling of beam radiation	✓	✓	✓	✓
	Adequate treatment of sky temperature	✗	✗	✗	✗
Weather input	Complete 'set'	✓	✓	✓	✓
Daylighting		✓	✓	✓	✗
Surface temperature for providing comfort temperatures		✓	difficult	✓	✓
Validation		†	†	†	†
Documentation		Very good	Poor	Good	Very good
Graphics output		Excellent	✗	Excellent	✗
Building input via digitising tablet		✓	✗	In principle	✗
Building input format		Cartesian	Cartesian	Assemble standard shapes	†
Internal tables of construction parameters such as insulation values		✓	✓	✗	✓
Is it continuing to be improved		✓	✓	✓	✓

† See reference given below

Permission to reproduce this Table(From: Littler,J.G.F 'Overview of some available models for passive solar design' CAD, Vol 14, No. 1, January 1982) is gratefully acknowledged.

Table 2 Summary of 4 models suitable for passive solar energy